W9-BBF-590

10/16- 10x

RIVER FOREST PUBLIC LIBRARY
735 Lathrop Avenue
River Forest, Illinois  60305
708 / 366-5205

2/16

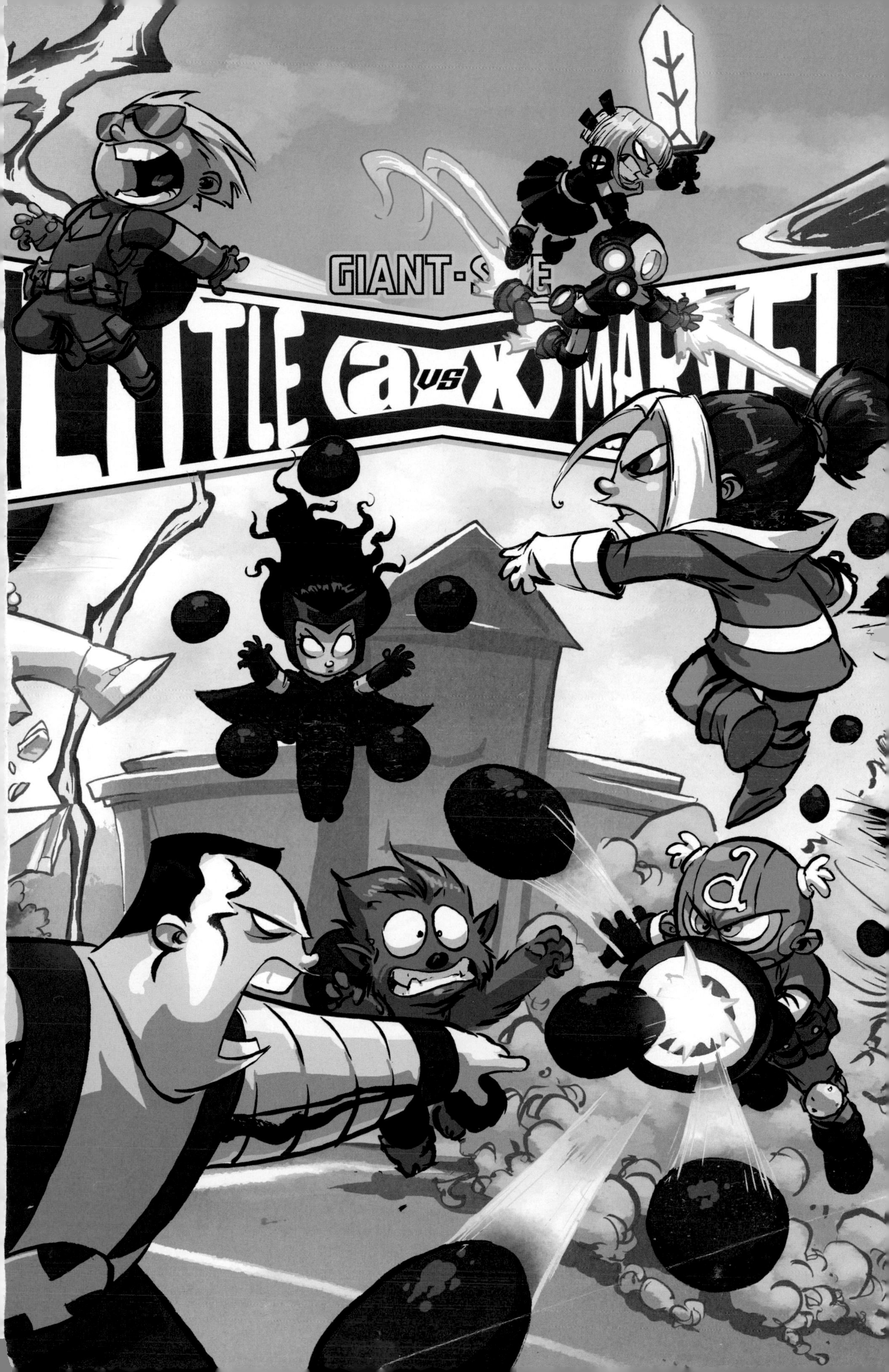

GIANT-S E
LITTLE A VS X

**GIANT-SIZE LITTLE MARVEL: AVX.** Contains material originally published in magazine form as GIANT-SIZE LITTLE MARVEL: AVX #1-4 and A-BABIES VS. X-BABIES #1. First printing 2016. ISBN# 978-0-7851-9870-3. Published by MARVEL WORLDWIDE, INC., a subsidiary of MARVEL ENTERTAINMENT, LLC. OFFICE OF PUBLICATION: 135 West 50th Street, New York, NY 10020. Copyright © 2016 MARVEL No similarity between any of the names, characters, persons, and/or institutions in this magazine with those of any living or dead person or institution is intended, and any such similarity which may exist is purely coincidental. **Printed in China.** ALAN FINE, President, Marvel Entertainment; DAN BUCKLEY, President, TV, Publishing and Brand Management; JOE QUESADA, Chief Creative Officer; TOM BREVOORT, SVP of Publishing; DAVID BOGART, SVP of Operations & Procurement, Publishing; C.B. CEBULSKI, VP of International Development & Brand Management; DAVID GABRIEL, SVP Print, Sales & Marketing; JIM O'KEEFE, VP of Operations & Logistics; DAN CARR, Executive Director of Publishing Technology; SUSAN CRESPI, Editorial Operations Manager; ALEX MORALES, Publishing Operations Manager; STAN LEE, Chairman Emeritus. For information regarding advertising in Marvel Comics or on Marvel.com, please contact Jonathan Rheingold, VP of Custom Solutions & Ad Sales, at jrheingold@marvel.com. For Marvel subscription inquiries, please call 800-217-9158. **Manufactured between 10/2/2015 and 12/14/2015 by R.R. DONNELLEY ASIA PRINTING SOLUTIONS, CHINA.**

10 9 8 7 6 5 4 3 2 1

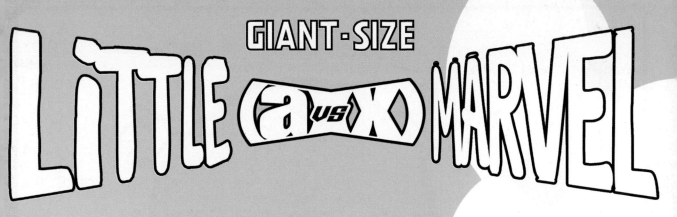

# GIANT·SIZE LITTLE (a) vs (x) MARVEL

WRITER/ARTIST
## Skottie Young

COLOR ARTIST
## Jean-Francois Beaulieu

LETTERER
## Jeff Eckleberry

COVER ART
## Skottie Young

EDITOR
## Charles Beacham

SUPERVISING EDITOR
## Sana Amanat

**A-BABIES VS. X-BABIES #1**
WRITER: Skottie Young
ARTIST: Gurihiru
LETTERER: VC's Clayton Cowles
EDITOR: Tom Brennan
EXECUTIVE EDITOR: Tom Brevoort

COLLECTION EDITOR: Jennifer Grünwald  ASSOCIATE MANAGING EDITOR: Alex Starbuck
EDITOR, SPECIAL PROJECTS: Mark D. Beazley  SENIOR EDITOR, SPECIAL PROJECTS: Jeff Youngquist
SVP OF PRINT & DIGITAL PUBLISHING SALES: David Gabriel

EDITOR IN CHIEF: Axel Alonso  CHIEF CREATIVE OFFICER: Joe Quesada
PUBLISHER: Dan Buckley  EXECUTIVE PRODUCER: Alan Fine

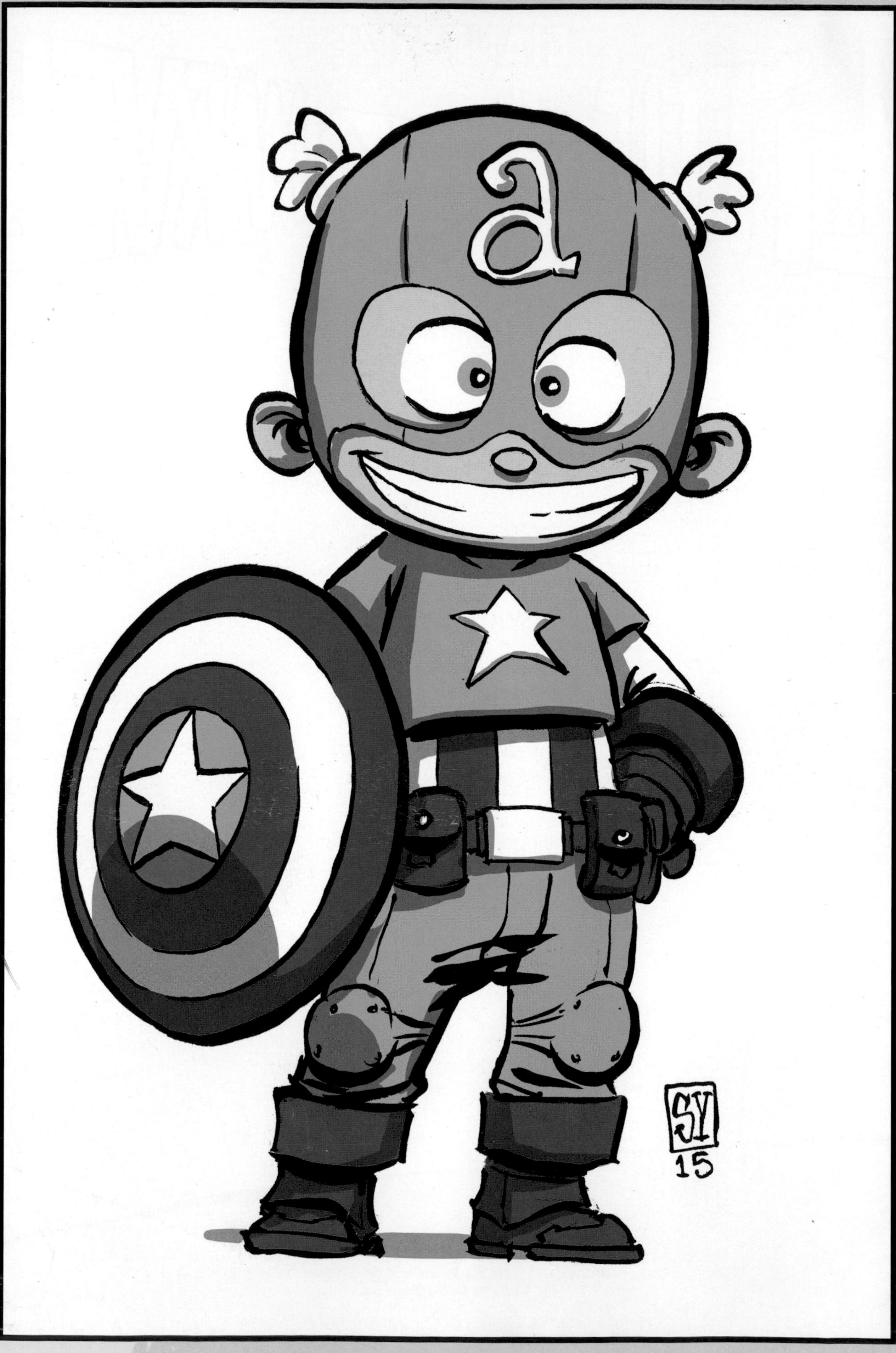
SY
15

GIANT-SIZE LITTLE MARVEL: AVX #1 ANT-SIZED VARIANT BY SKOTTIE YOUNG

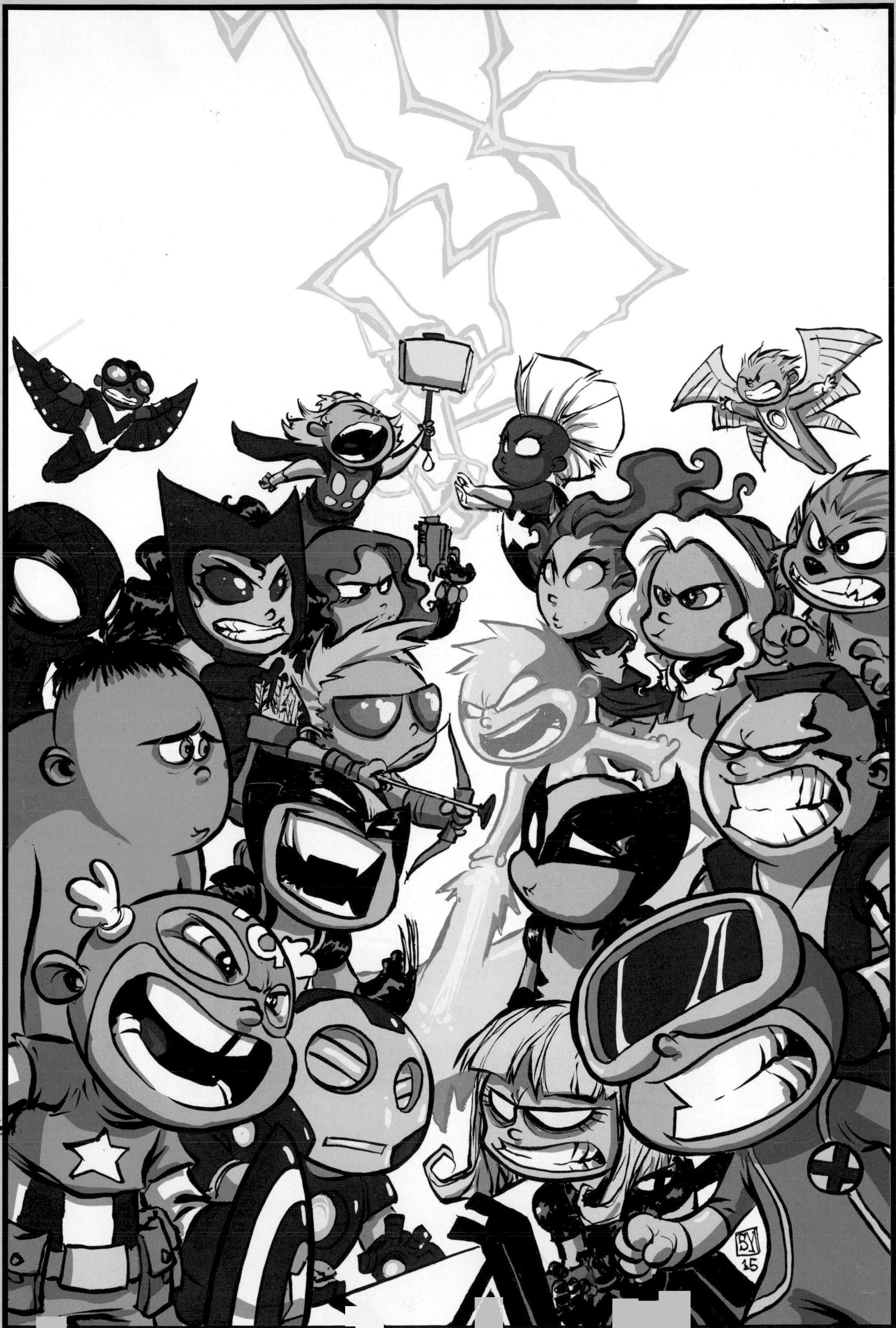

GIANT-SIZE LITTLE MARVEL: AVX #1

# SECRET WARS

THE MULTIVERSE WAS DESTROYED!

•

THE HEROES OF EARTH-616 AND EARTH-1610
WERE POWERLESS TO SAVE IT!

•

NOW, ALL THAT REMAINS...IS **BATTLEWORLD:**
A MASSIVE, PATCHWORK PLANET COMPOSED OF THE FRAGMENTS OF
WORLDS THAT NO LONGER EXIST, MAINTAINED BY THE IRON WILL OF ITS
GOD AND MASTER, VICTOR VON DOOM!

•

EACH REGION IS A DOMAIN UNTO ITSELF!

GIANT-SIZE

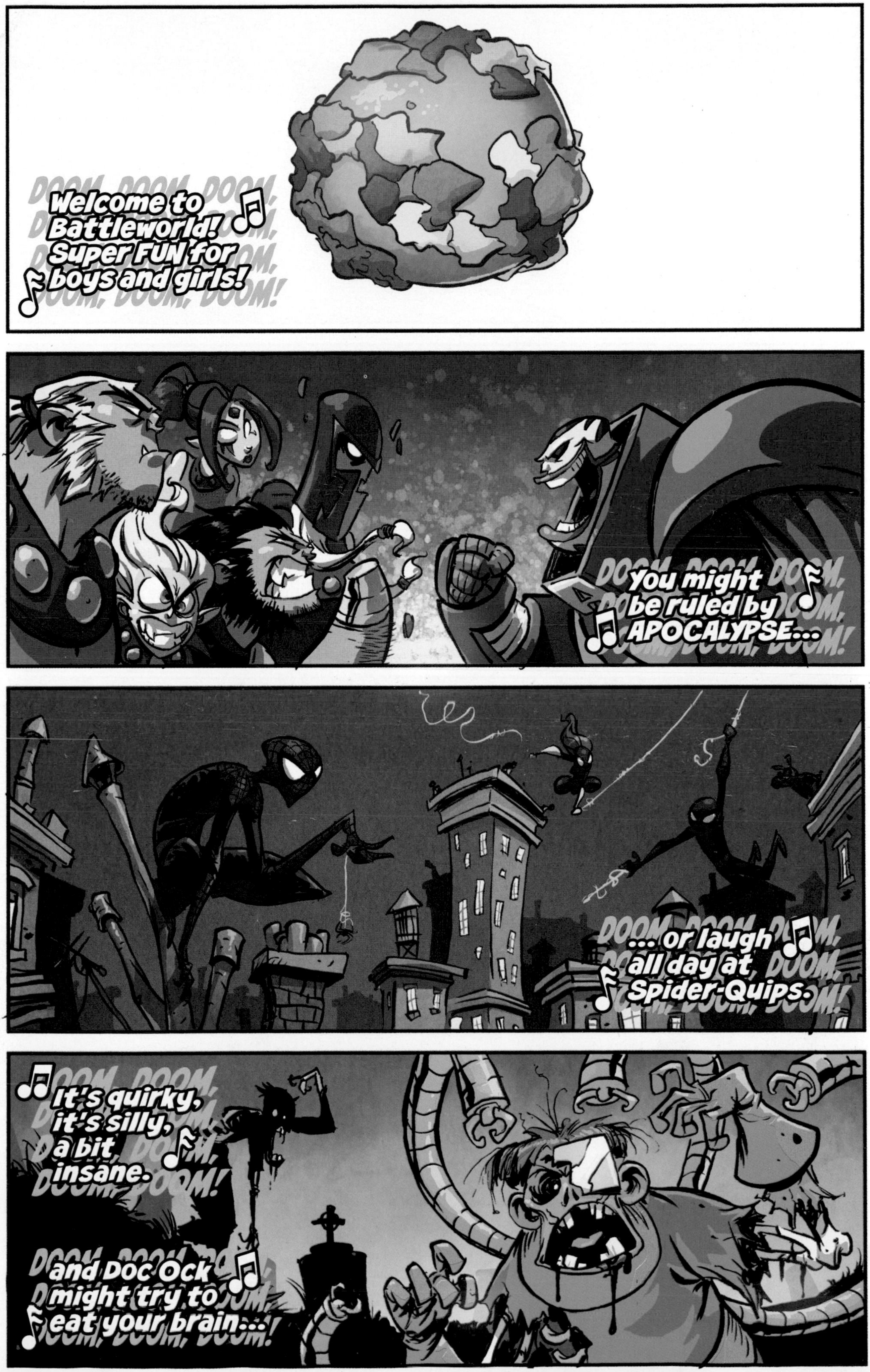
Welcome to Battleworld! Super FUN for boys and girls!
You might be ruled by APOCALYPSE...
... or laugh all day at Spider-Quips.
It's quirky, it's silly, a bit insane.
and Doc Ock might try to eat your brain...

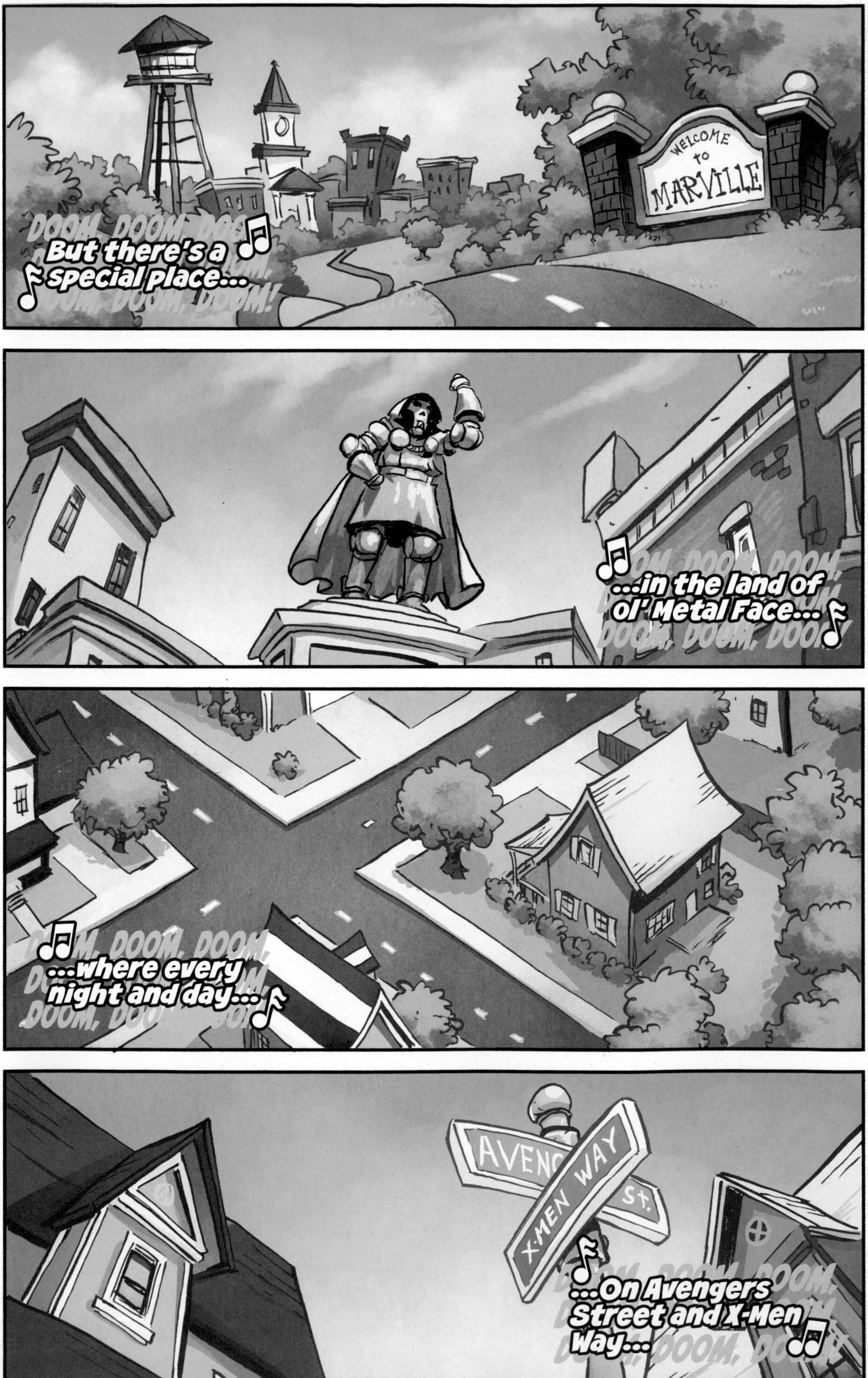
WELCOME to MARVILLE
But there's a special place...
...in the land of ol' Metal Face...
...where every night and day...
X-MEN WAY
St.
...On Avengers Street and X-Men Way...

COME ON, MAGIK! I SAID IT WAS AN ACCIDENT.

*...the kids all jump for joy...*

DOOM, DOOM, DOOM, DOOM, DOOM, DOO

DON'T GIVE ME THAT, STARK!

SAYING "HEY, CAP, WATCH ME MELT THIS EVIL PONY PAL WITH MY NEW HAND-BLASTERS AND SEE IF WE CAN MAKE MAGIK CRY" BEFORE YOU DO EXACTLY THAT...

...IS NO ACCIDENT!

*...but never share their toys...*

DOOM, DOOM, DOOM, DOOM, DOOM!

SHE HAS YOU THERE, IRON MAN.

DO ME A FAVOR, CAP-- DON'T HELP HER OUT.

*...they're all the best of friends...*

DOOM, DOOM, DOOM, DOOM, DOOM!

DON'T WORRY...

*...they're sure to make you grinnnnnn...*

DOOM, DOOM, DOOM, DOOM, DOOM!

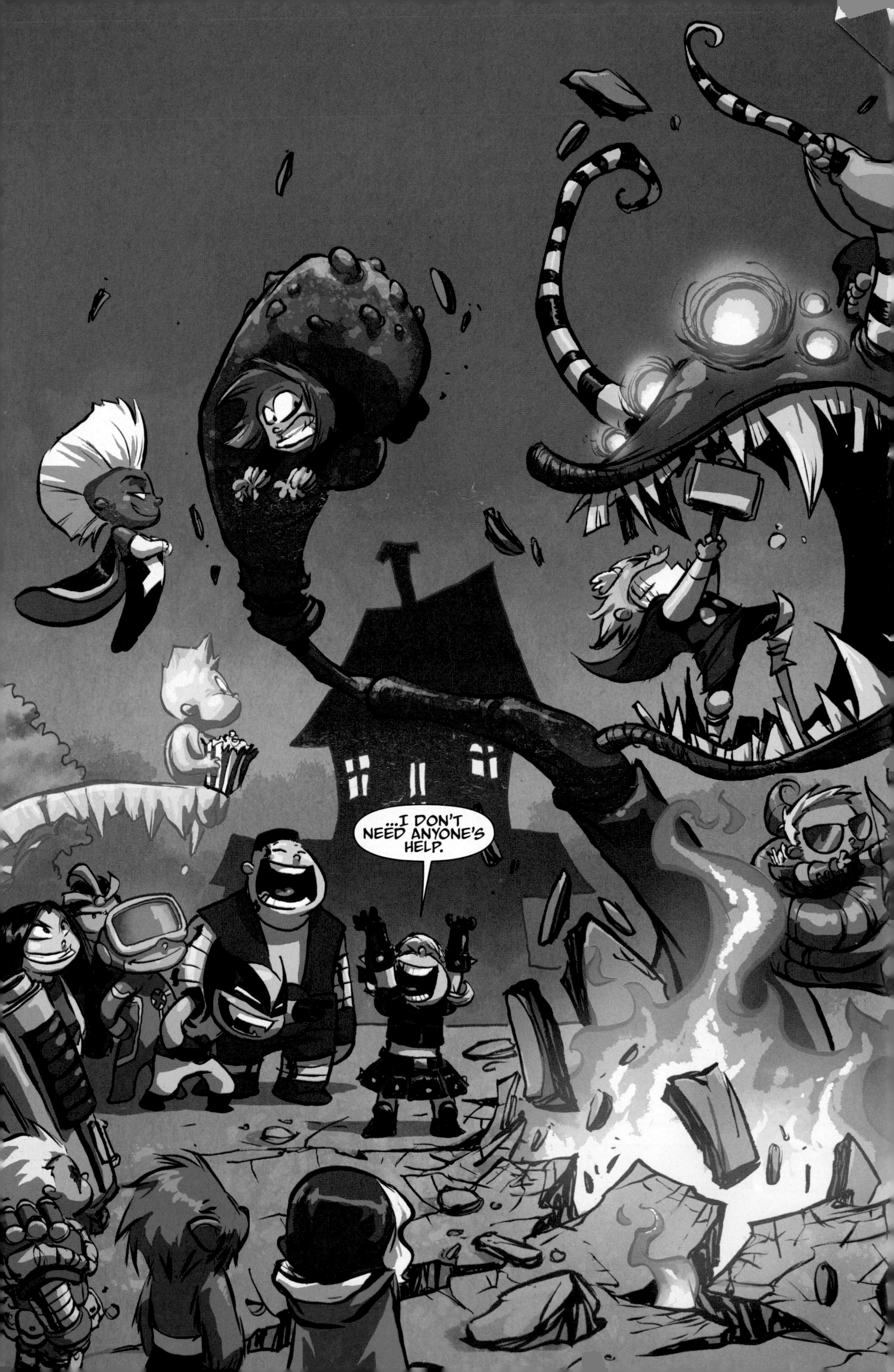
...I DON'T NEED ANYONE'S HELP.

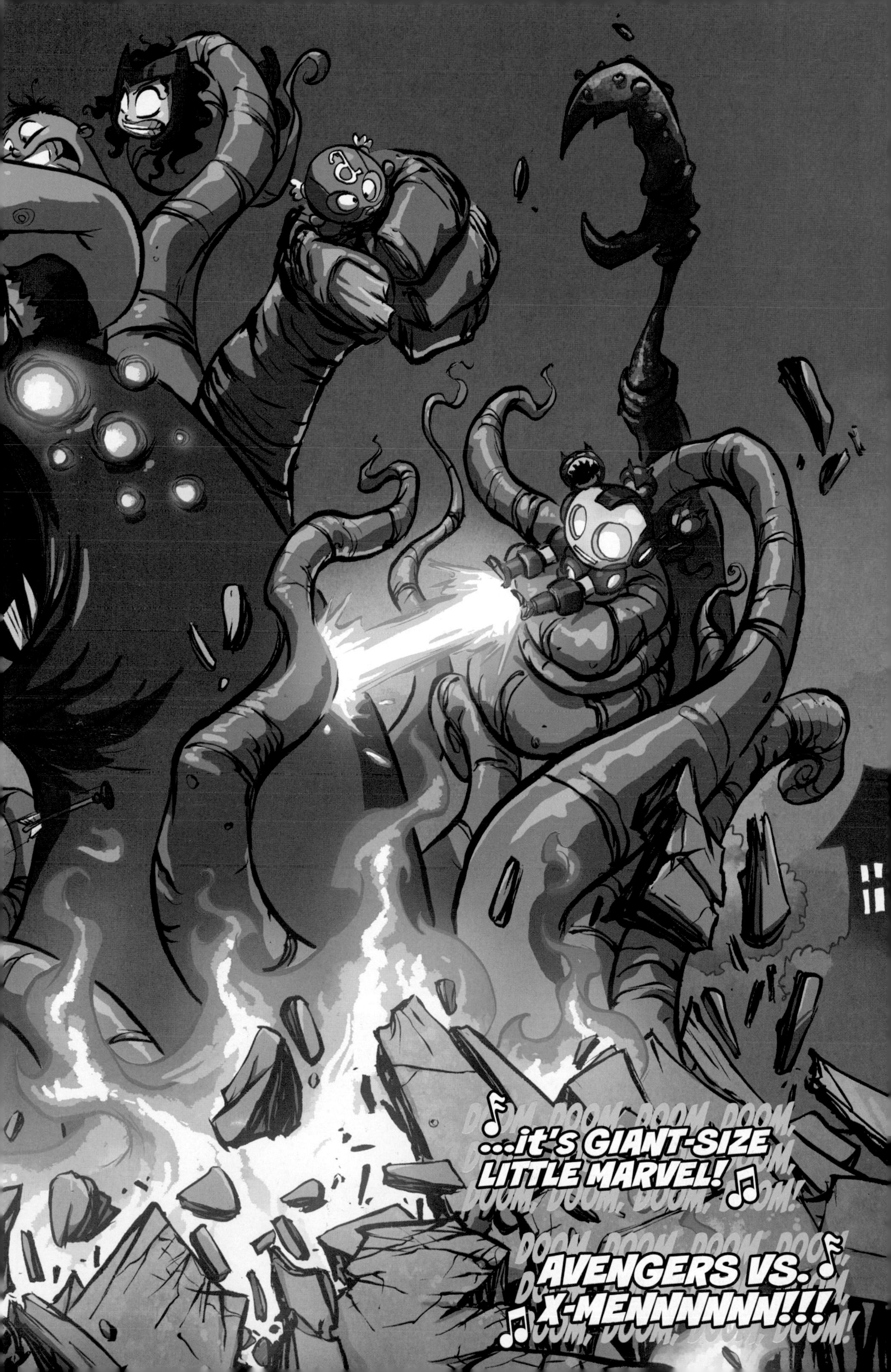

DOOM, DOOM, DOOM, DOOM,
DOOM, DOOM, DOOM, DOOM!
...it's GIANT-SIZE LITTLE MARVEL!
DOOM, DOOM, DOOM, DOOM,
DOOM, DOOM, DOOM, DOOM!
AVENGERS VS. X-MENNNNNN!!!

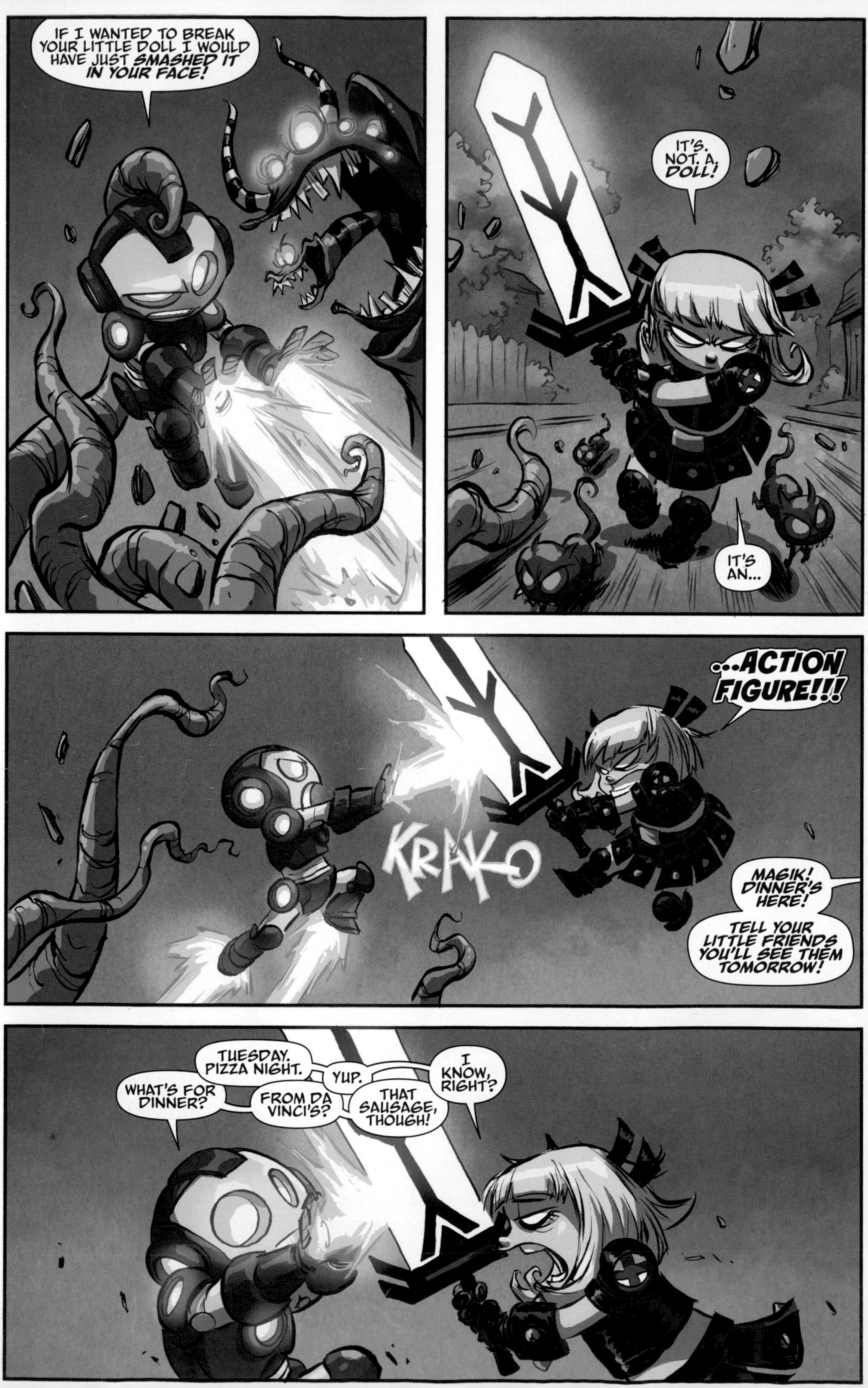

IF I WANTED TO BREAK YOUR LITTLE DOLL I WOULD HAVE JUST SMASHED IT IN YOUR FACE!
IT'S. NOT. A. DOLL!
IT'S AN...
...ACTION FIGURE!!!
KRAKO
MAGIK! DINNER'S HERE!
TELL YOUR LITTLE FRIENDS YOU'LL SEE THEM TOMORROW!
WHAT'S FOR DINNER?
TUESDAY. PIZZA NIGHT.
FROM DA VINCI'S?
YUP.
THAT SAUSAGE, THOUGH!
I KNOW, RIGHT?

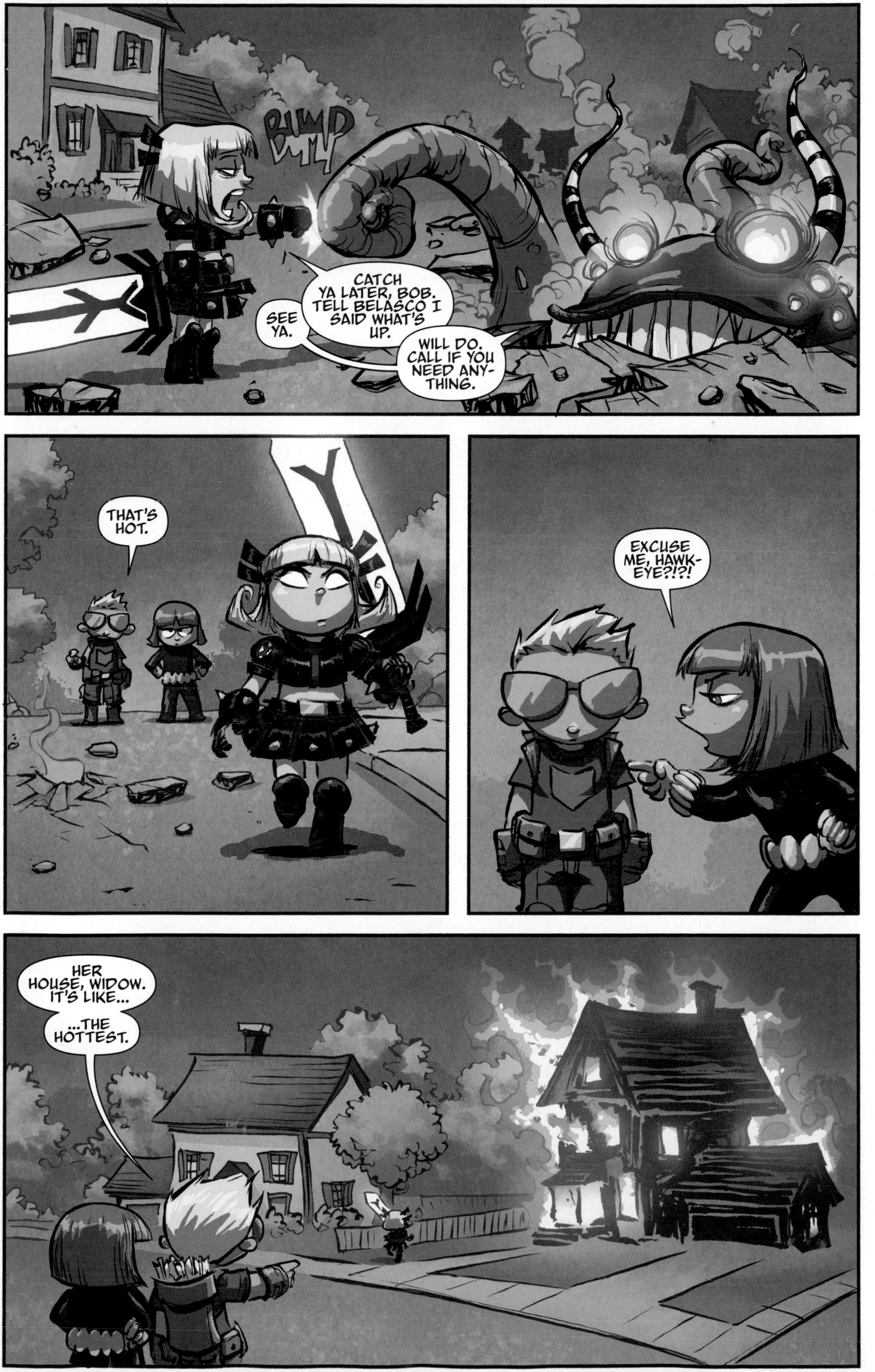
BUMP
CATCH YA LATER, BOB. TELL BELASCO I SAID WHAT'S UP.
SEE YA.
WILL DO. CALL IF YOU NEED ANY-THING.
THAT'S HOT.
EXCUSE ME, HAWK-EYE?!?!
HER HOUSE, WIDOW. IT'S LIKE...
...THE HOTTEST.

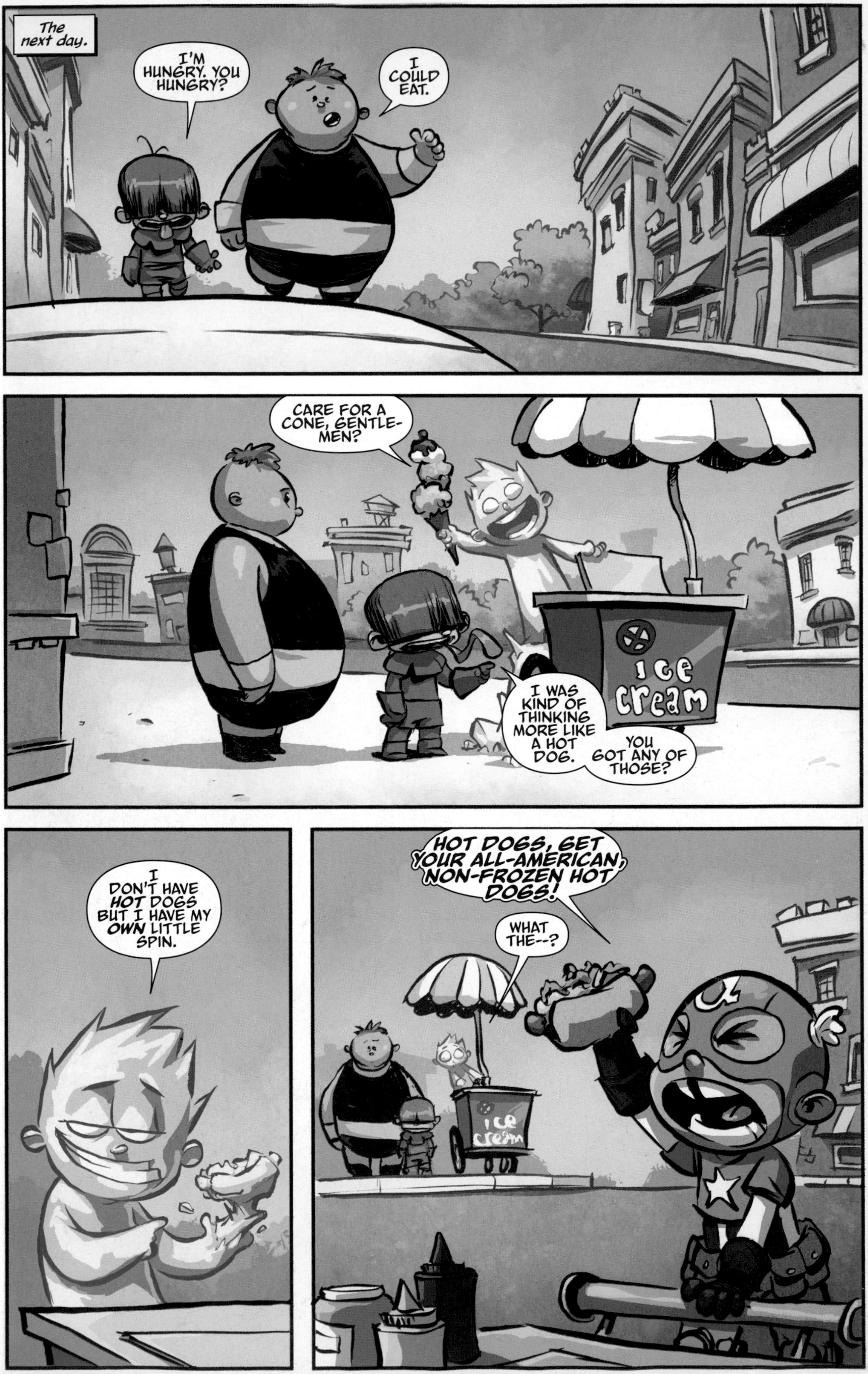
The next day.
I'M HUNGRY. YOU HUNGRY?
I COULD EAT.
CARE FOR A CONE, GENTLE-MEN?
I WAS KIND OF THINKING MORE LIKE A HOT DOG.
YOU GOT ANY OF THOSE?
ice cream
I DON'T HAVE HOT DOGS BUT I HAVE MY OWN LITTLE SPIN.
HOT DOGS, GET YOUR ALL-AMERICAN, NON-FROZEN HOT DOGS!
WHAT THE--?
ice cream

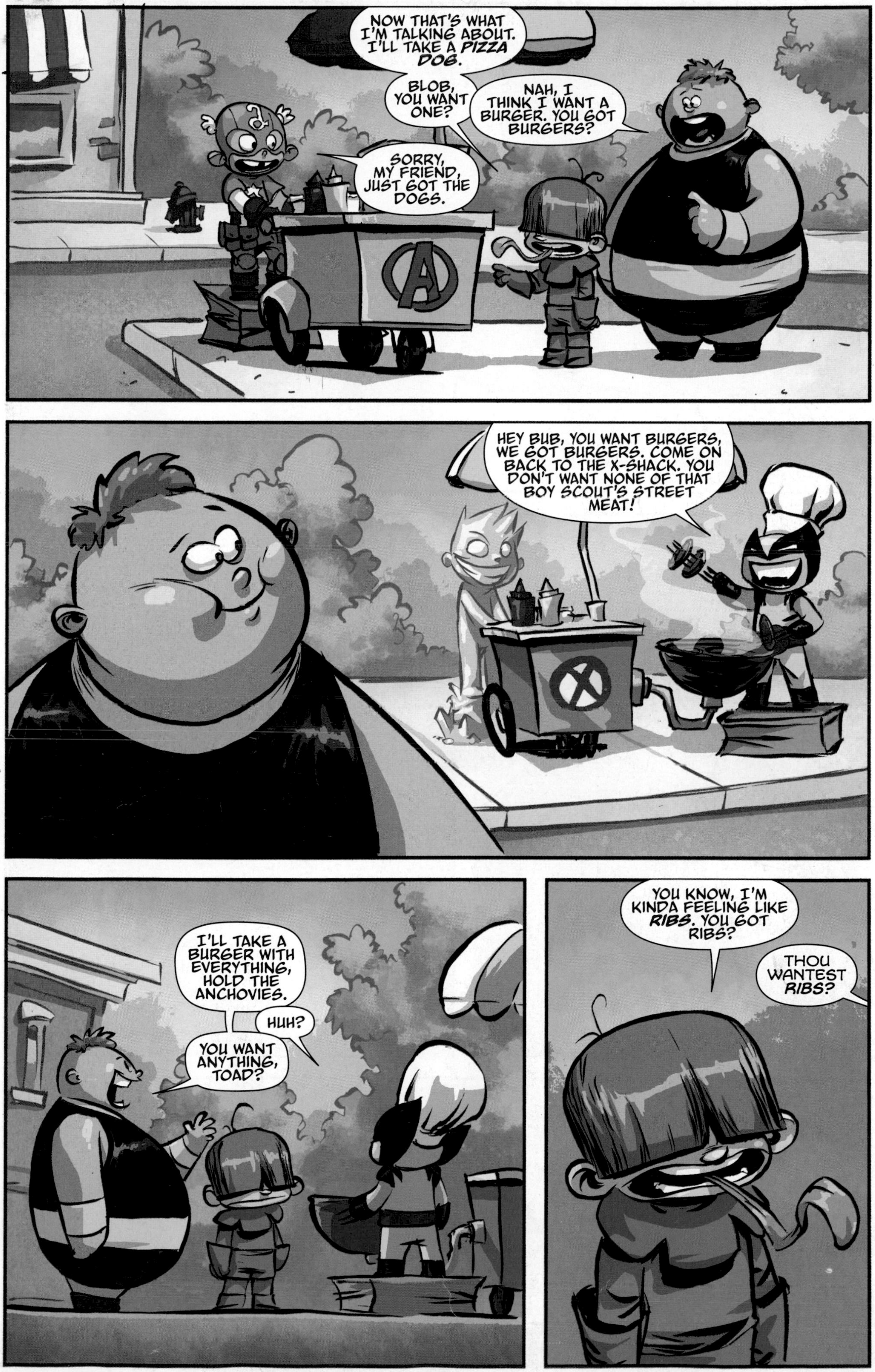
NOW THAT'S WHAT I'M TALKING ABOUT. I'LL TAKE A PIZZA DOG.
BLOB, YOU WANT ONE?
NAH, I THINK I WANT A BURGER. YOU GOT BURGERS?
SORRY, MY FRIEND, JUST GOT THE DOGS.
HEY BUB, YOU WANT BURGERS, WE GOT BURGERS. COME ON BACK TO THE X-SHACK. YOU DON'T WANT NONE OF THAT BOY SCOUT'S STREET MEAT!
I'LL TAKE A BURGER WITH EVERYTHING, HOLD THE ANCHOVIES.
HUH?
YOU WANT ANYTHING, TOAD?
YOU KNOW, I'M KINDA FEELING LIKE RIBS. YOU GOT RIBS?
THOU WANTEST RIBS?

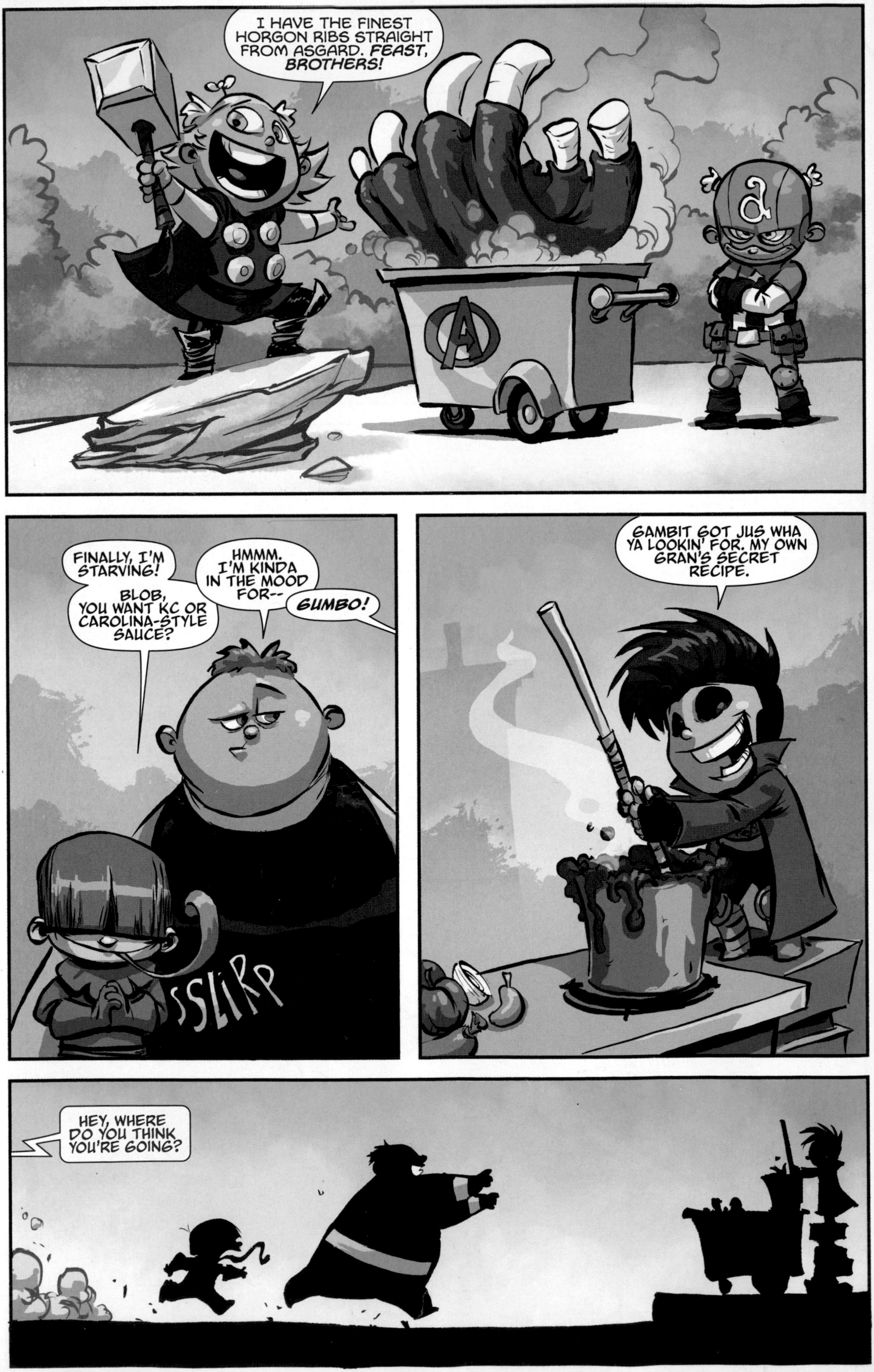
I HAVE THE FINEST HORGON RIBS STRAIGHT FROM ASGARD. FEAST, BROTHERS!
FINALLY, I'M STARVING!
BLOB, YOU WANT KC OR CAROLINA-STYLE SAUCE?
HMMM. I'M KINDA IN THE MOOD FOR--
GUMBO!
SSLIRP
GAMBIT GOT JUS WHA YA LOOKIN' FOR. MY OWN GRAN'S SECRET RECIPE.
HEY, WHERE DO YOU THINK YOU'RE GOING?

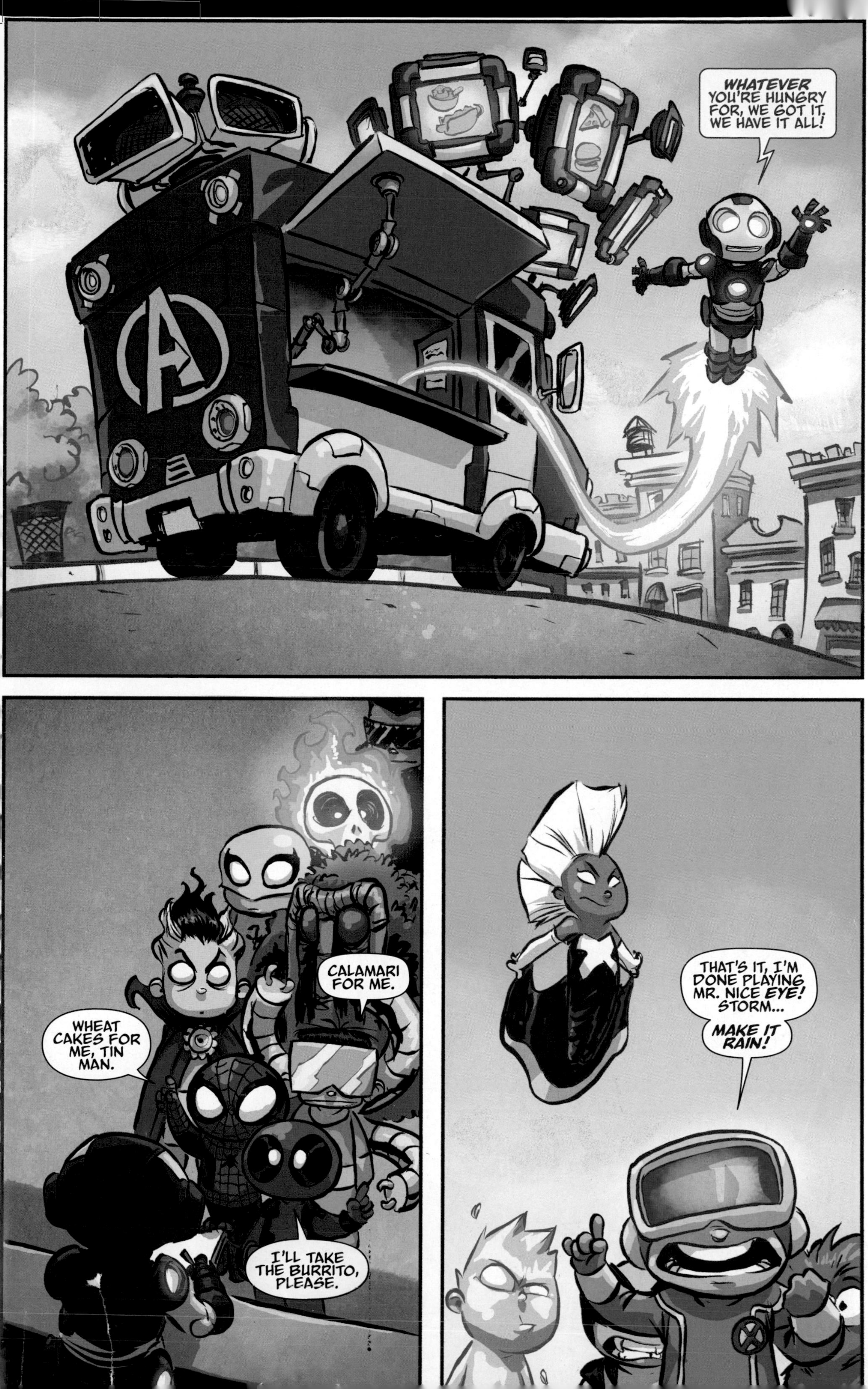
WHATEVER YOU'RE HUNGRY FOR, WE GOT IT. WE HAVE IT ALL!
WHEAT CAKES FOR ME, TIN MAN.
CALAMARI FOR ME.
I'LL TAKE THE BURRITO, PLEASE.
THAT'S IT, I'M DONE PLAYING MR. NICE EYE! STORM...
MAKE IT RAIN!

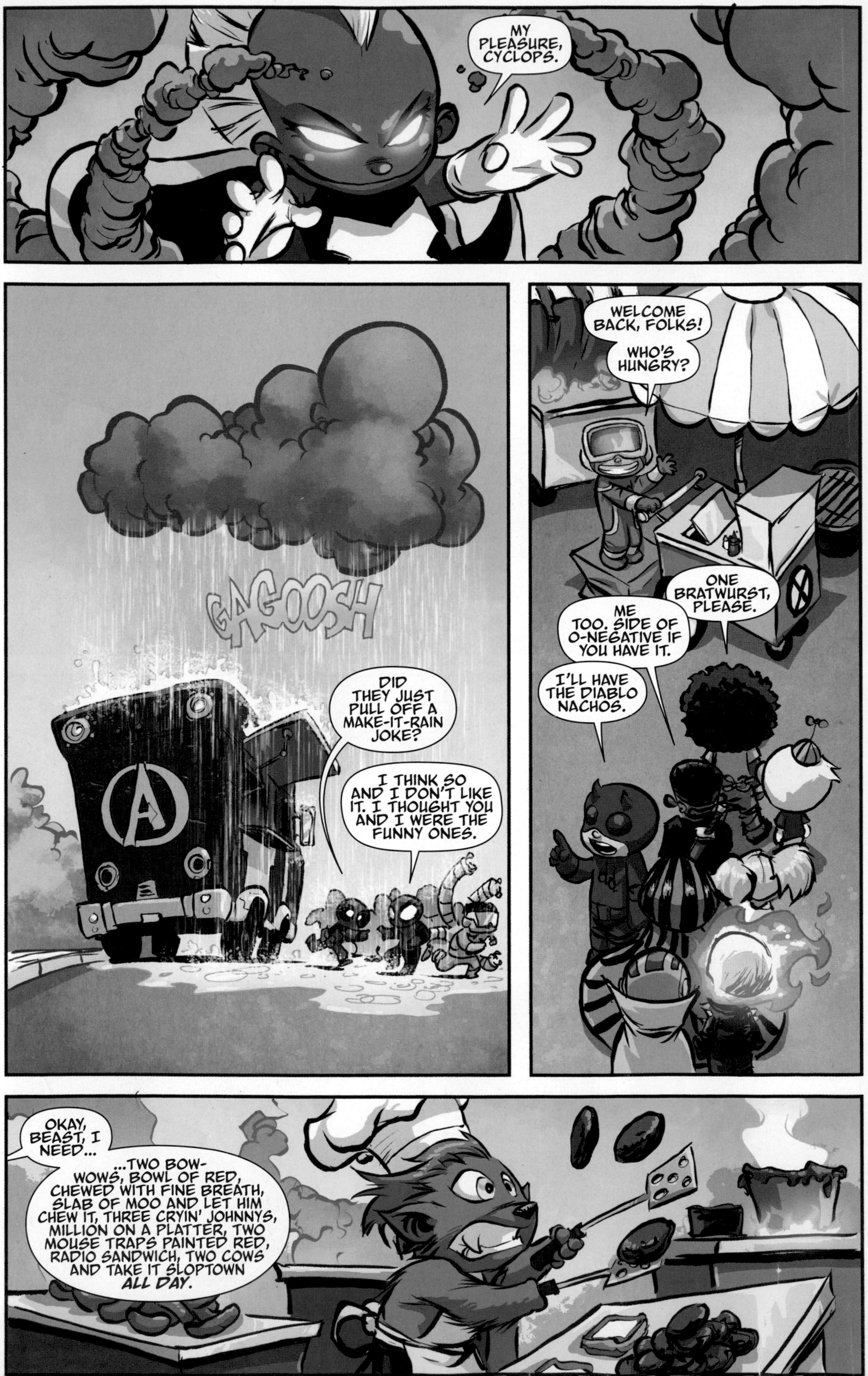
MY PLEASURE, CYCLOPS.
GAGOOSH
DID THEY JUST PULL OFF A MAKE-IT-RAIN JOKE?
I THINK SO AND I DON'T LIKE IT. I THOUGHT YOU AND I WERE THE FUNNY ONES.
WELCOME BACK, FOLKS!
WHO'S HUNGRY?
ONE BRATWURST, PLEASE.
ME TOO. SIDE OF O-NEGATIVE IF YOU HAVE IT.
I'LL HAVE THE DIABLO NACHOS.
OKAY, BEAST, I NEED...
...TWO BOW-WOWS, BOWL OF RED, CHEWED WITH FINE BREATH, SLAB OF MOO AND LET HIM CHEW IT, THREE CRYIN' JOHNNYS, MILLION ON A PLATTER, TWO MOUSE TRAPS PAINTED RED, RADIO SANDWICH, TWO COWS AND TAKE IT SLOPTOWN ALL DAY.

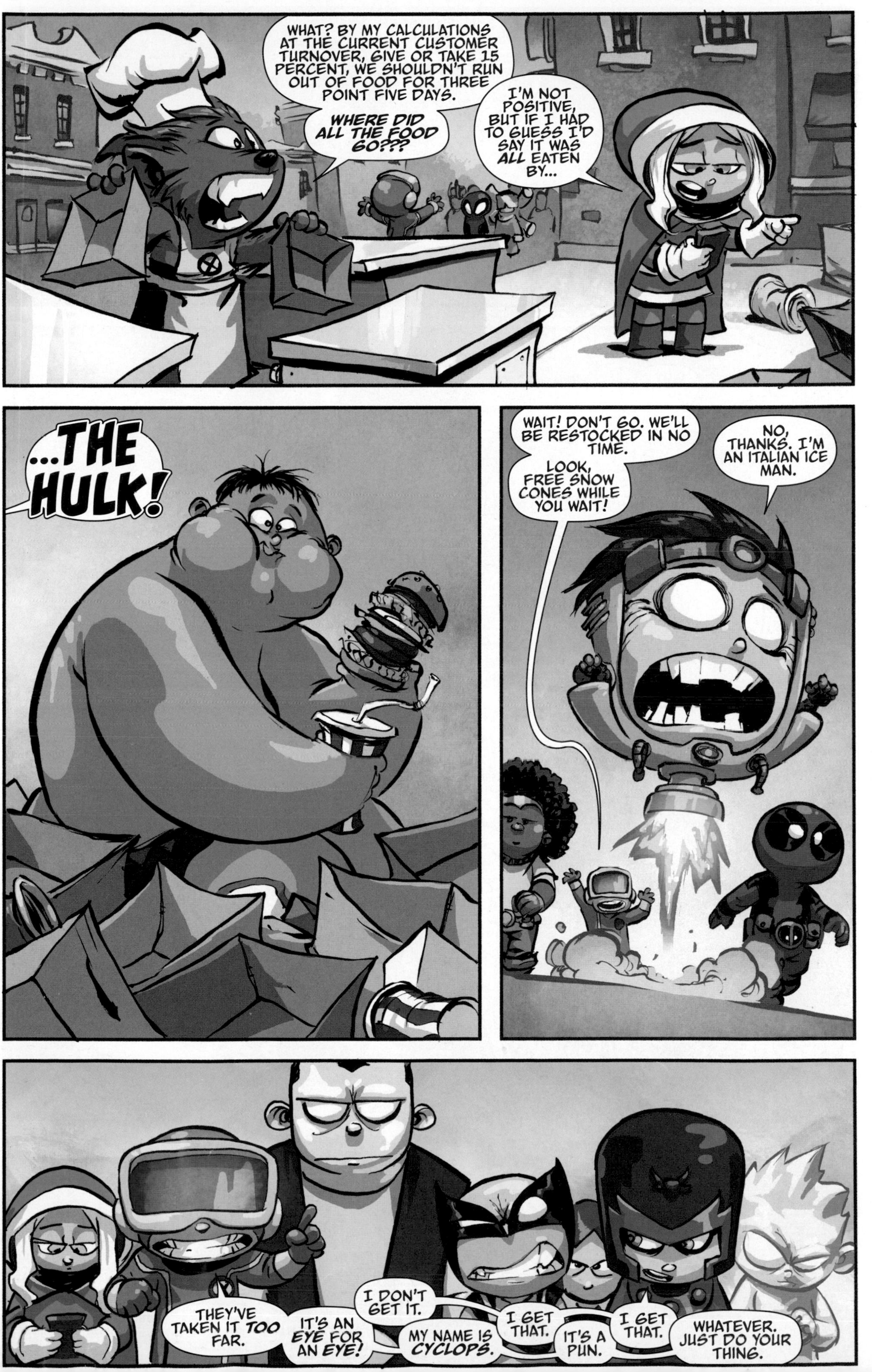
WHAT? BY MY CALCULATIONS AT THE CURRENT CUSTOMER TURNOVER, GIVE OR TAKE 15 PERCENT, WE SHOULDN'T RUN OUT OF FOOD FOR THREE POINT FIVE DAYS.
WHERE DID ALL THE FOOD GO???
I'M NOT POSITIVE, BUT IF I HAD TO GUESS I'D SAY IT WAS ALL EATEN BY...
...THE HULK!
WAIT! DON'T GO. WE'LL BE RESTOCKED IN NO TIME.
LOOK, FREE SNOW CONES WHILE YOU WAIT!
NO, THANKS. I'M AN ITALIAN ICE MAN.
THEY'VE TAKEN IT TOO FAR.
IT'S AN EYE FOR AN EYE!
I DON'T GET IT.
MY NAME IS CYCLOPS.
I GET THAT.
IT'S A PUN.
I GET THAT.
WHATEVER. JUST DO YOUR THING.

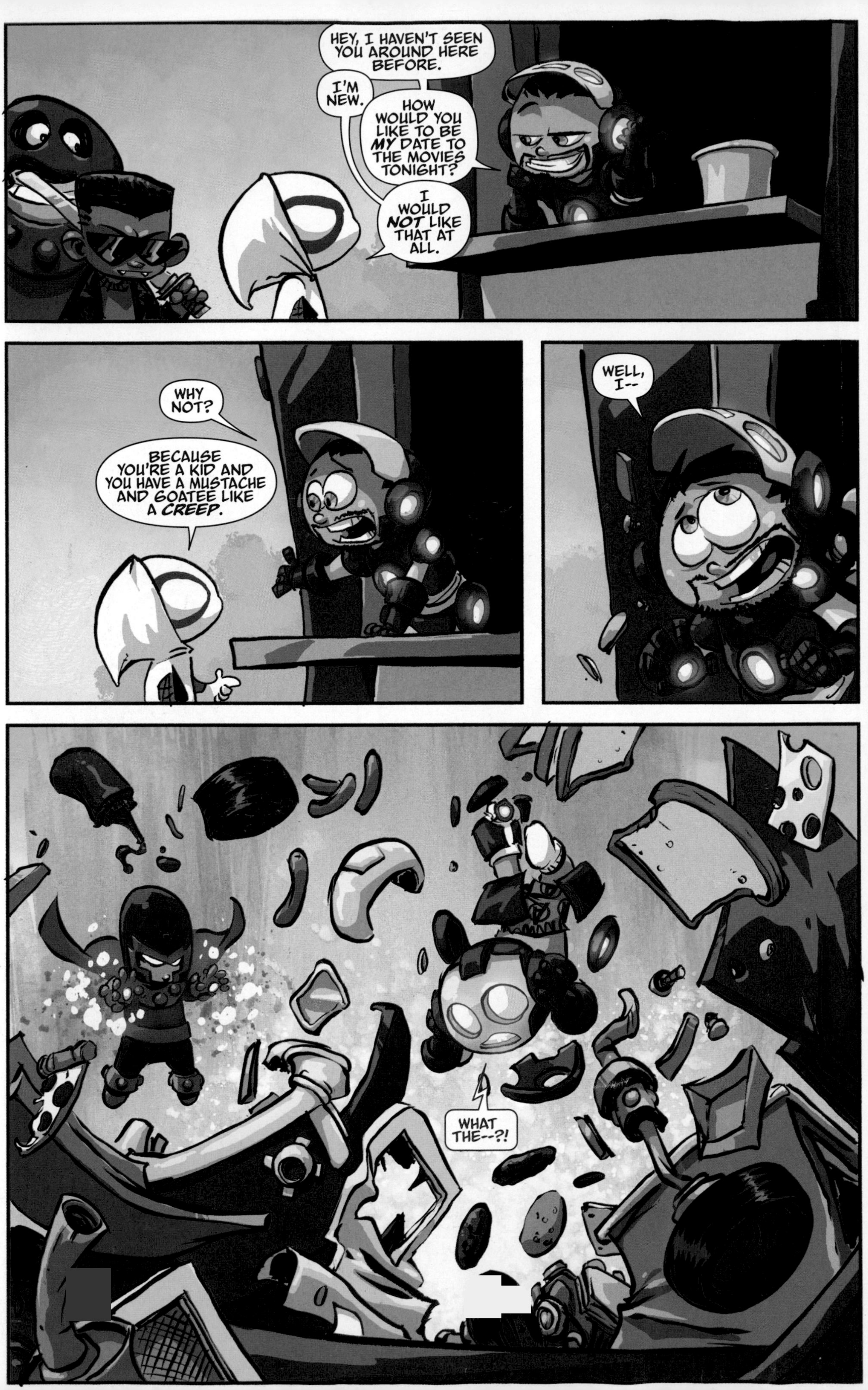

HEY, I HAVEN'T SEEN YOU AROUND HERE BEFORE.
I'M NEW.
HOW WOULD YOU LIKE TO BE MY DATE TO THE MOVIES TONIGHT?
I WOULD NOT LIKE THAT AT ALL.
WHY NOT?
BECAUSE YOU'RE A KID AND YOU HAVE A MUSTACHE AND GOATEE LIKE A CREEP.
WELL, I--
WHAT THE--?!

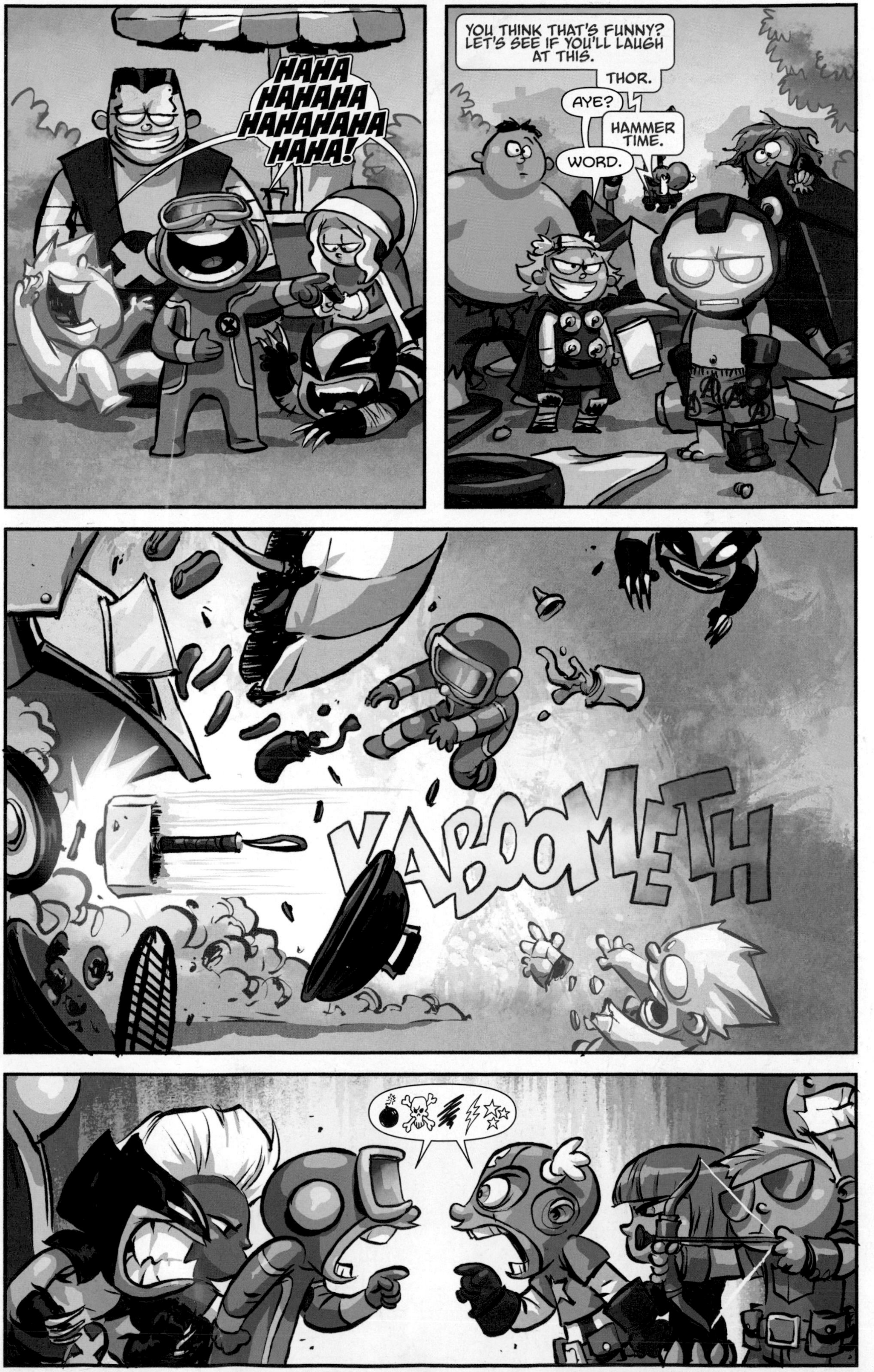
HAHA
HAHAHA
HAHAHAHA
HAHA!
YOU THINK THAT'S FUNNY? LET'S SEE IF YOU'LL LAUGH AT THIS.
THOR.
AYE?
HAMMER TIME.
WORD.
KABOOMETH

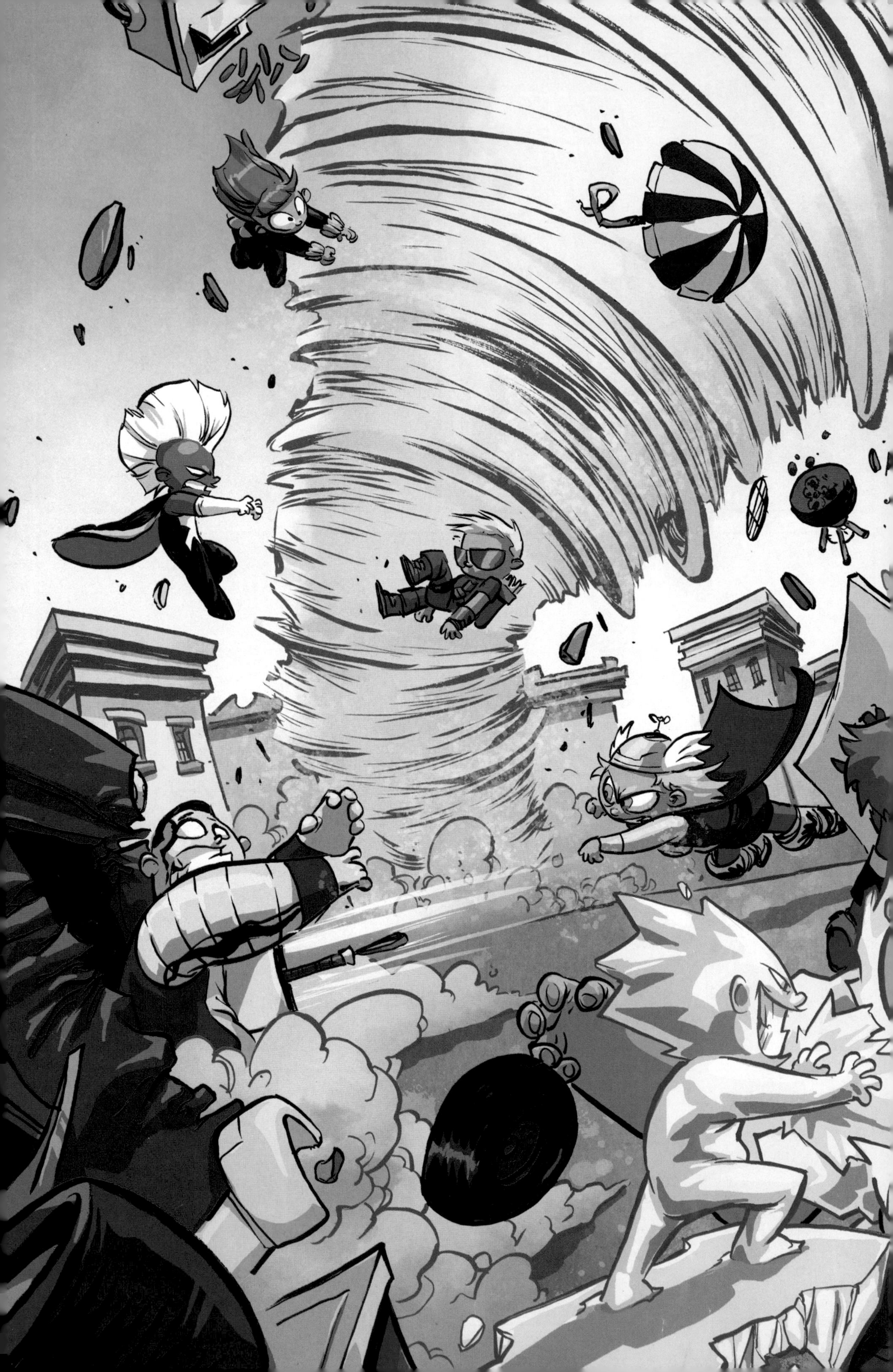

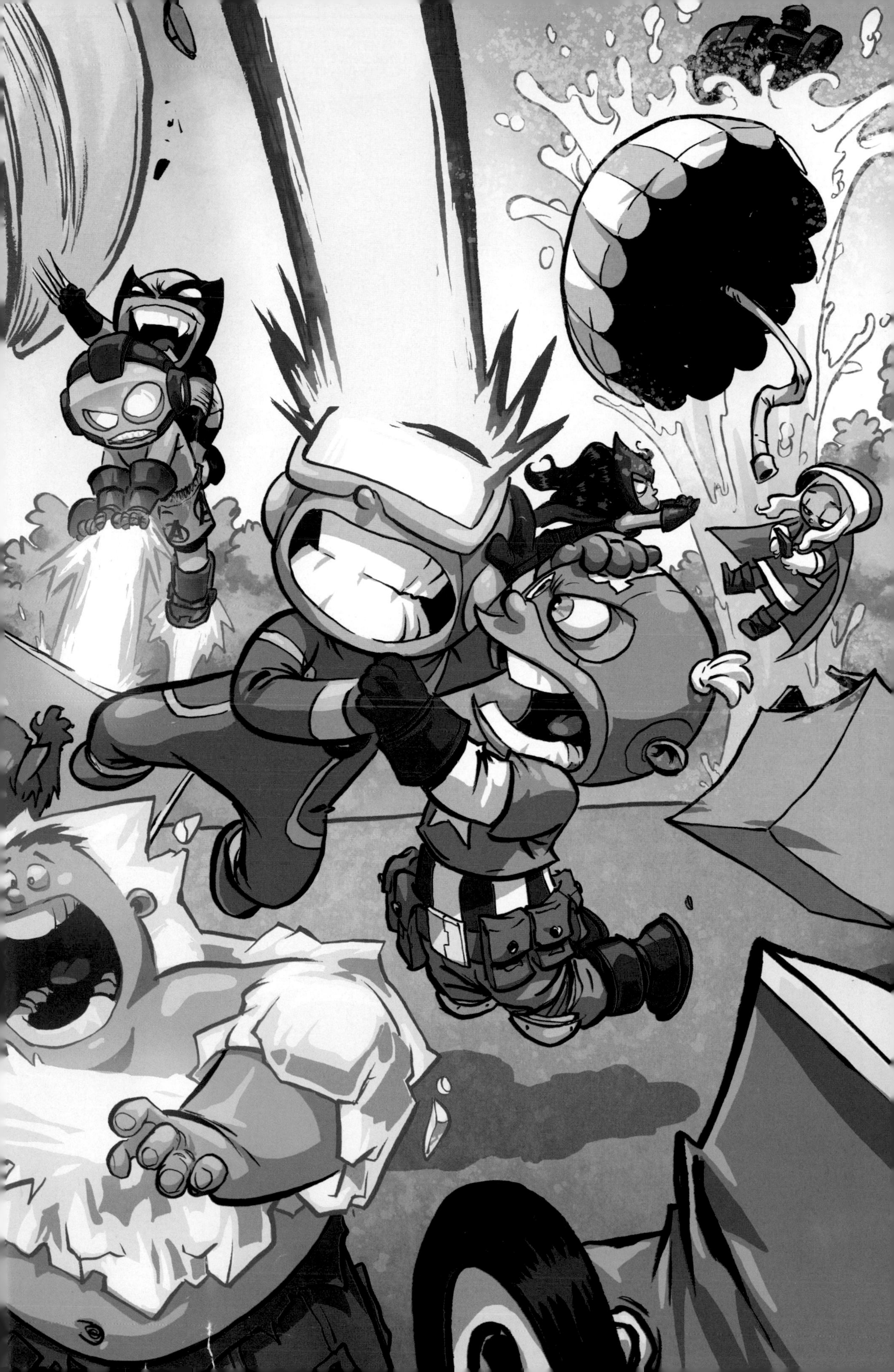

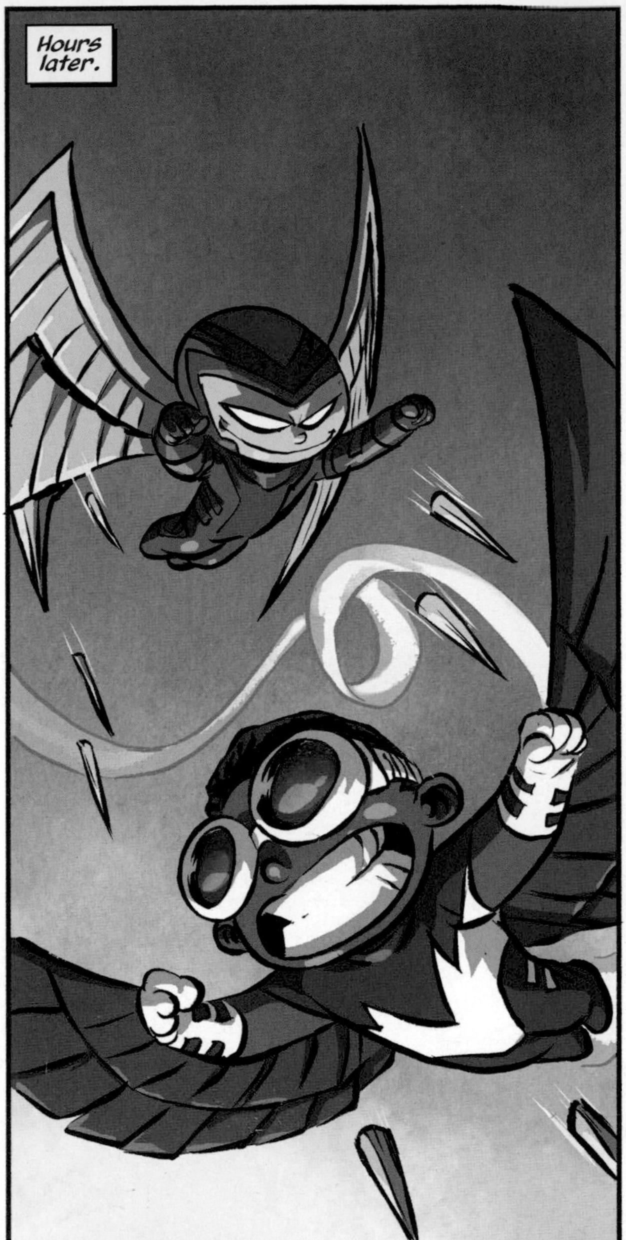
Hours later.

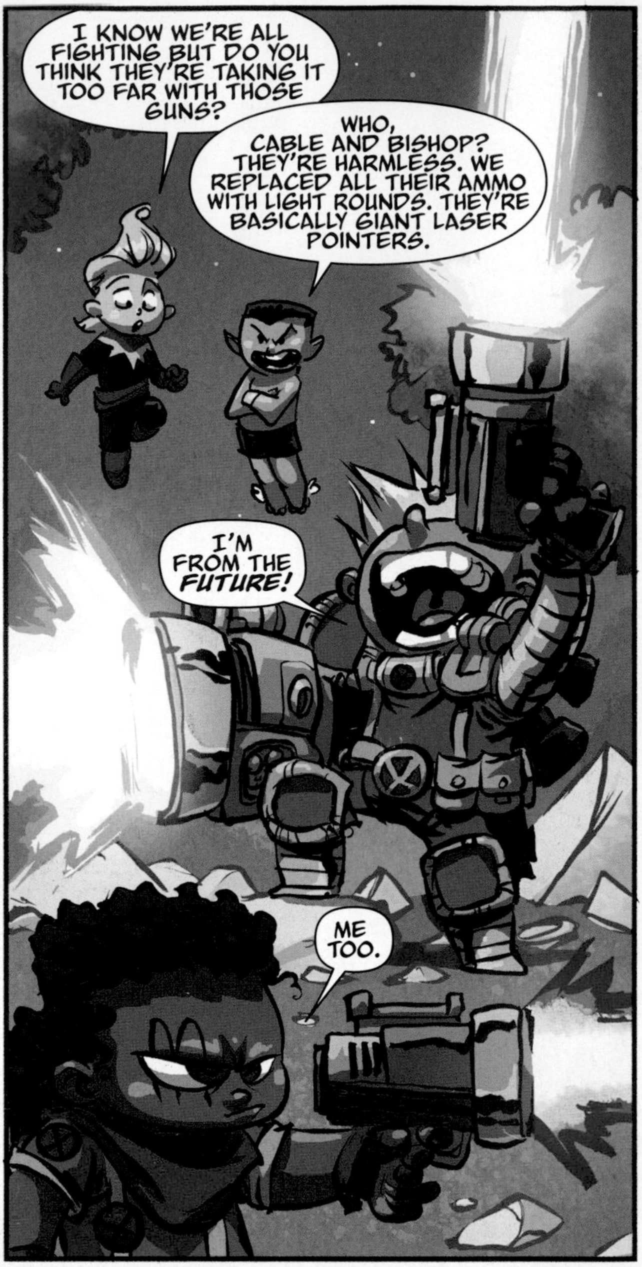
I KNOW WE'RE ALL FIGHTING BUT DO YOU THINK THEY'RE TAKING IT TOO FAR WITH THOSE GUNS?
WHO, CABLE AND BISHOP? THEY'RE HARMLESS. WE REPLACED ALL THEIR AMMO WITH LIGHT ROUNDS. THEY'RE BASICALLY GIANT LASER POINTERS.
I'M FROM THE *FUTURE!*
ME TOO.

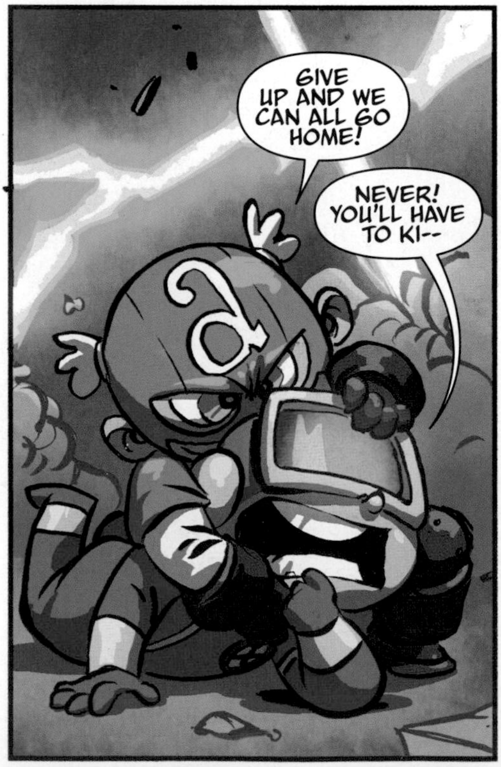
GIVE UP AND WE CAN ALL GO HOME!
NEVER! YOU'LL HAVE TO KI--

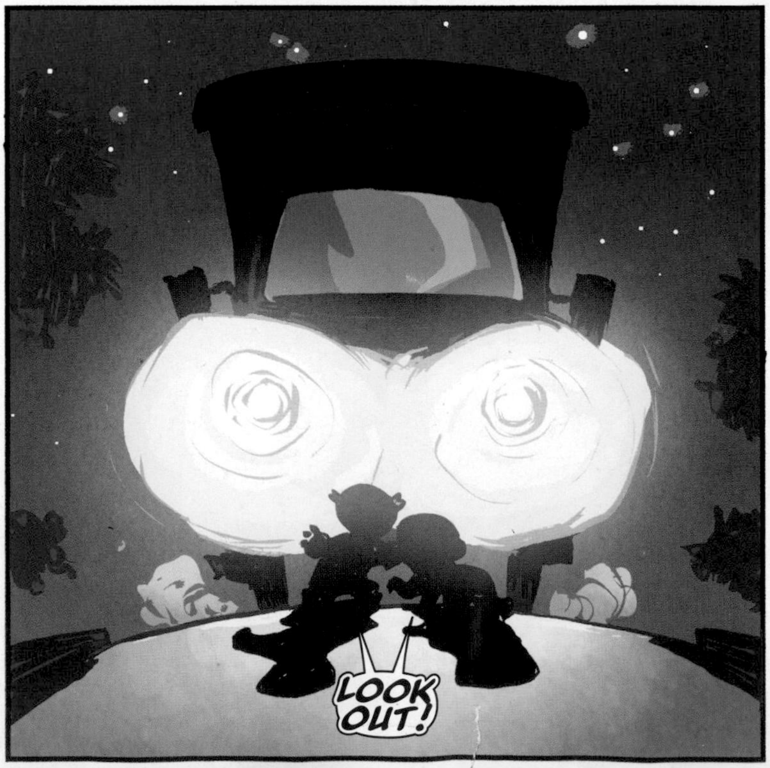
LOOK OUT!

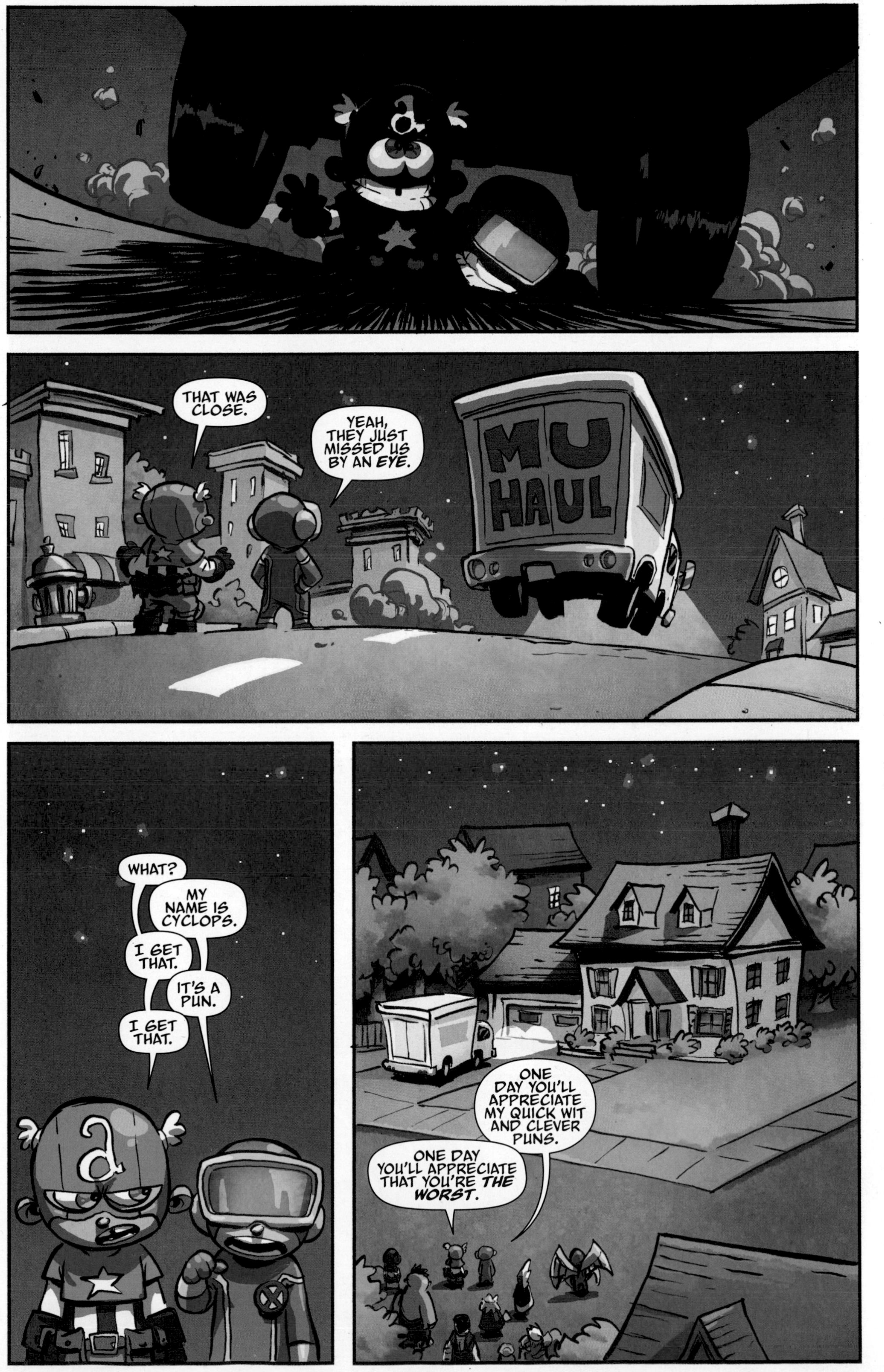
MU HAUL
THAT WAS CLOSE.
YEAH, THEY JUST MISSED US BY AN *EYE*.
WHAT?
MY NAME IS CYCLOPS.
I GET THAT.
IT'S A PUN.
I GET THAT.
ONE DAY YOU'LL APPRECIATE MY QUICK WIT AND CLEVER PUNS.
ONE DAY YOU'LL APPRECIATE THAT YOU'RE ***THE WORST***.

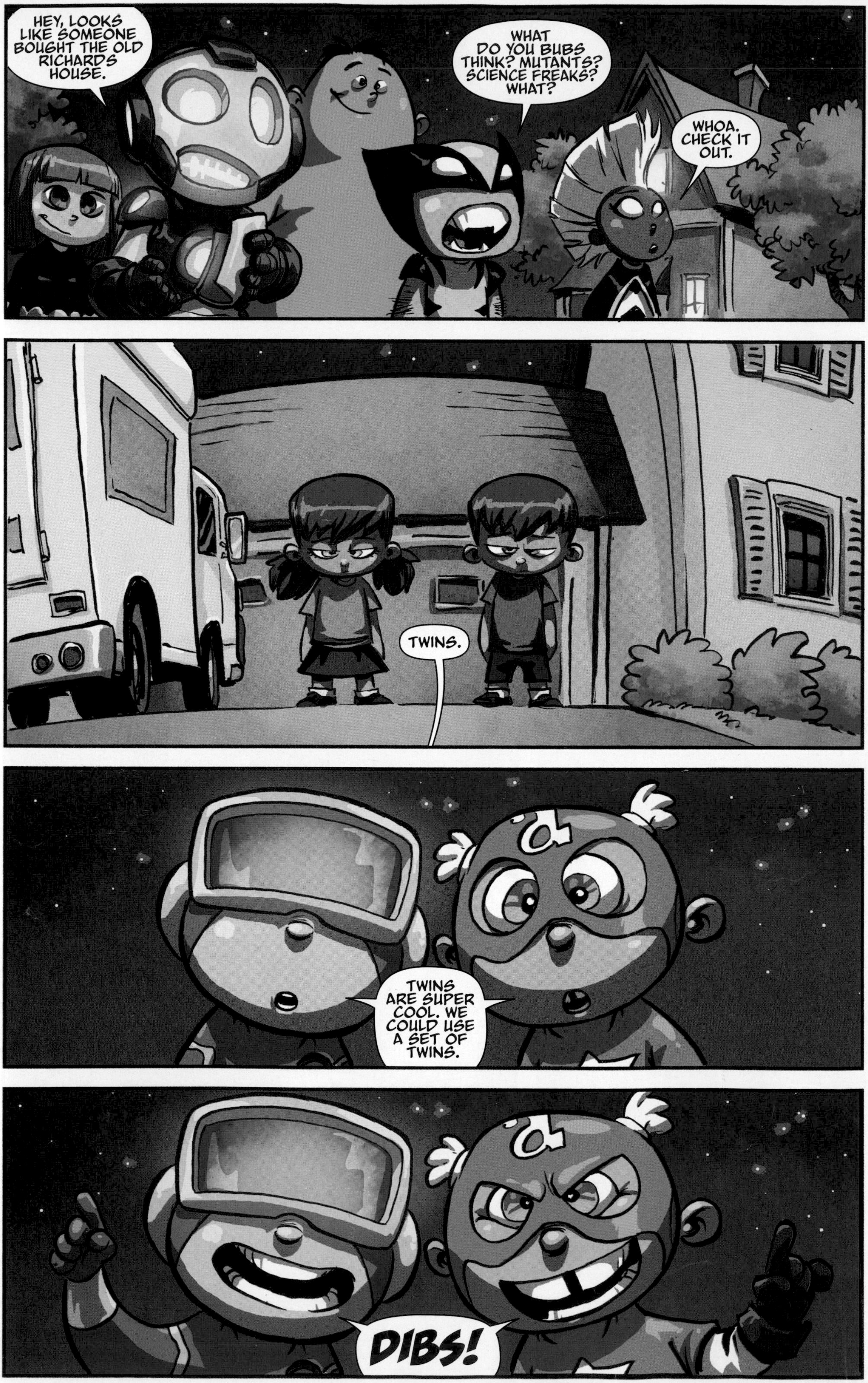
HEY, LOOKS LIKE SOMEONE BOUGHT THE OLD RICHARDS HOUSE.
WHAT DO YOU BUBS THINK? MUTANTS? SCIENCE FREAKS? WHAT?
WHOA. CHECK IT OUT.
TWINS.
TWINS ARE SUPER COOL. WE COULD USE A SET OF TWINS.
DIBS!

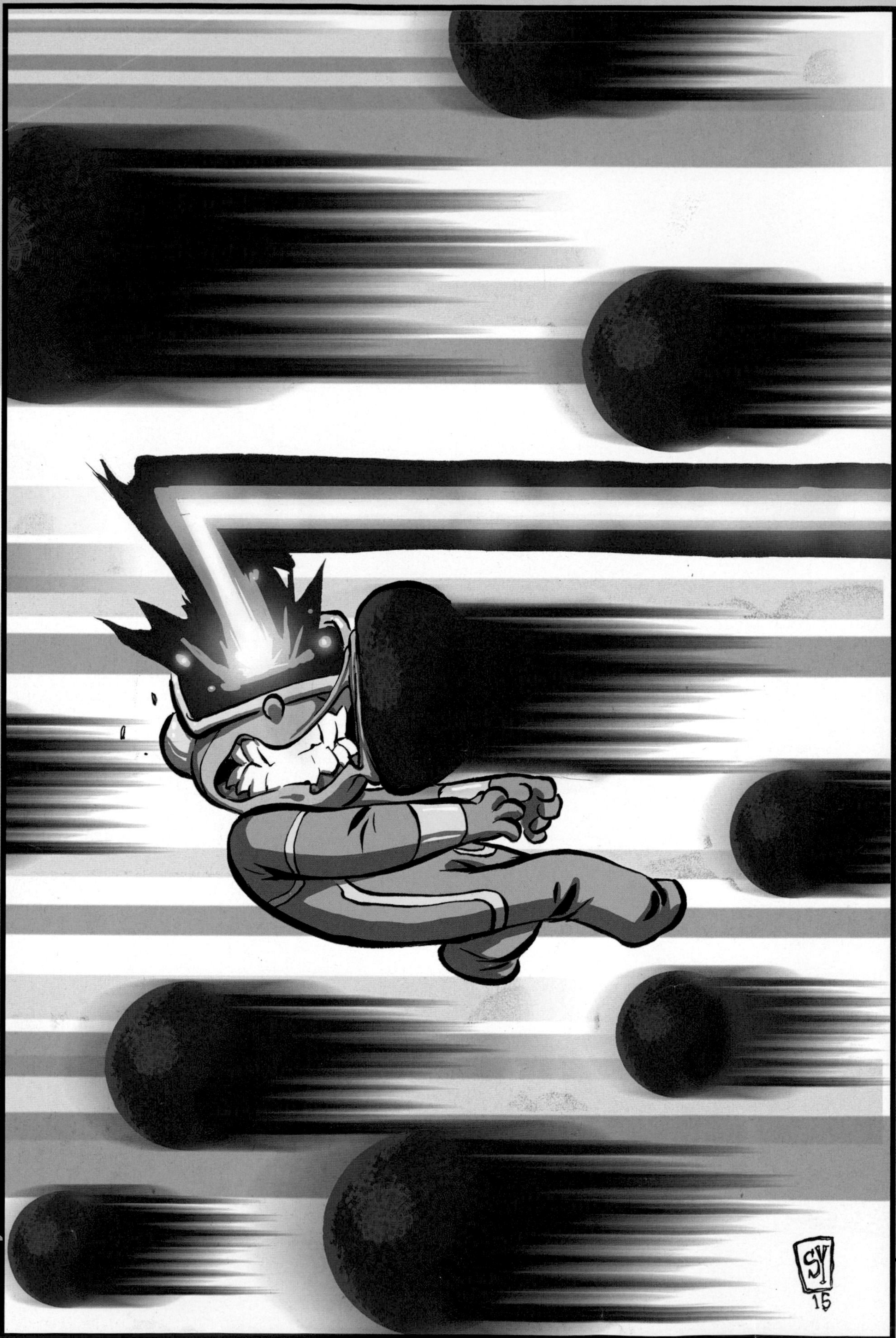
SY
15

GIANT-SIZE LITTLE MARVEL: AVX #2

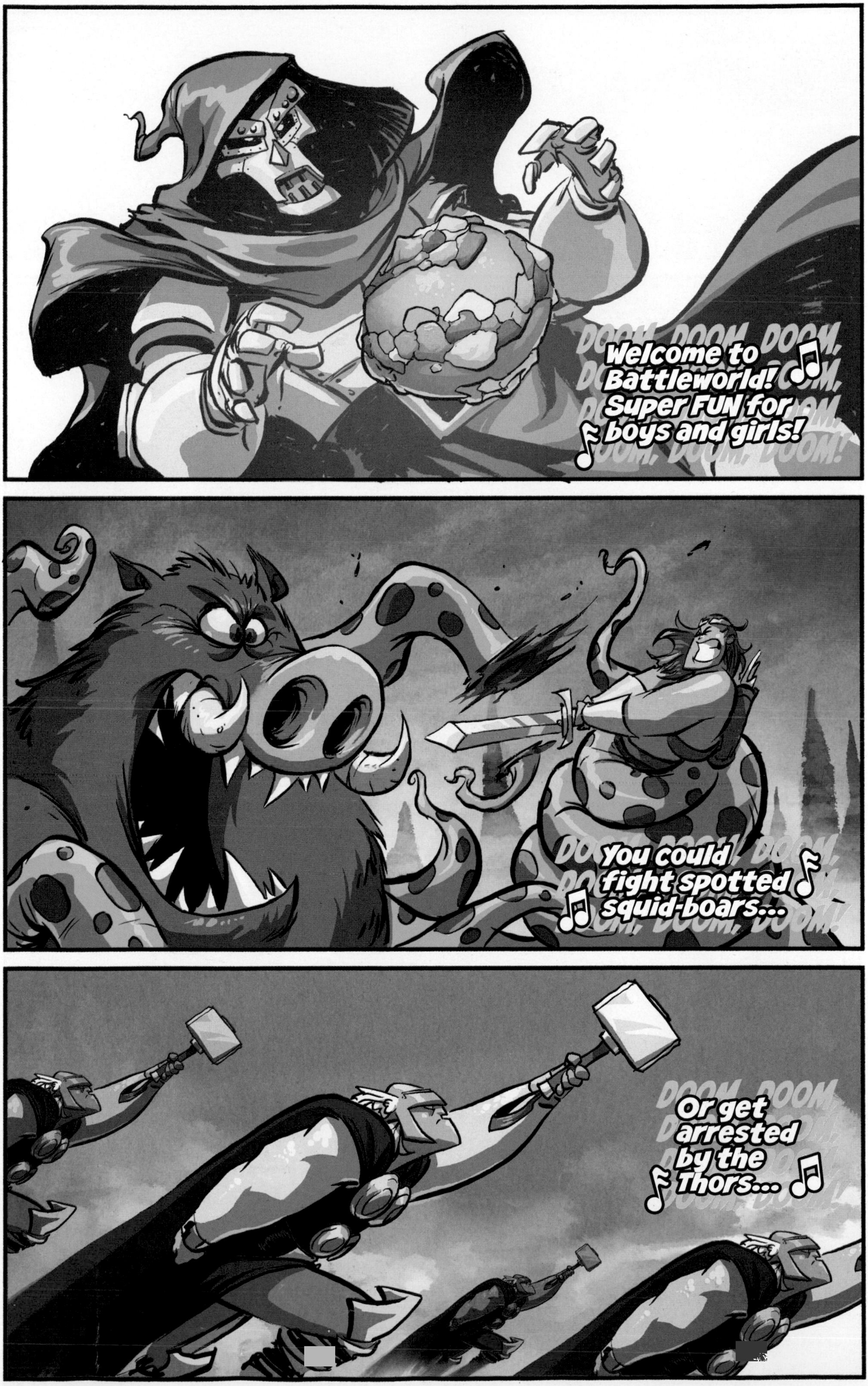
Welcome to Battleworld! Super FUN for boys and girls!
You could fight spotted squid-boars...
Or get arrested by the Thors...

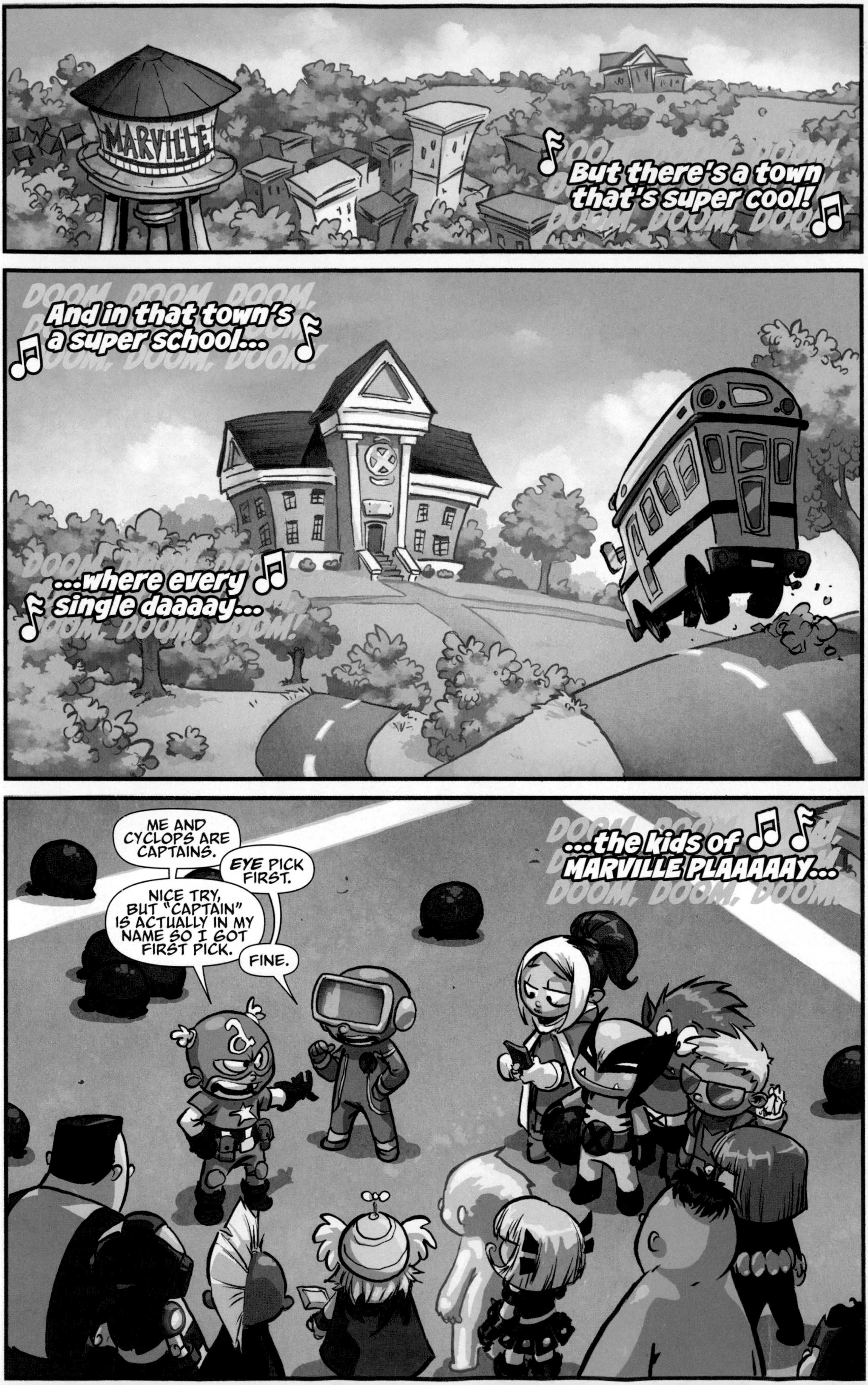
MARVILLE
But there's a town that's super cool!
DOOM, DOOM, DOOM,
And in that town's a super school...
...where every single daaaay...
...the kids of MARVILLE PLAAAAAY...
ME AND CYCLOPS ARE CAPTAINS.
EYE PICK FIRST.
NICE TRY, BUT "CAPTAIN" IS ACTUALLY IN MY NAME SO I GOT FIRST PICK.
FINE.

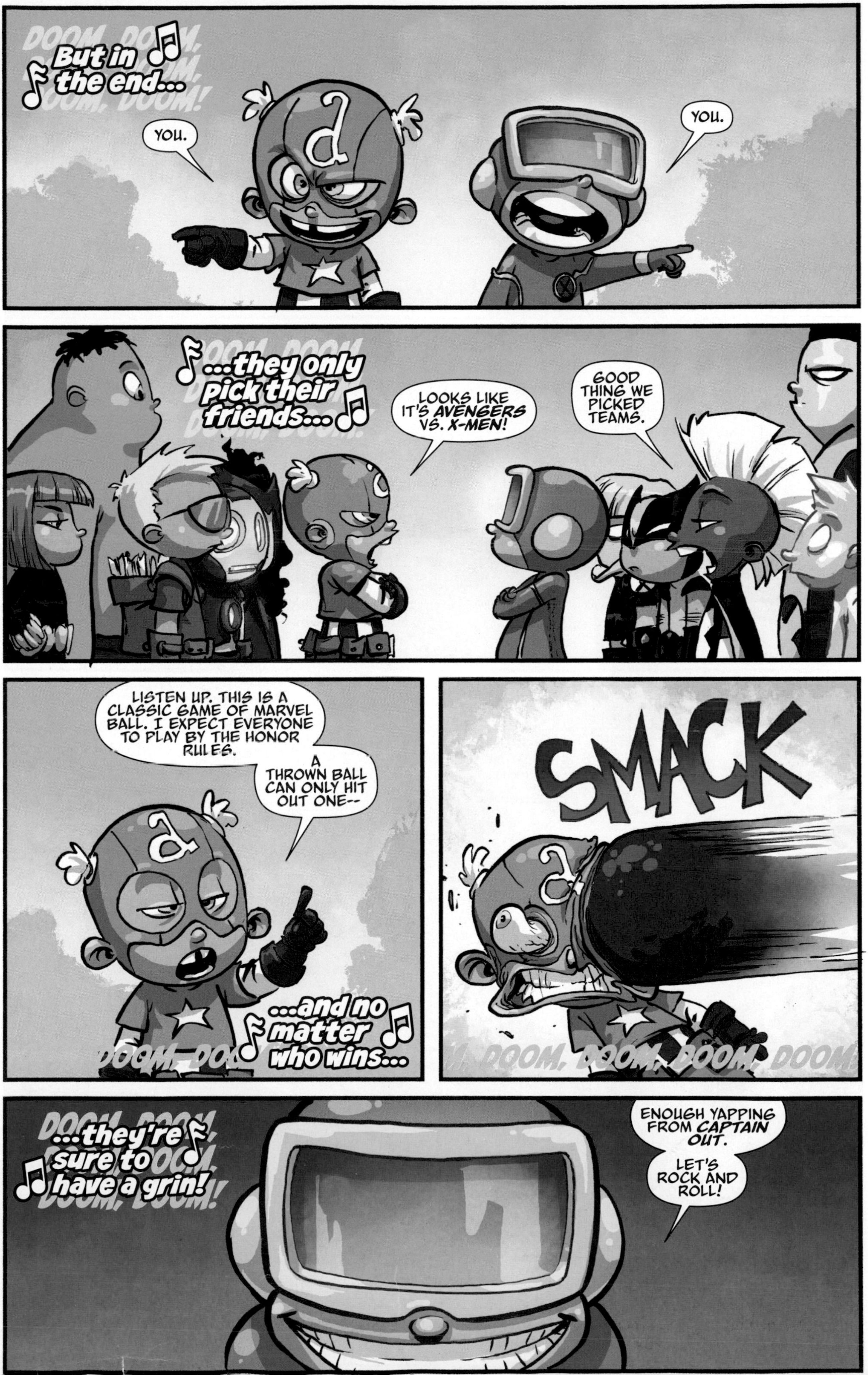
DOOM, DOOM, DOOM, DOOM, DOOM, DOOM!
But in the end...
YOU.
YOU.
...they only pick their friends...
LOOKS LIKE IT'S AVENGERS VS. X-MEN!
GOOD THING WE PICKED TEAMS.
LISTEN UP. THIS IS A CLASSIC GAME OF MARVEL BALL. I EXPECT EVERYONE TO PLAY BY THE HONOR RULES.
A THROWN BALL CAN ONLY HIT OUT ONE--
...and no matter who wins...
SMACK
DOOM, DOOM, DOOM, DOOM!
...they're sure to have a grin!
ENOUGH YAPPING FROM CAPTAIN OUT.
LET'S ROCK AND ROLL!

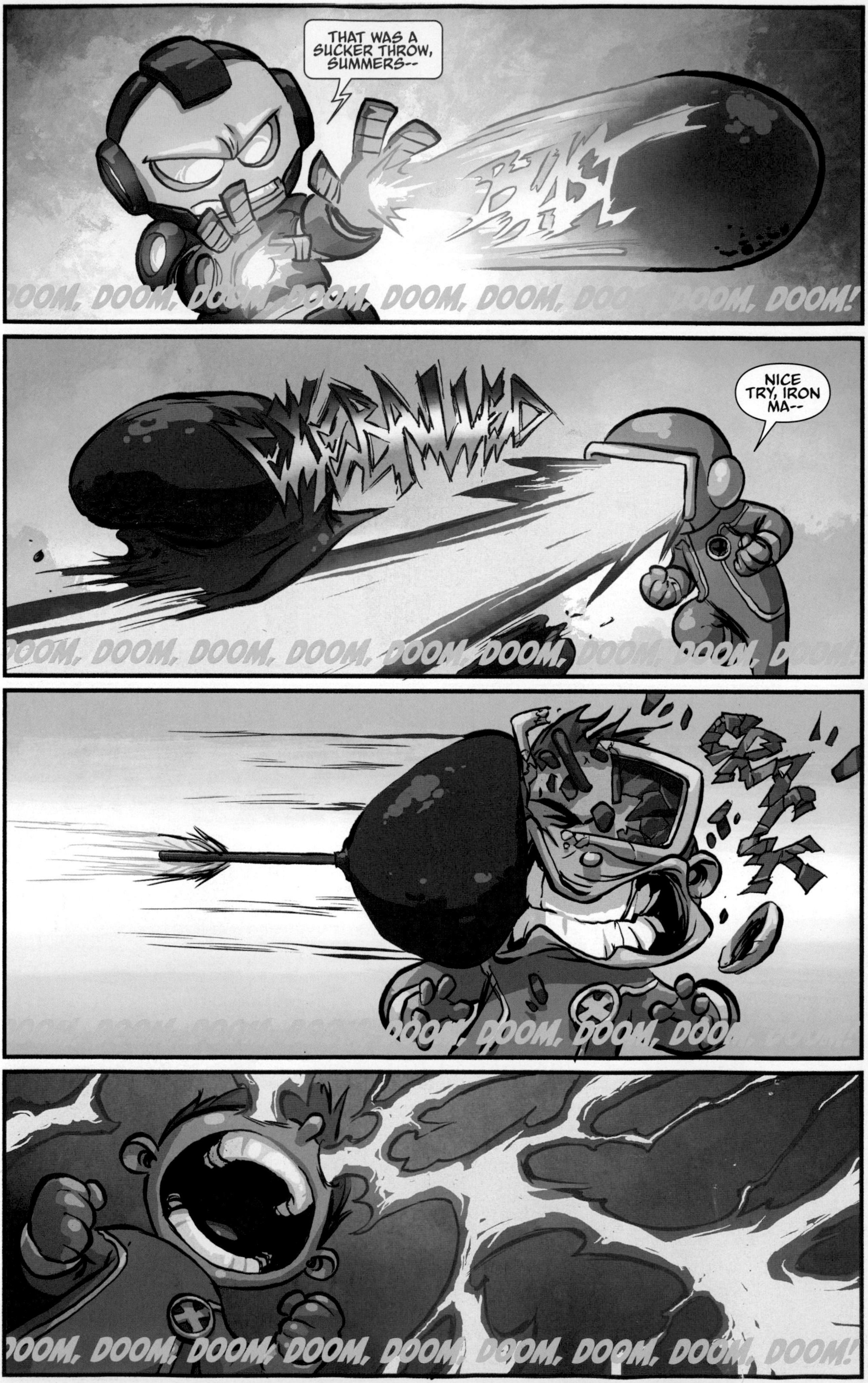
THAT WAS A SUCKER THROW, SUMMERS--
NICE TRY, IRON MA--

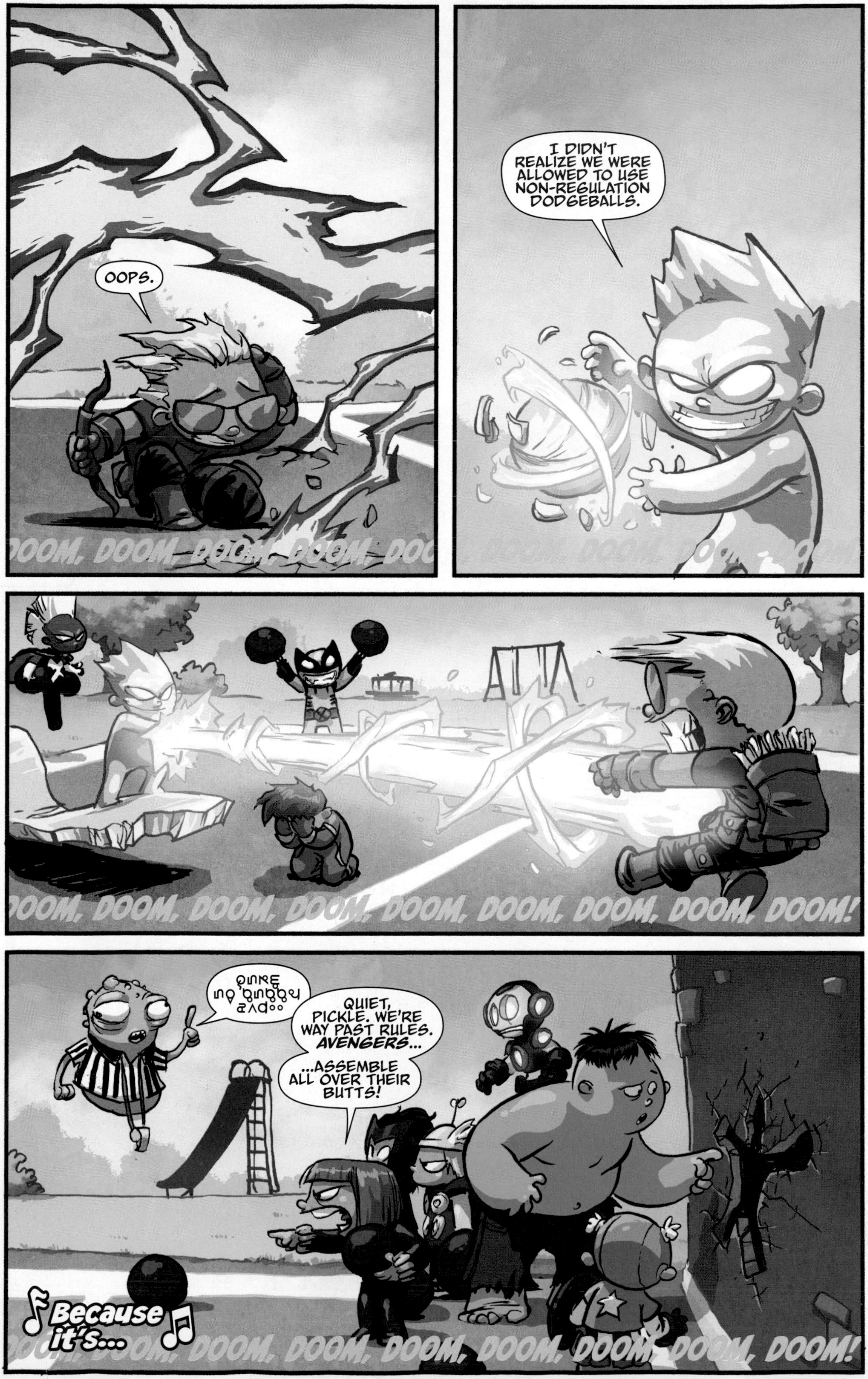
OOPS.
DOOM, DOOM, DOOM, DOOM, DOO
I DIDN'T REALIZE WE WERE ALLOWED TO USE NON-REGULATION DODGEBALLS.
DOOM, DOOM, DOOM, DOOM, DOOM, DOOM, DOOM, DOOM, DOOM!
QUIET, PICKLE. WE'RE WAY PAST RULES. AVENGERS...
...ASSEMBLE ALL OVER THEIR BUTTS!
Because it's...
DOOM, DOOM, DOOM, DOOM, DOOM, DOOM, DOOM, DOOM!

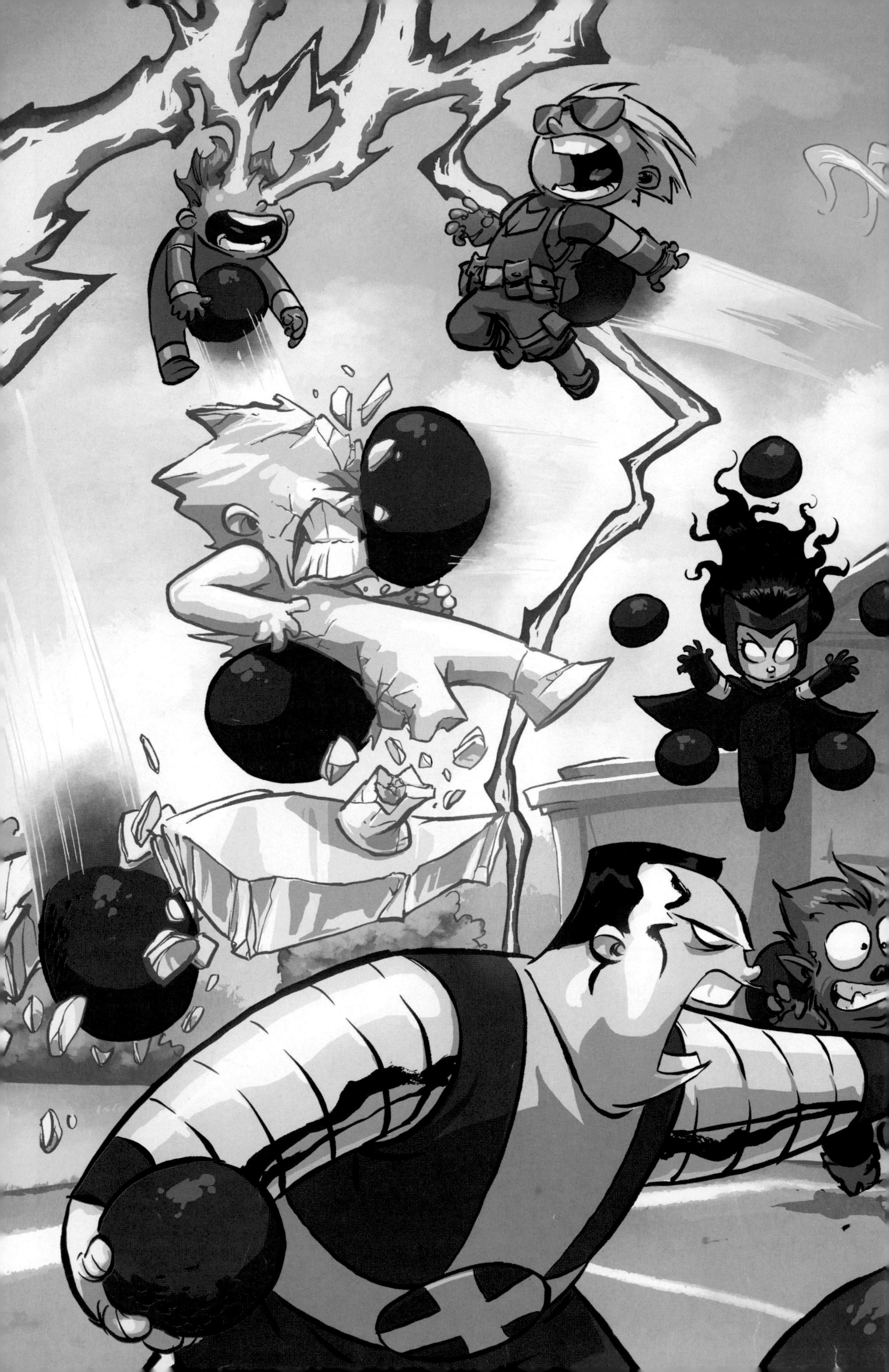

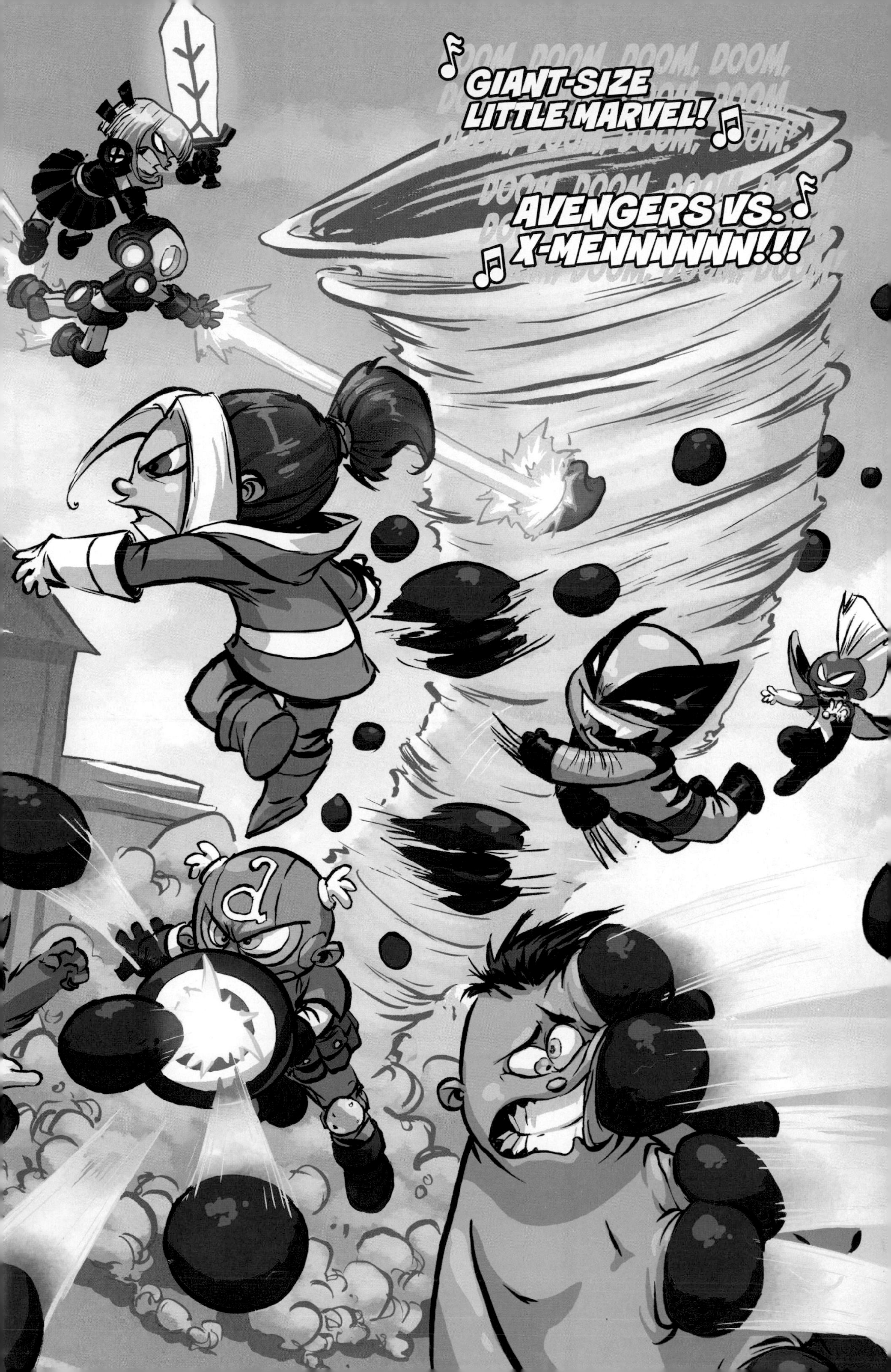
GIANT-SIZE LITTLE MARVEL!
AVENGERS VS. X-MENNNNNNN!!!

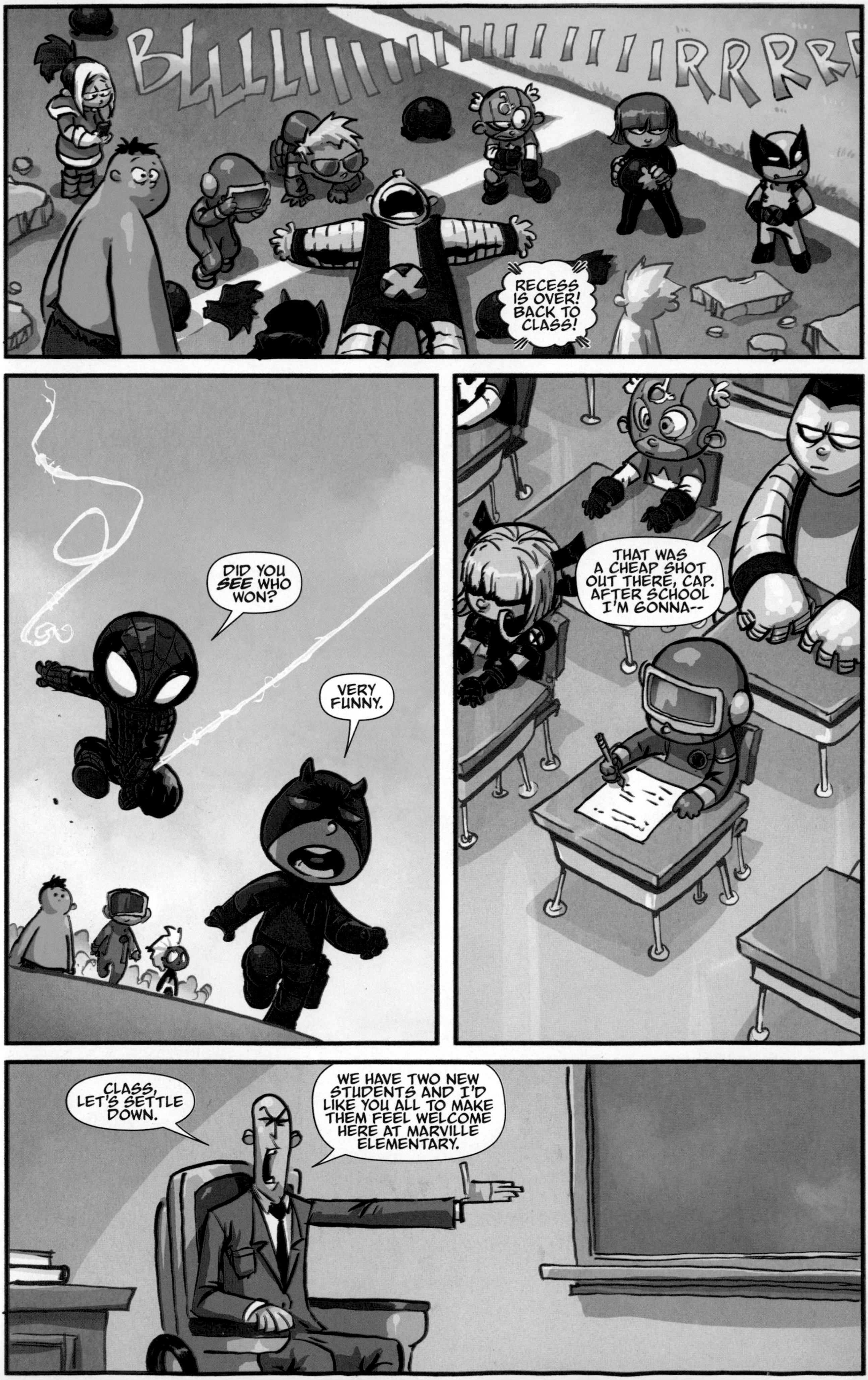
BLLLIIIIIIIIIIIIIIRRRRR
RECESS IS OVER! BACK TO CLASS!
DID YOU SEE WHO WON?
VERY FUNNY.
THAT WAS A CHEAP SHOT OUT THERE, CAP. AFTER SCHOOL I'M GONNA--
CLASS, LET'S SETTLE DOWN.
WE HAVE TWO NEW STUDENTS AND I'D LIKE YOU ALL TO MAKE THEM FEEL WELCOME HERE AT MARVILLE ELEMENTARY.

MEET ZACHARY AND ZOE.

I'D LIKE YOU ALL TO TAKE A FEW MINUTES TO GET TO KNOW EACH OTHER.

SO, WHO HAS QUESTIONS?

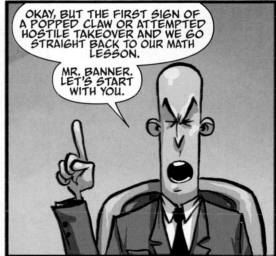

OKAY, BUT THE FIRST SIGN OF A POPPED CLAW OR ATTEMPTED HOSTILE TAKEOVER AND WE GO STRAIGHT BACK TO OUR MATH LESSON.

MR. BANNER. LET'S START WITH YOU.

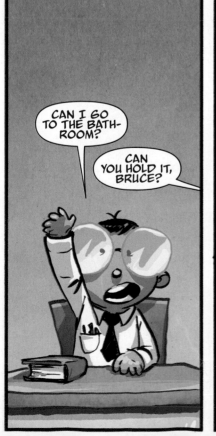

CAN I GO TO THE BATH-ROOM?

CAN YOU HOLD IT, BRUCE?

I'LL TAKE THAT AS A NO. COME GET A HALL PASS.

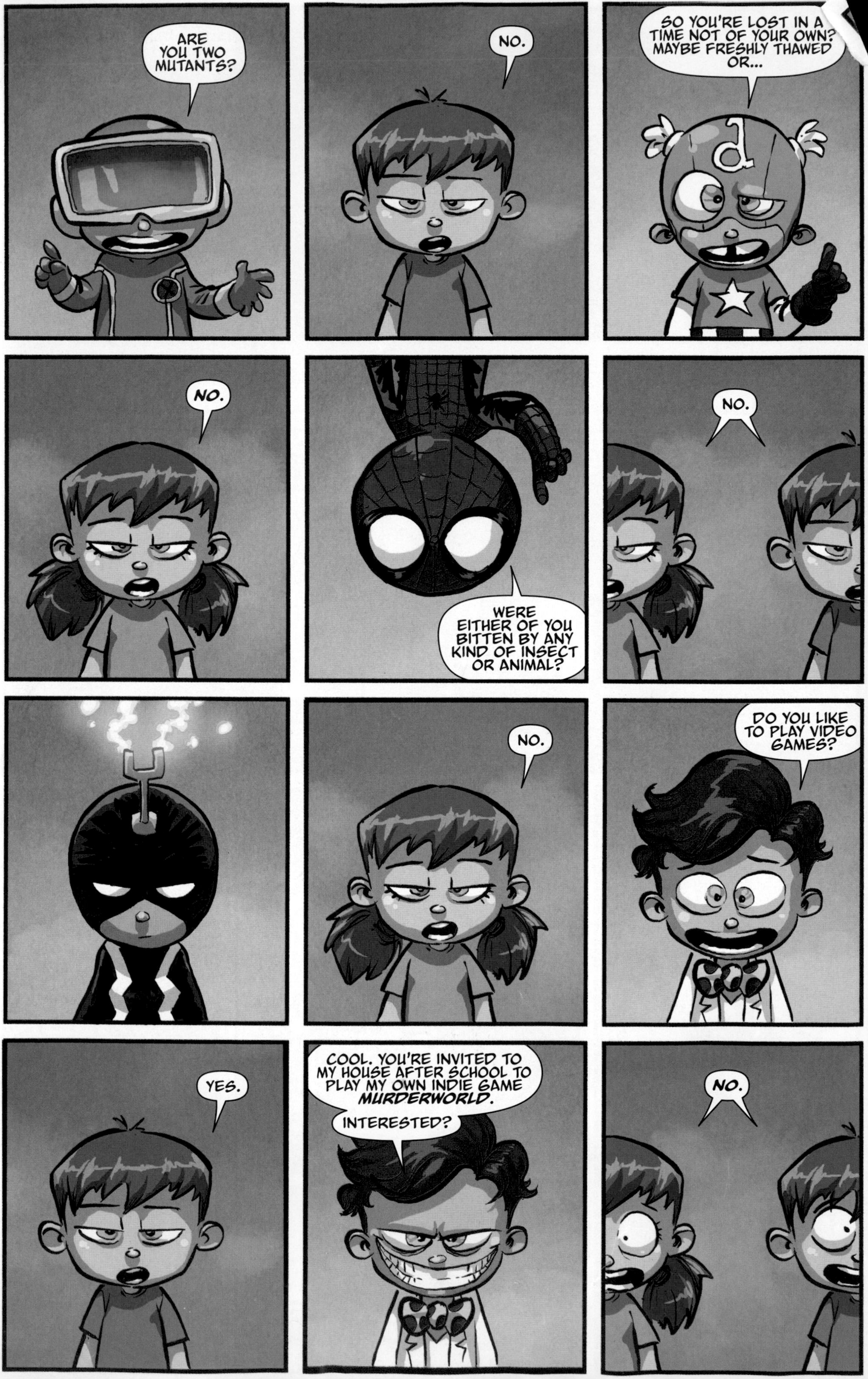
ARE YOU TWO MUTANTS?
NO.
SO YOU'RE LOST IN A TIME NOT OF YOUR OWN? MAYBE FRESHLY THAWED OR...
NO.
WERE EITHER OF YOU BITTEN BY ANY KIND OF INSECT OR ANIMAL?
NO.
NO.
DO YOU LIKE TO PLAY VIDEO GAMES?
YES.
COOL. YOU'RE INVITED TO MY HOUSE AFTER SCHOOL TO PLAY MY OWN INDIE GAME MURDERWORLD.
INTERESTED?
NO.

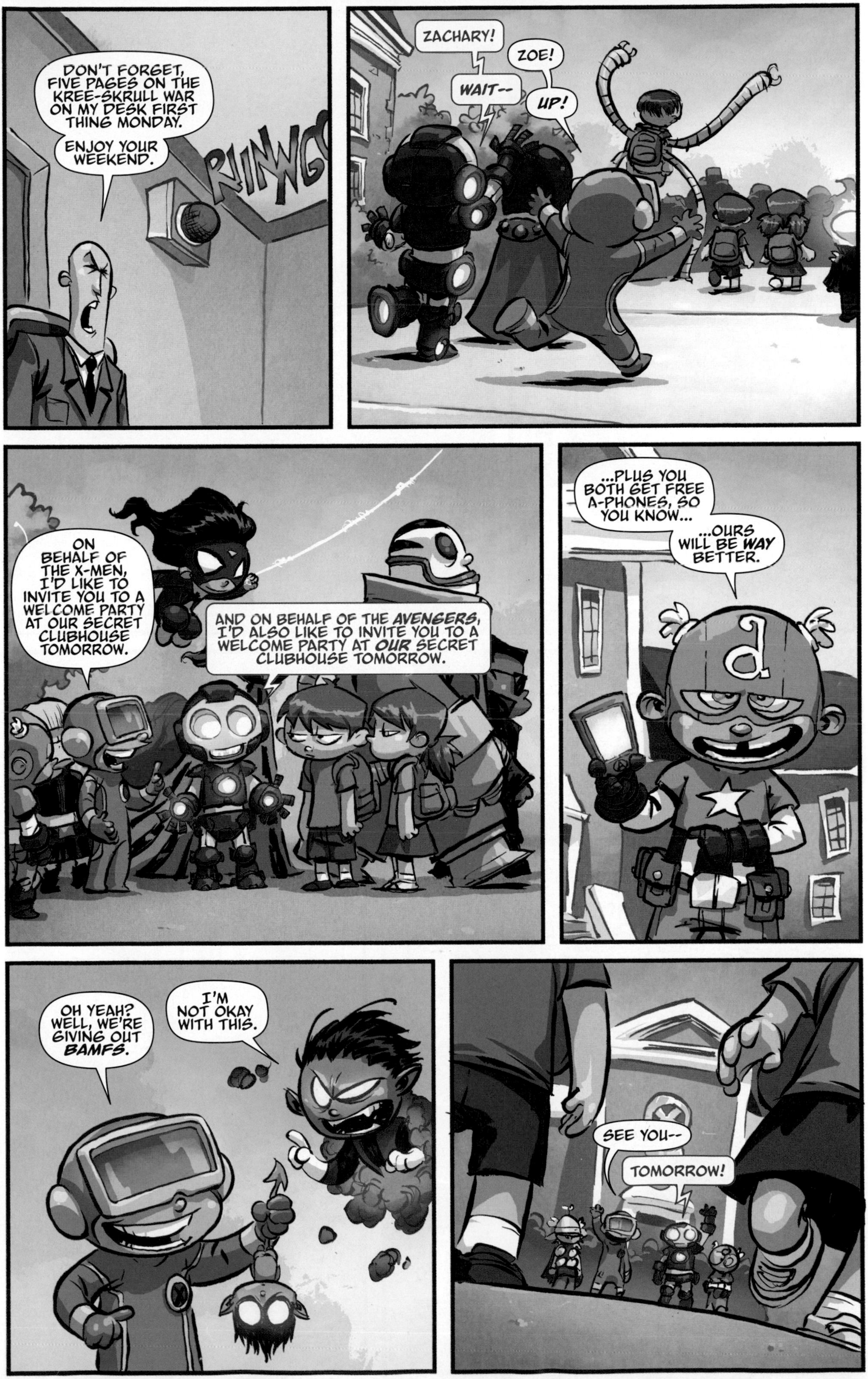
DON'T FORGET, FIVE PAGES ON THE KREE-SKRULL WAR ON MY DESK FIRST THING MONDAY.
ENJOY YOUR WEEKEND.
RINNNG
ZACHARY!
WAIT--
ZOE!
UP!
ON BEHALF OF THE X-MEN, I'D LIKE TO INVITE YOU TO A WELCOME PARTY AT OUR SECRET CLUBHOUSE TOMORROW.
AND ON BEHALF OF THE *AVENGERS*, I'D ALSO LIKE TO INVITE YOU TO A WELCOME PARTY AT *OUR* SECRET CLUBHOUSE TOMORROW.
...PLUS YOU BOTH GET FREE A-PHONES, SO YOU KNOW...
...OURS WILL BE *WAY* BETTER.
OH YEAH? WELL, WE'RE GIVING OUT *BAMFS*.
I'M NOT OKAY WITH THIS.
SEE YOU--
TOMORROW!

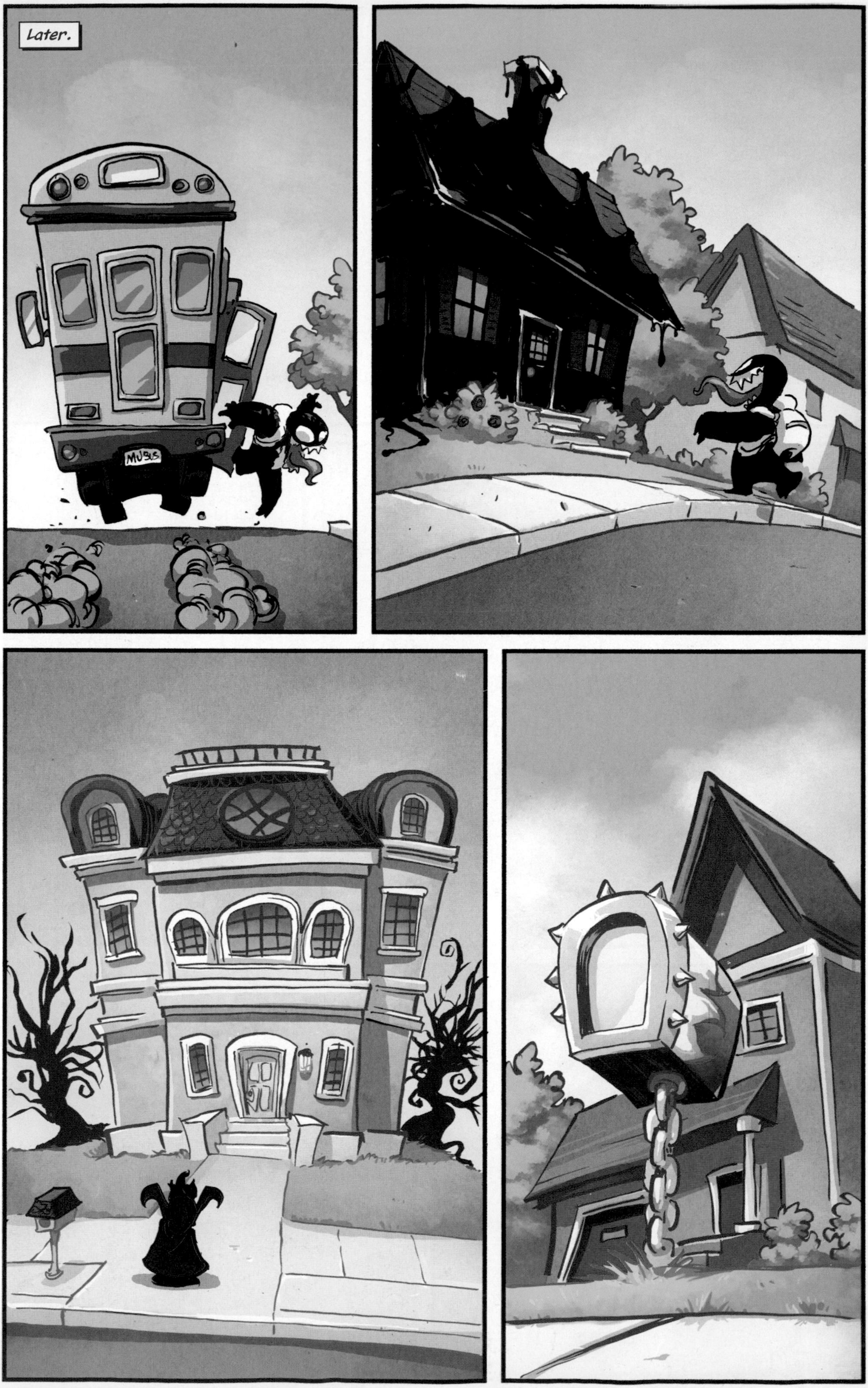

Later.
MUBUS

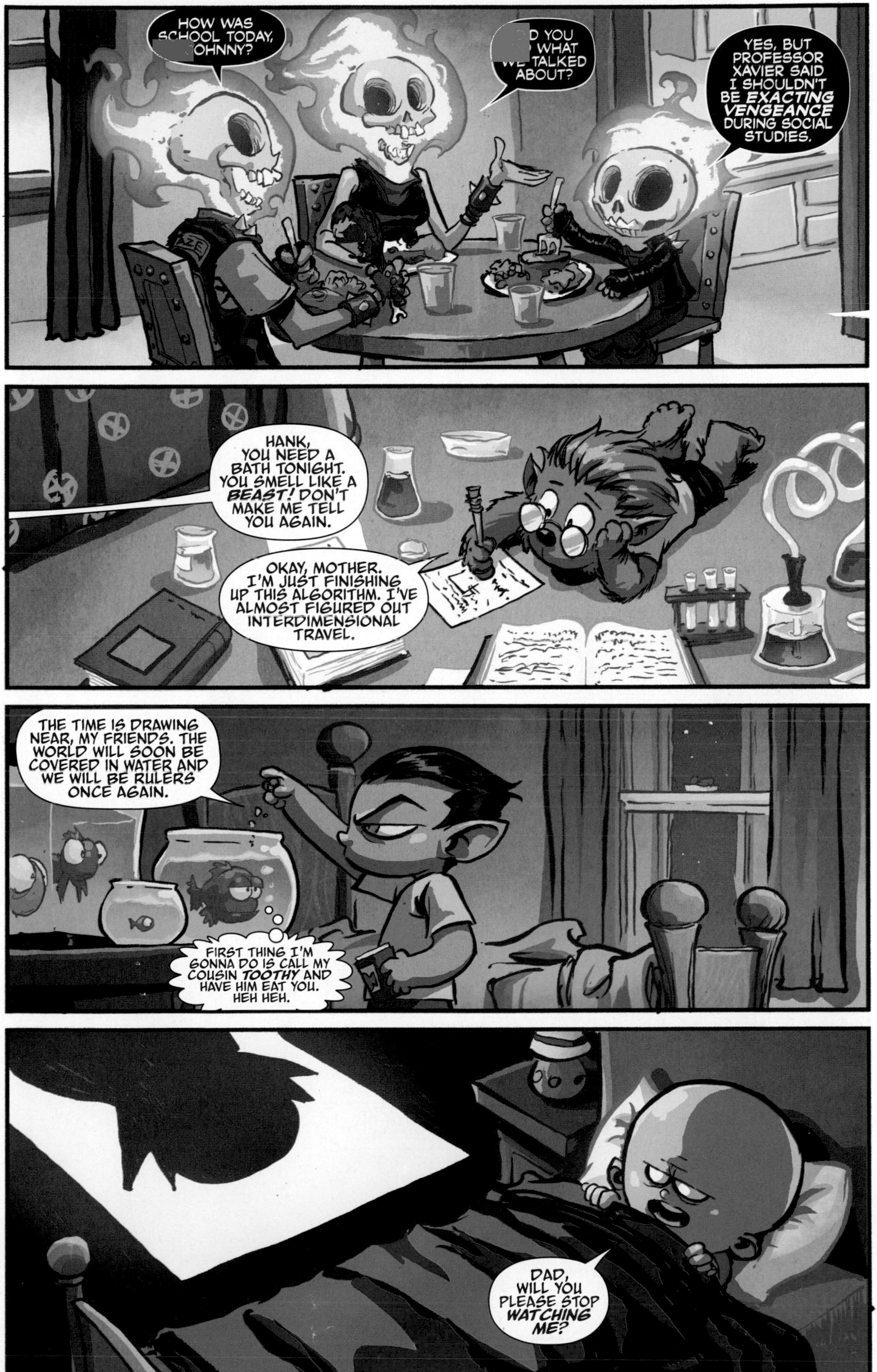
HOW WAS SCHOOL TODAY, OHNNY?
D YOU D WHAT WE TALKED ABOUT?
YES, BUT PROFESSOR XAVIER SAID I SHOULDN'T BE EXACTING VENGEANCE DURING SOCIAL STUDIES.
HANK, YOU NEED A BATH TONIGHT. YOU SMELL LIKE A BEAST! DON'T MAKE ME TELL YOU AGAIN.
OKAY, MOTHER. I'M JUST FINISHING UP THIS ALGORITHM. I'VE ALMOST FIGURED OUT INTERDIMENSIONAL TRAVEL.
THE TIME IS DRAWING NEAR, MY FRIENDS. THE WORLD WILL SOON BE COVERED IN WATER AND WE WILL BE RULERS ONCE AGAIN.
FIRST THING I'M GONNA DO IS CALL MY COUSIN TOOTHY AND HAVE HIM EAT YOU. HEH HEH.
DAD, WILL YOU PLEASE STOP WATCHING ME?

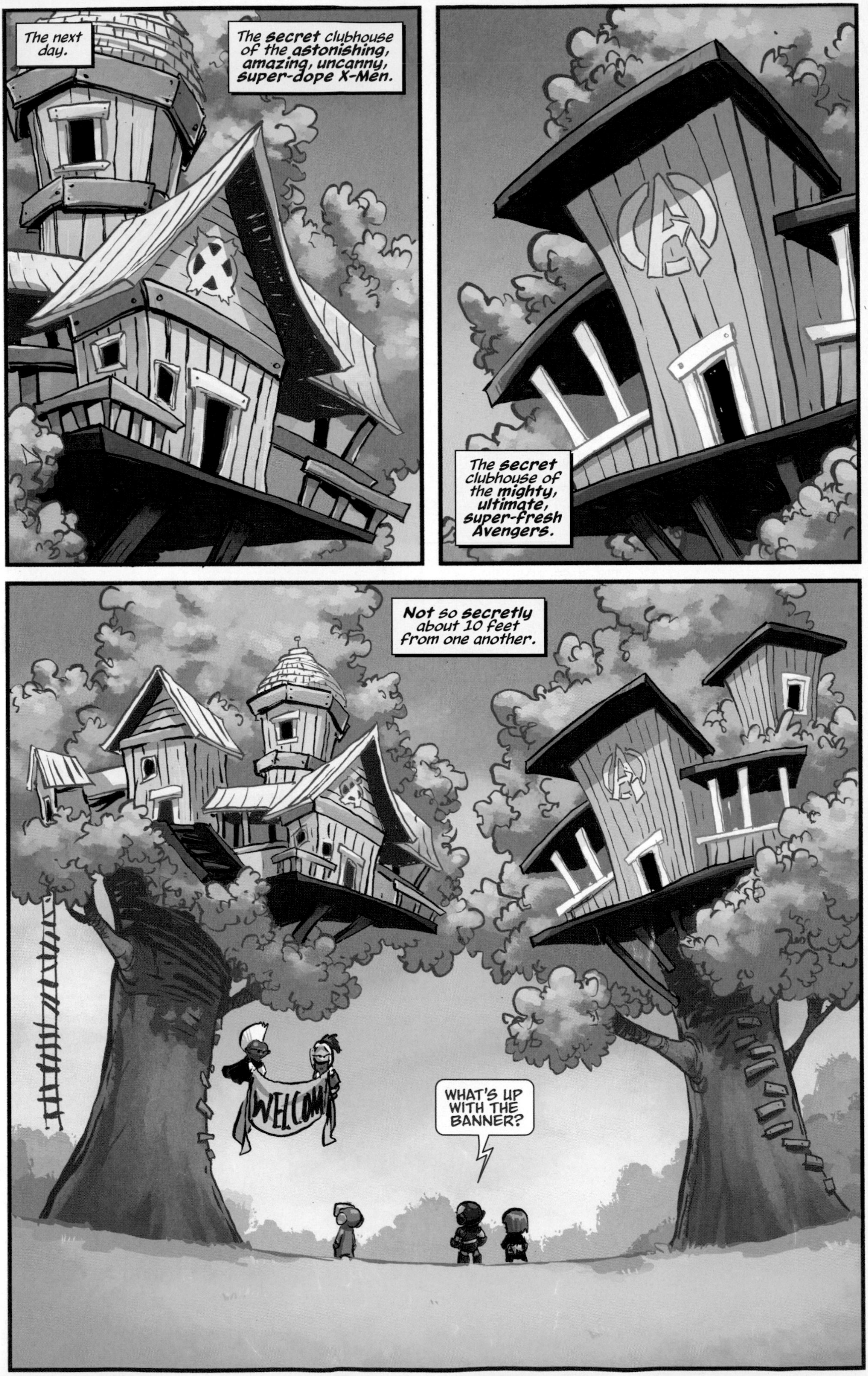
The next day.
The secret clubhouse of the astonishing, amazing, uncanny, super-dope X-Men.
The secret clubhouse of the mighty, ultimate, super-fresh Avengers.
Not so secretly about 10 feet from one another.
WELCOM
WHAT'S UP WITH THE BANNER?

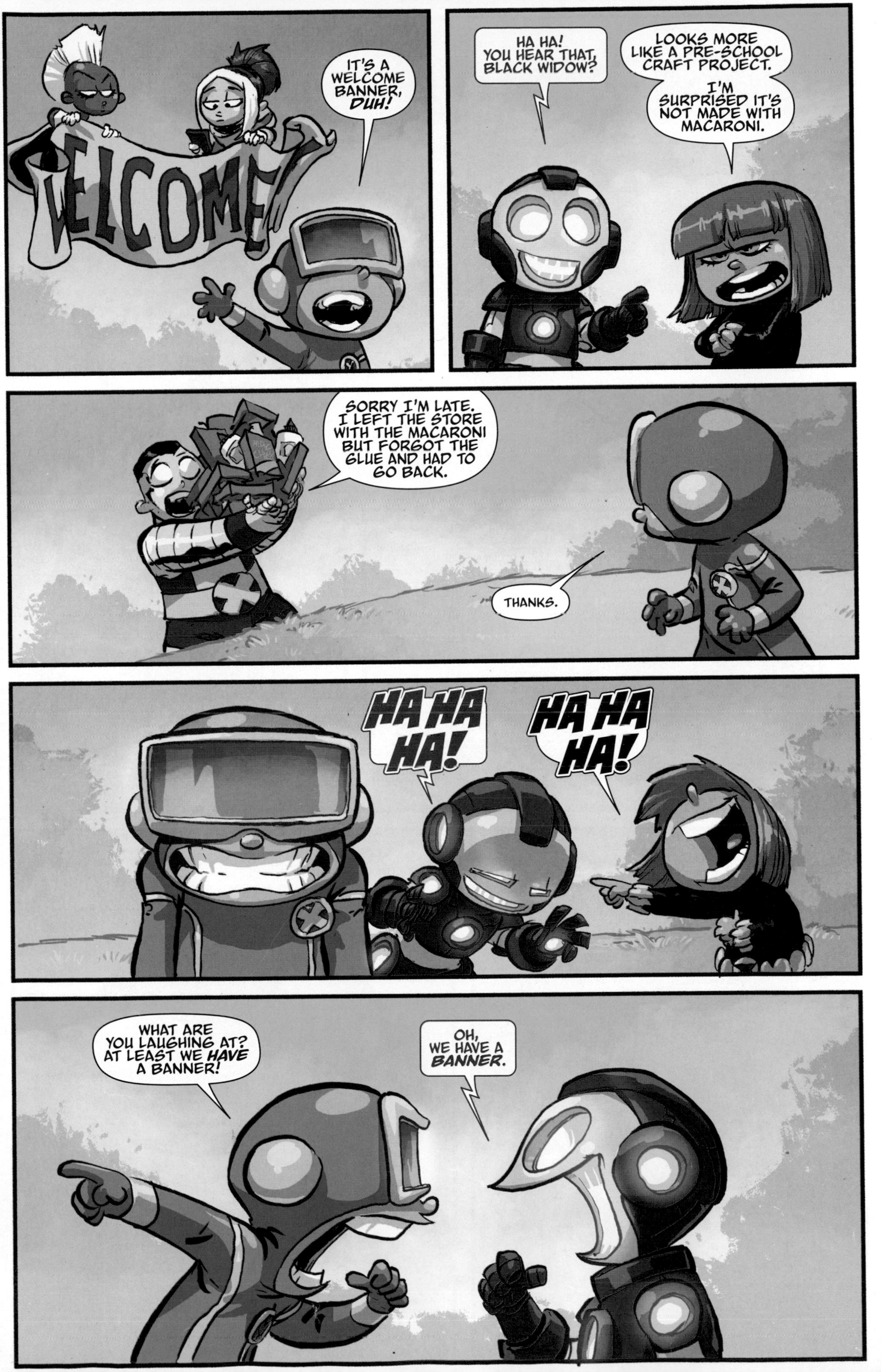
IT'S A WELCOME BANNER, *DUH!*
HA HA! YOU HEAR THAT, BLACK WIDOW?
LOOKS MORE LIKE A PRE-SCHOOL CRAFT PROJECT.
I'M SURPRISED IT'S NOT MADE WITH MACARONI.
SORRY I'M LATE. I LEFT THE STORE WITH THE MACARONI BUT FORGOT THE GLUE AND HAD TO GO BACK.
THANKS.
HA HA HA!
HA HA HA!
WHAT ARE YOU LAUGHING AT? AT LEAST WE *HAVE* A BANNER!
OH, WE HAVE A *BANNER*.

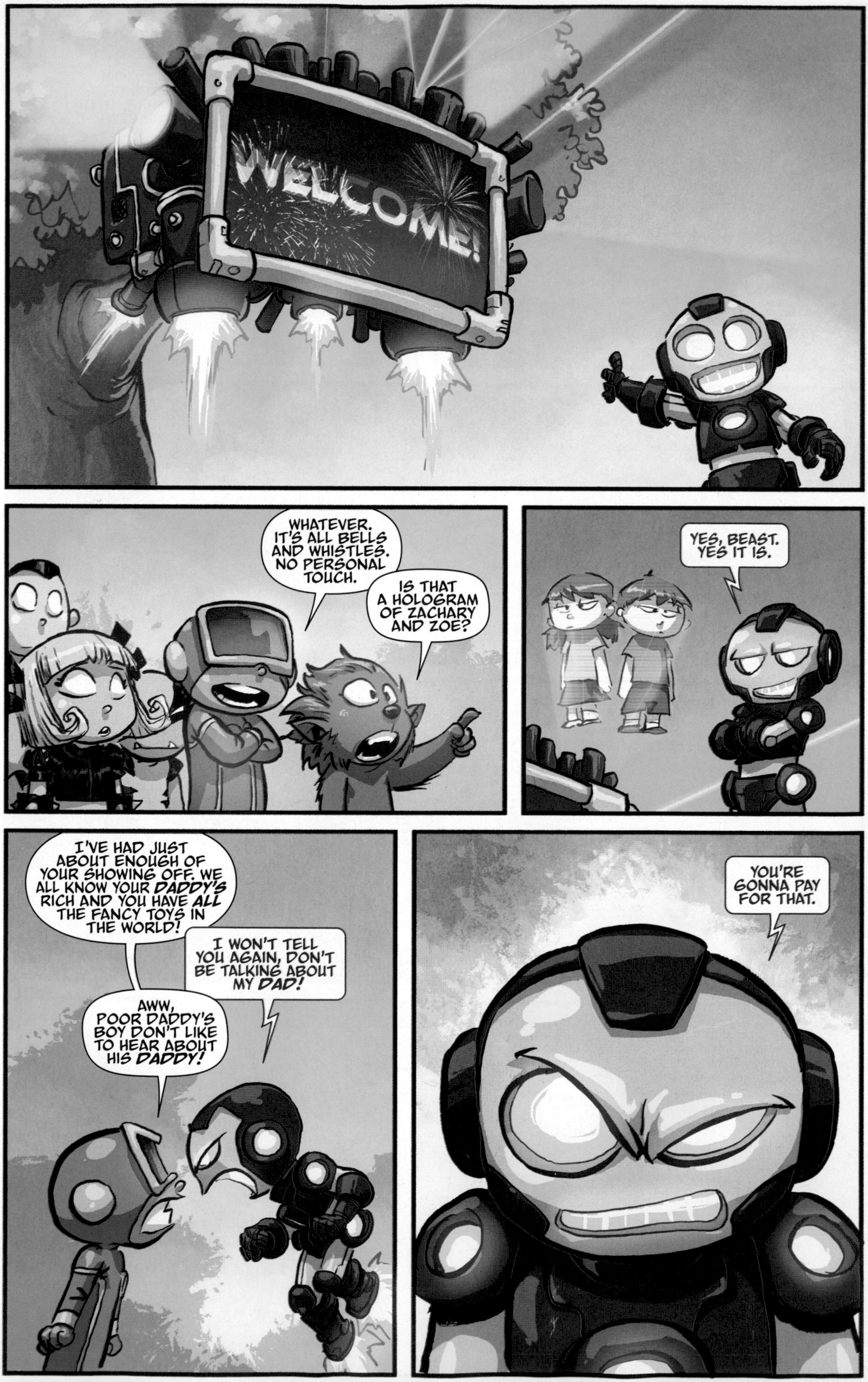
WELCOME!
WHATEVER. IT'S ALL BELLS AND WHISTLES. NO PERSONAL TOUCH.
IS THAT A HOLOGRAM OF ZACHARY AND ZOE?
YES, BEAST. YES IT IS.
I'VE HAD JUST ABOUT ENOUGH OF YOUR SHOWING OFF. WE ALL KNOW YOUR *DADDY'S* RICH AND YOU HAVE *ALL* THE FANCY TOYS IN THE WORLD!
I WON'T TELL YOU AGAIN, DON'T BE TALKING ABOUT MY *DAD!*
AWW, POOR DADDY'S BOY DON'T LIKE TO HEAR ABOUT HIS *DADDY!*
YOU'RE GONNA PAY FOR THAT.

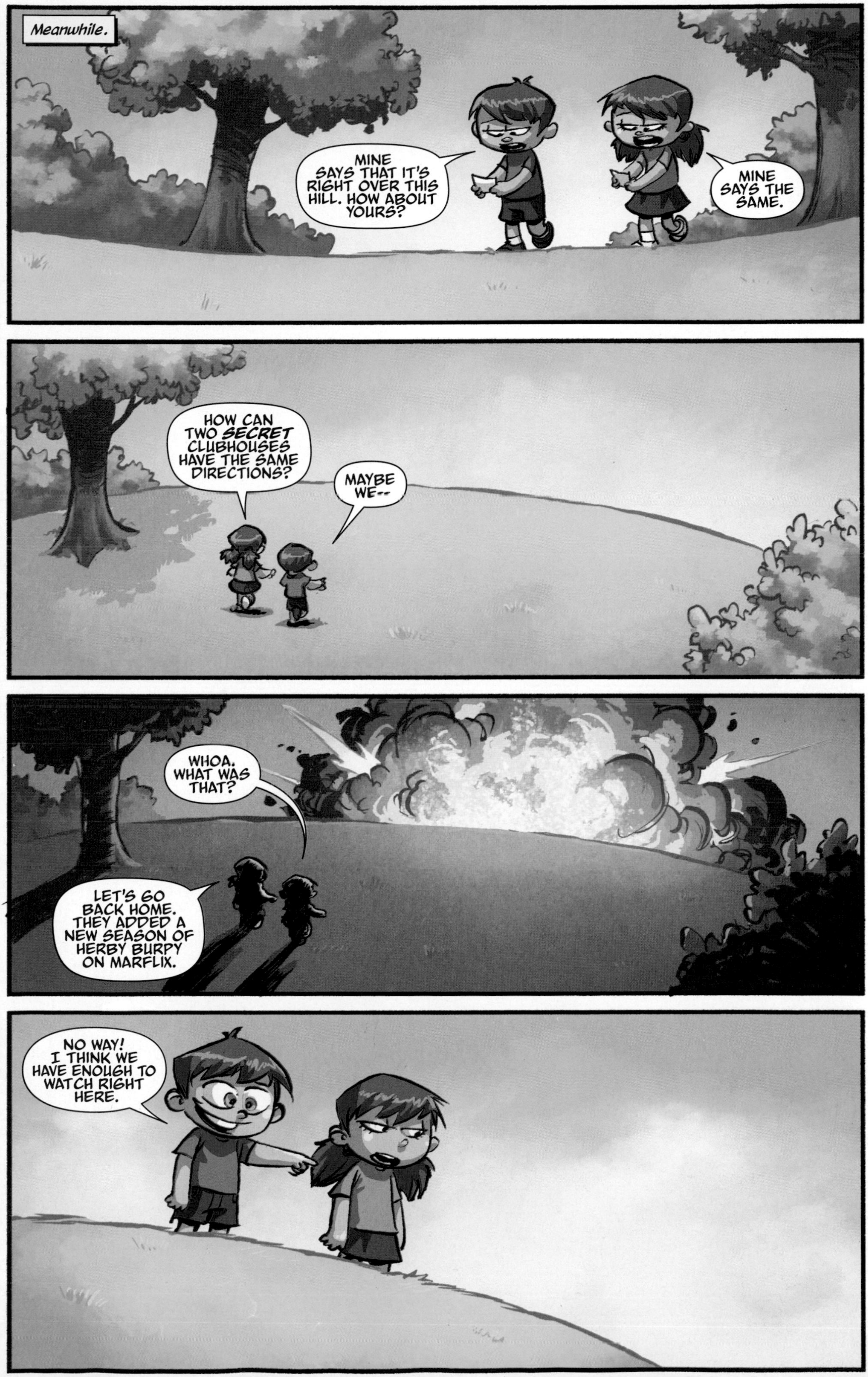
Meanwhile.
MINE SAYS THAT IT'S RIGHT OVER THIS HILL. HOW ABOUT YOURS?
MINE SAYS THE SAME.
HOW CAN TWO SECRET CLUBHOUSES HAVE THE SAME DIRECTIONS?
MAYBE WE--
WHOA. WHAT WAS THAT?
LET'S GO BACK HOME. THEY ADDED A NEW SEASON OF HERBY BURPY ON MARFLIX.
NO WAY! I THINK WE HAVE ENOUGH TO WATCH RIGHT HERE.

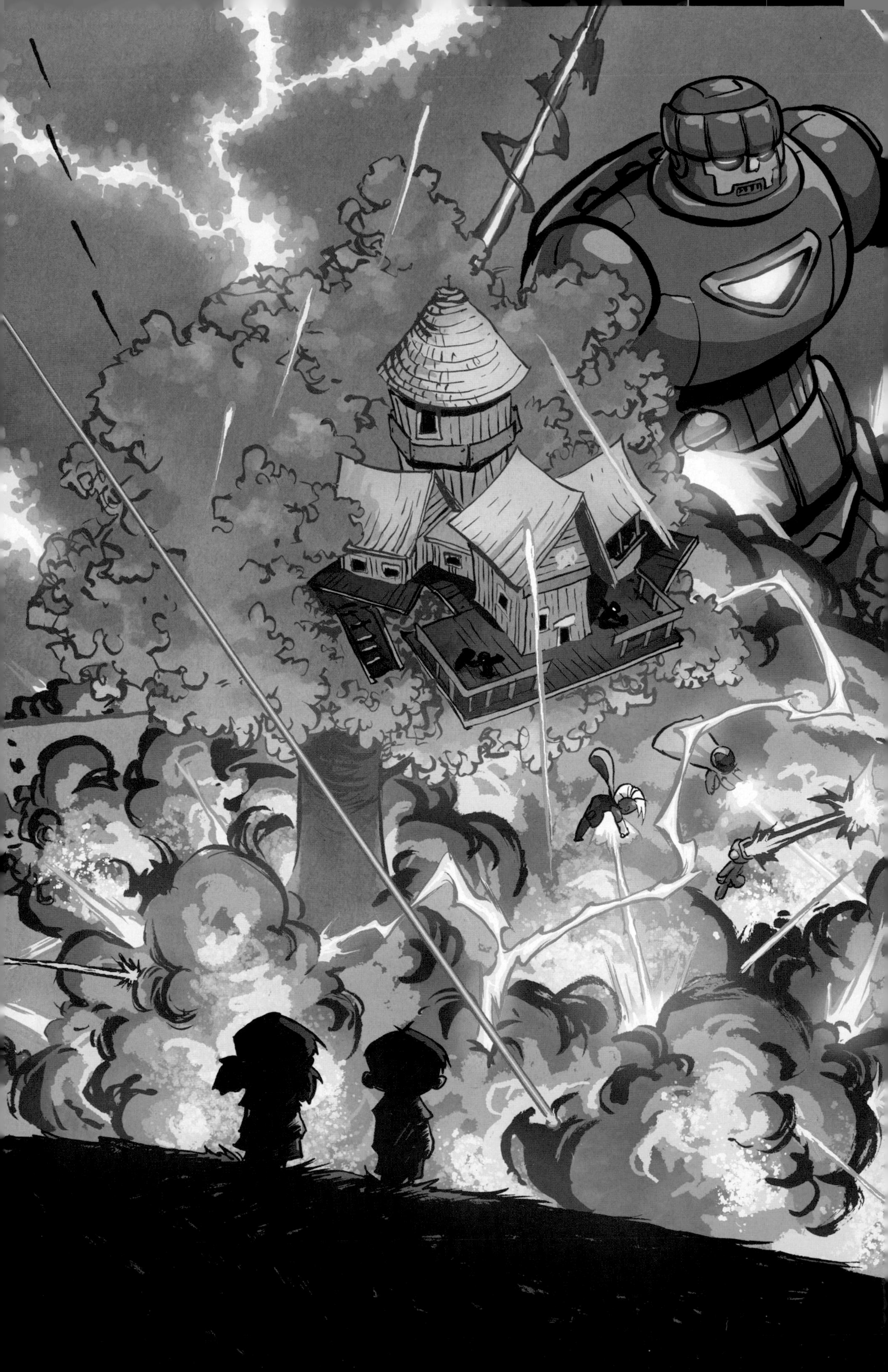

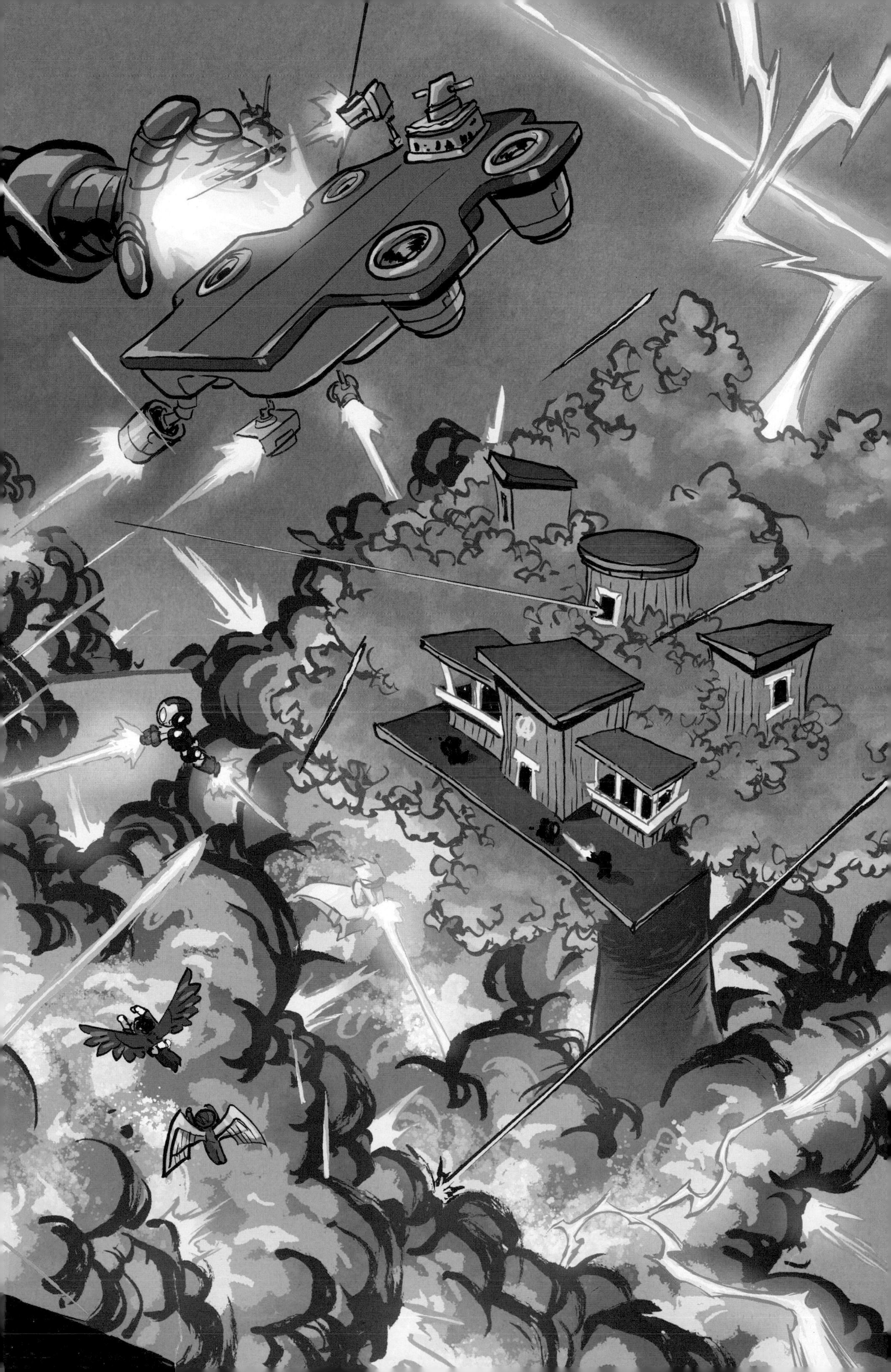

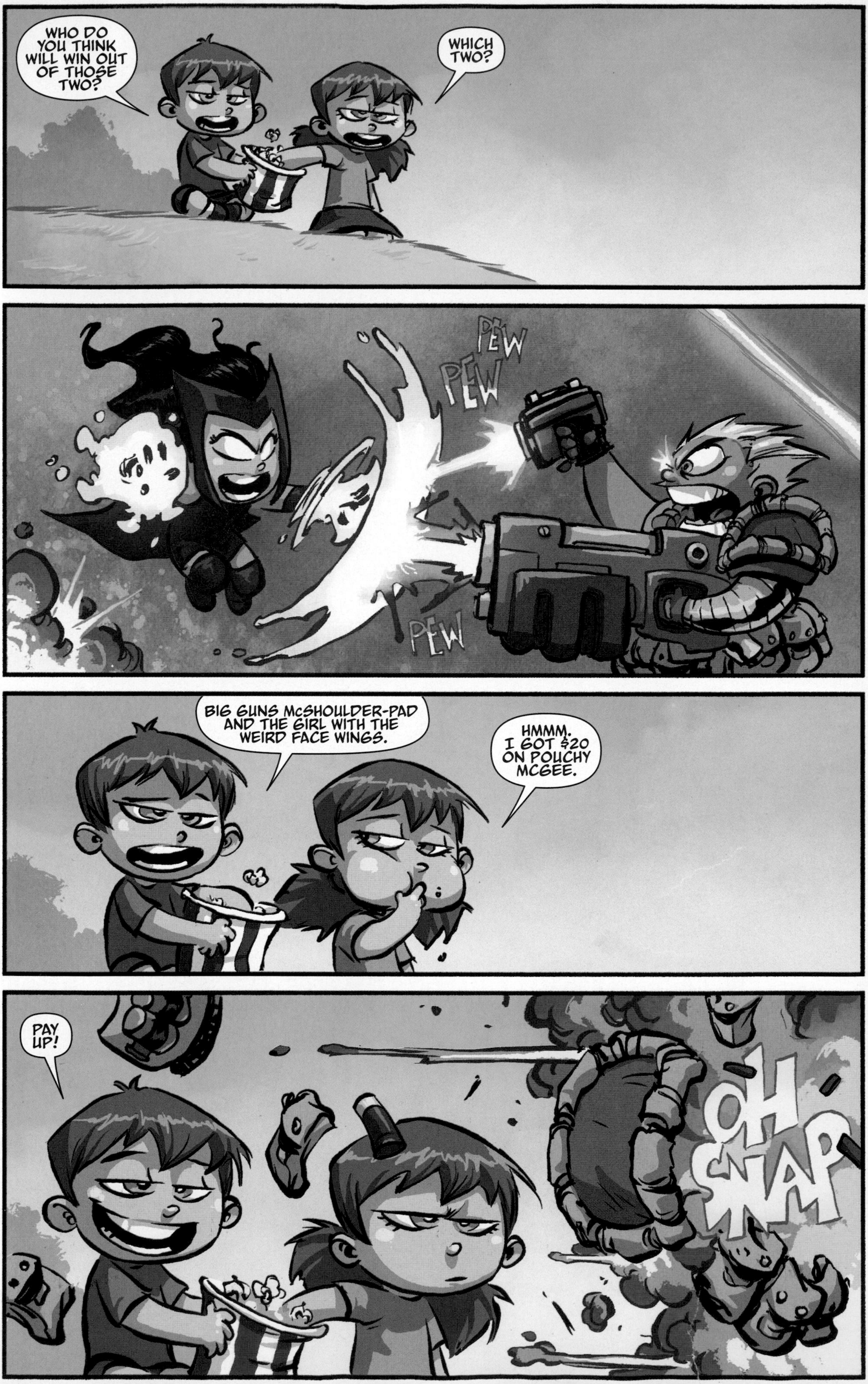
WHO DO YOU THINK WILL WIN OUT OF THOSE TWO?
WHICH TWO?
PEW
PEW
PEW
BIG GUNS McSHOULDER-PAD AND THE GIRL WITH THE WEIRD FACE WINGS.
HMMM. I GOT $20 ON POUCHY McGEE.
PAY UP!
OH SNAP

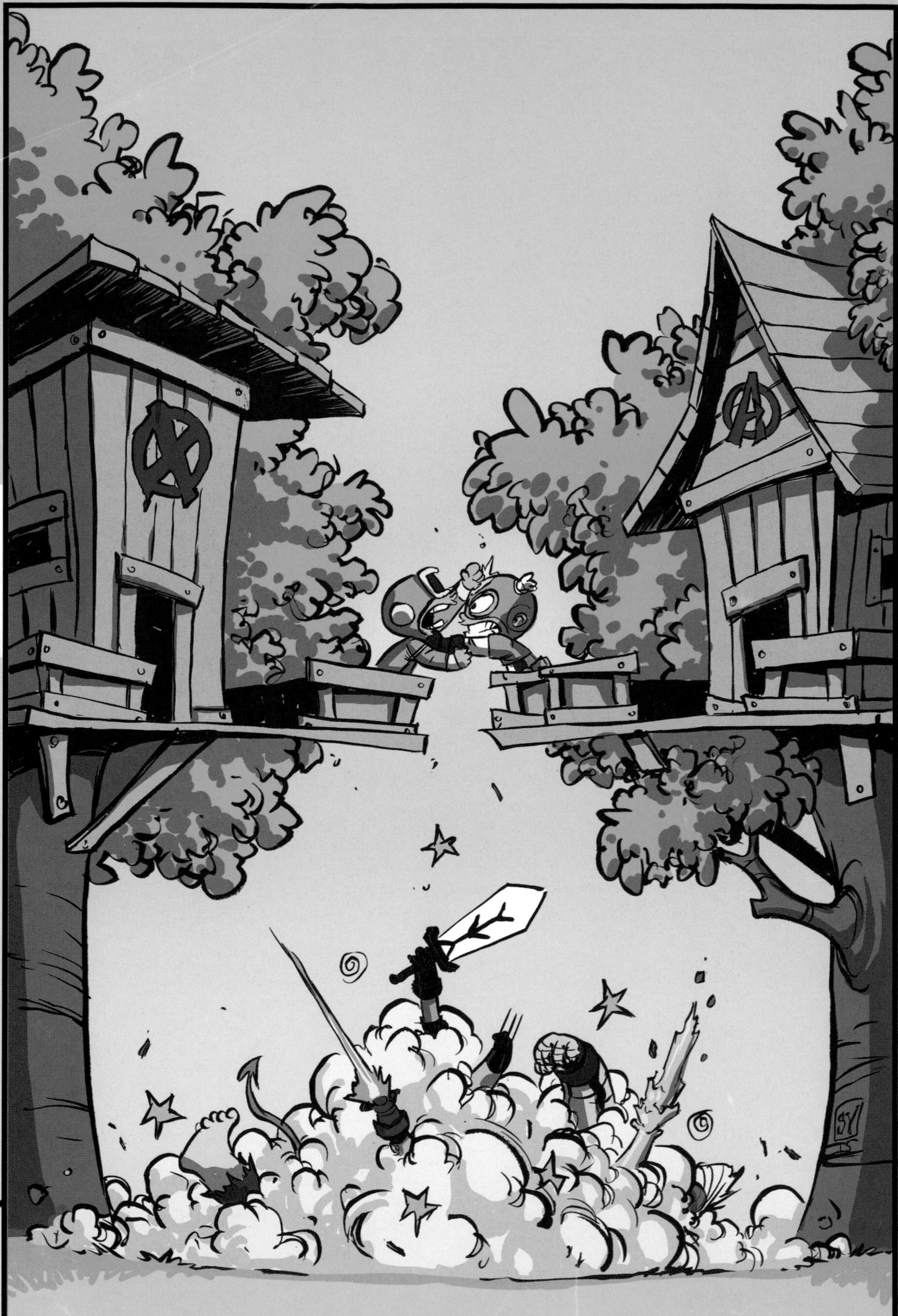

GIANT-SIZE LITTLE MARVEL: AVX #3

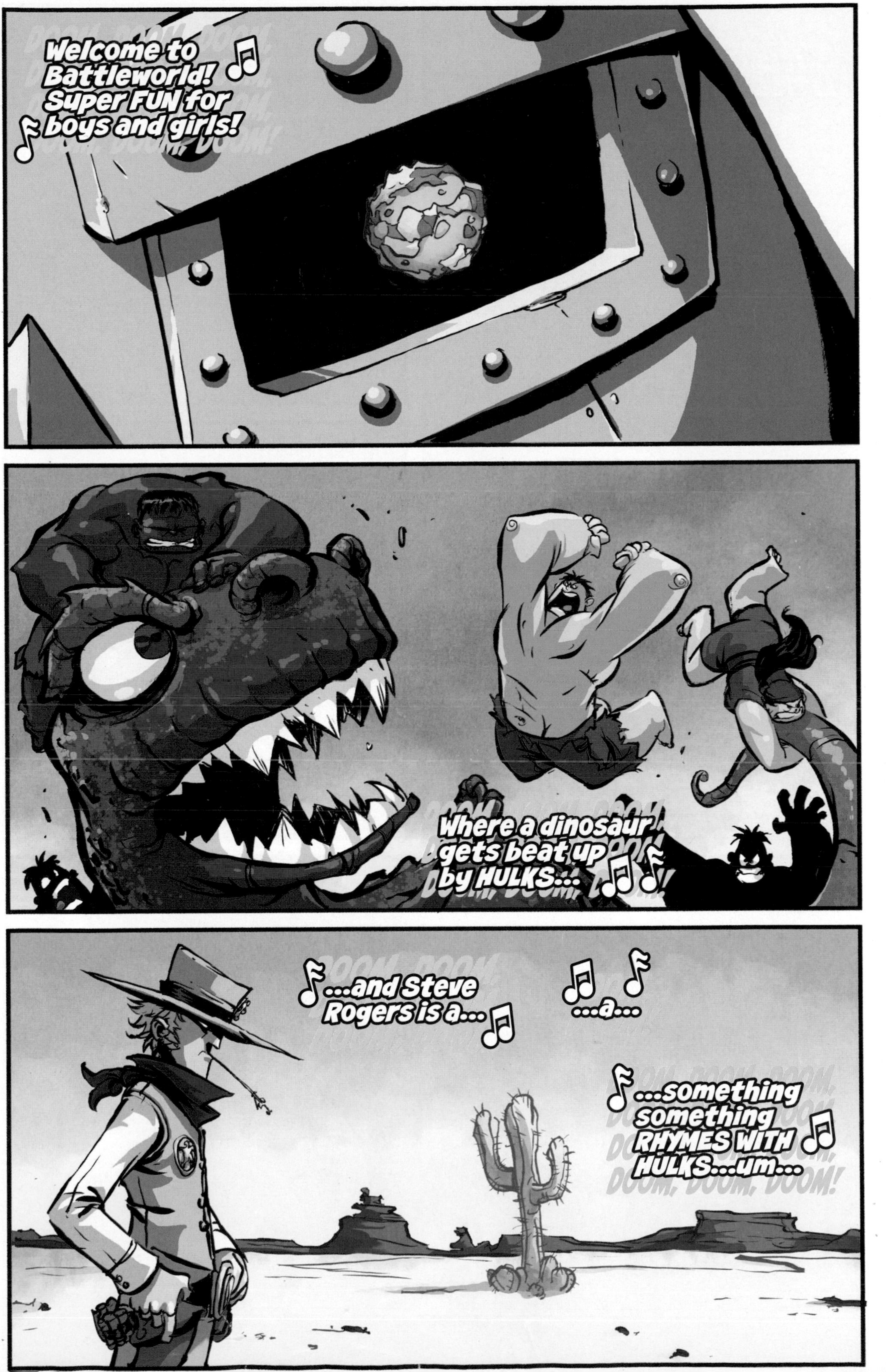
Welcome to Battleworld! Super FUN for boys and girls!
Where a dinosaur gets beat up by HULKS...
...and Steve Rogers is a...
...a...
...something something RHYMES WITH HULKS...um...

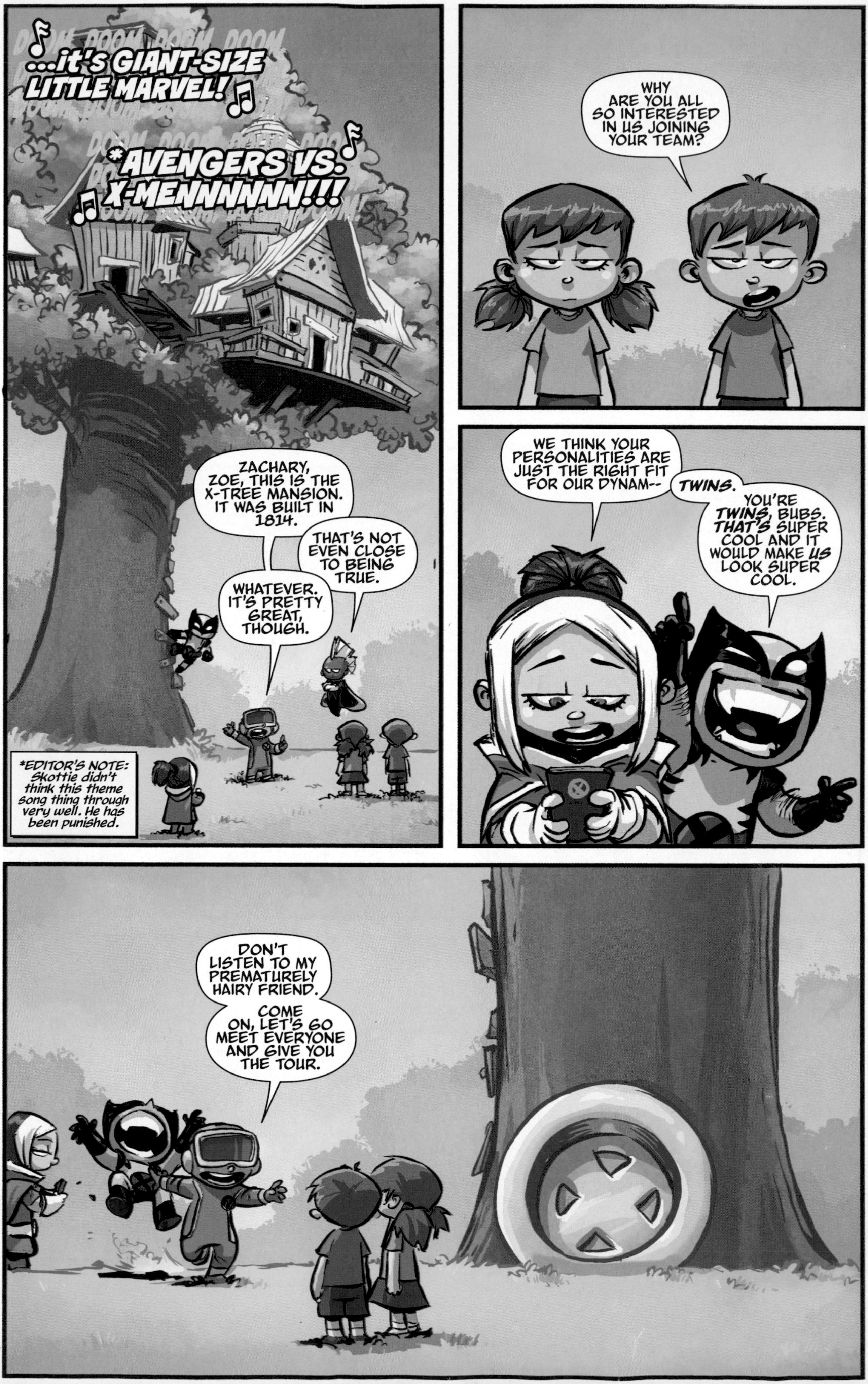
DOOM DOOM DOOM DOOM
...it's GIANT-SIZE LITTLE MARVEL!
*AVENGERS VS. X-MENNNNNN!!!
ZACHARY, ZOE, THIS IS THE X-TREE MANSION. IT WAS BUILT IN 1814.
THAT'S NOT EVEN CLOSE TO BEING TRUE.
WHATEVER. IT'S PRETTY GREAT, THOUGH.
*EDITOR'S NOTE: Skottie didn't think this theme song thing through very well. He has been punished.
WHY ARE YOU ALL SO INTERESTED IN US JOINING YOUR TEAM?
WE THINK YOUR PERSONALITIES ARE JUST THE RIGHT FIT FOR OUR DYNAM--
TWINS.
YOU'RE TWINS, BUBS. THAT'S SUPER COOL AND IT WOULD MAKE US LOOK SUPER COOL.
DON'T LISTEN TO MY PREMATURELY HAIRY FRIEND.
COME ON, LET'S GO MEET EVERYONE AND GIVE YOU THE TOUR.

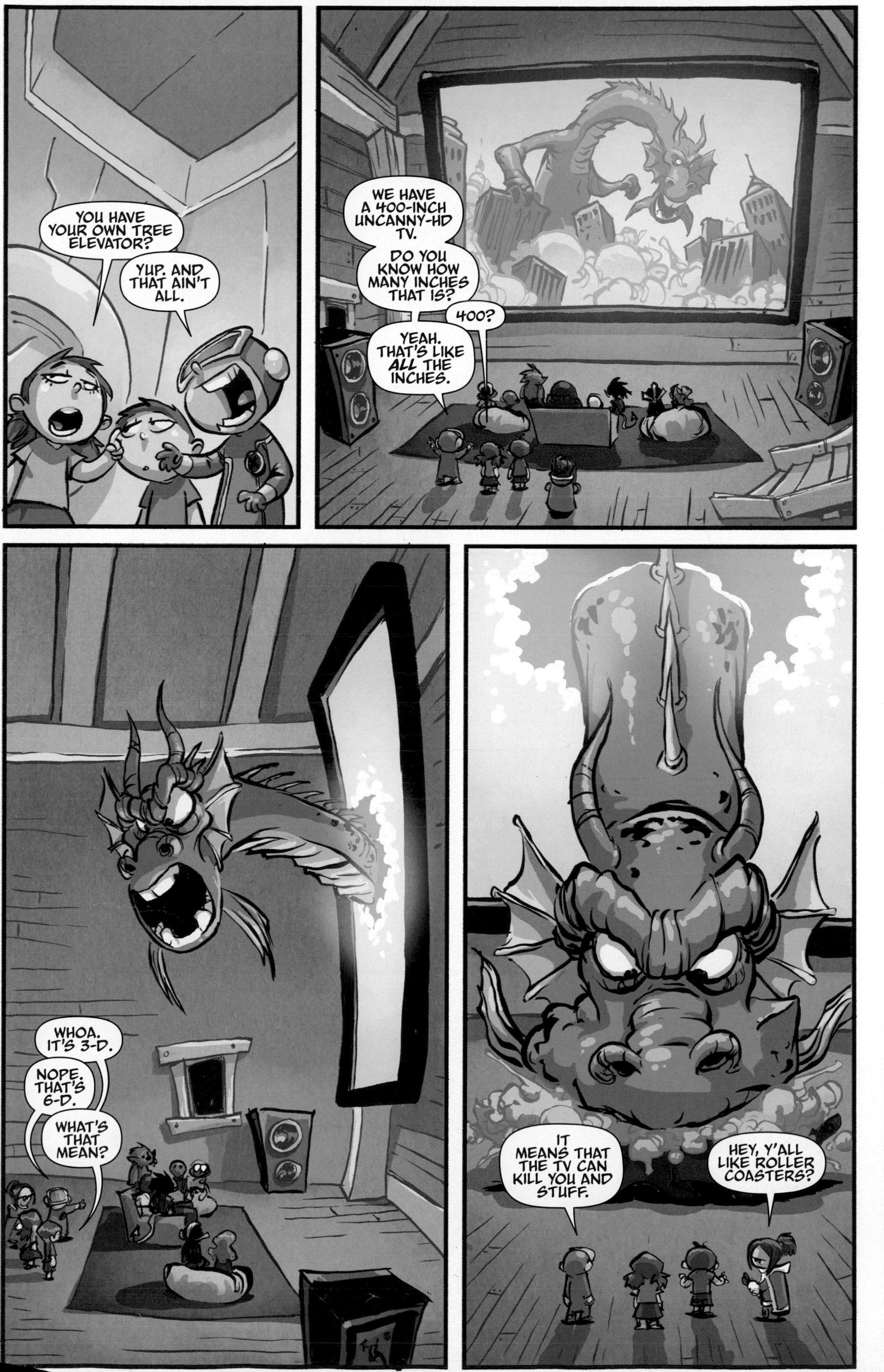
YOU HAVE YOUR OWN TREE ELEVATOR?
YUP. AND THAT AIN'T ALL.
WE HAVE A 400-INCH UNCANNY-HD TV.
DO YOU KNOW HOW MANY INCHES THAT IS?
400?
YEAH. THAT'S LIKE *ALL* THE INCHES.
WHOA. IT'S 3-D.
NOPE. THAT'S 6-D.
WHAT'S THAT MEAN?
IT MEANS THAT THE TV CAN KILL YOU AND STUFF.
HEY, Y'ALL LIKE ROLLER COASTERS?

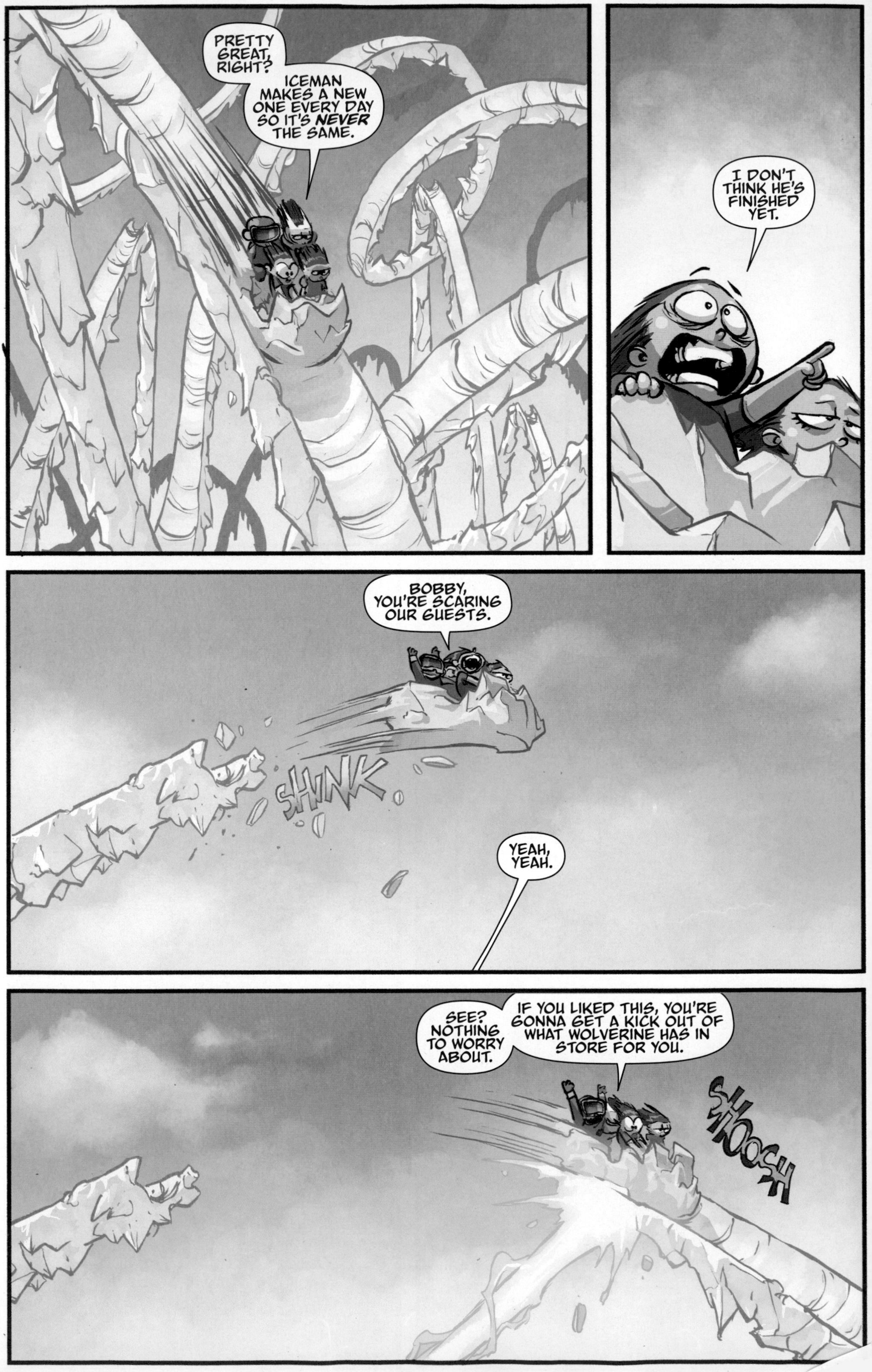
PRETTY GREAT, RIGHT?
ICEMAN MAKES A NEW ONE EVERY DAY SO IT'S *NEVER* THE SAME.
I DON'T THINK HE'S FINISHED YET.
BOBBY, YOU'RE SCARING OUR GUESTS.
SHINK
YEAH, YEAH.
SEE? NOTHING TO WORRY ABOUT.
IF YOU LIKED THIS, YOU'RE GONNA GET A KICK OUT OF WHAT WOLVERINE HAS IN STORE FOR YOU.
SHOOSH

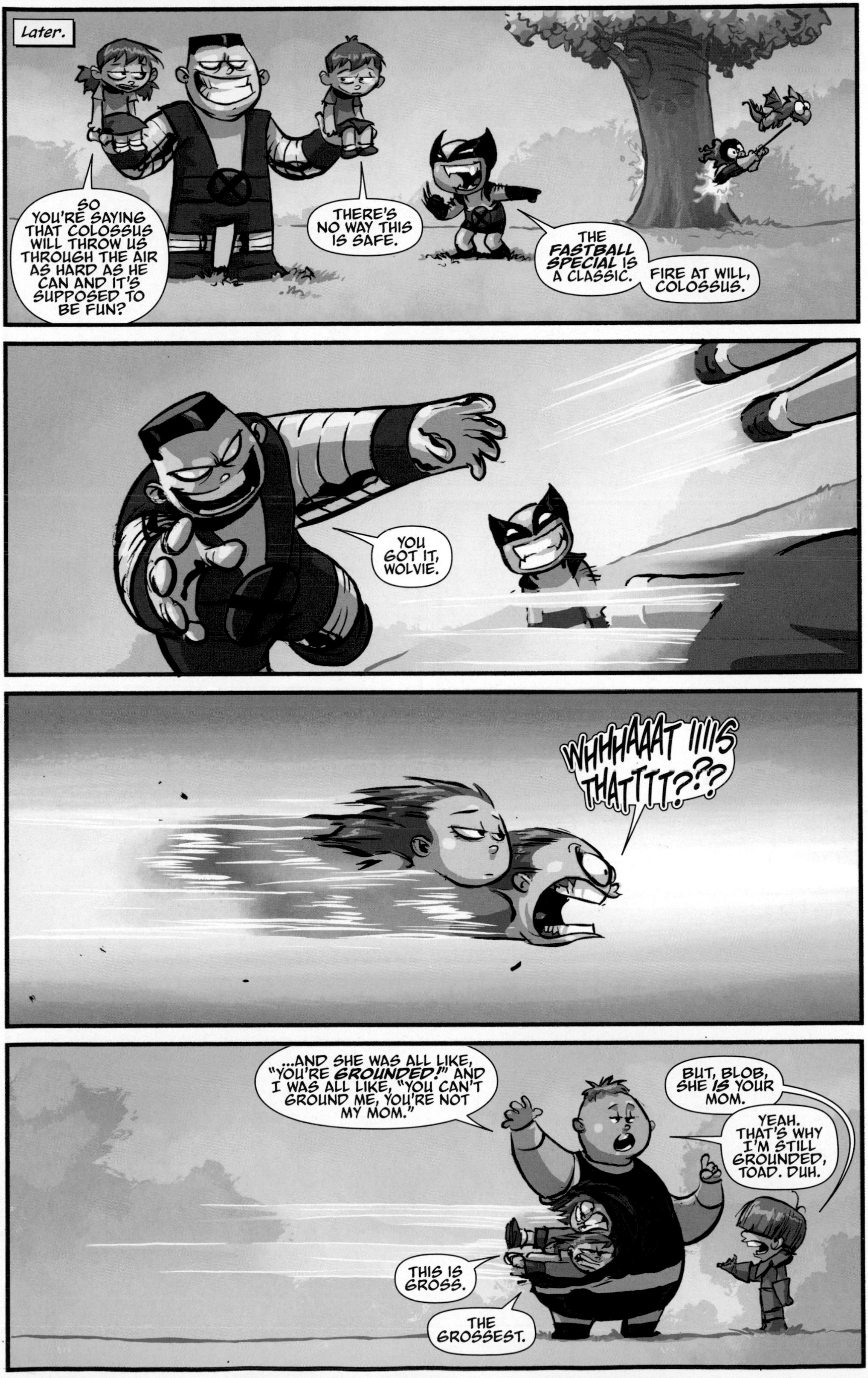
Later.
SO YOU'RE SAYING THAT COLOSSUS WILL THROW US THROUGH THE AIR AS HARD AS HE CAN AND IT'S SUPPOSED TO BE FUN?
THERE'S NO WAY THIS IS SAFE.
THE FASTBALL SPECIAL IS A CLASSIC.
FIRE AT WILL, COLOSSUS.
YOU GOT IT, WOLVIE.
WHHHAAAT IIIIS THATTTT???
...AND SHE WAS ALL LIKE, "YOU'RE GROUNDED!" AND I WAS ALL LIKE, "YOU CAN'T GROUND ME, YOU'RE NOT MY MOM."
BUT, BLOB, SHE IS YOUR MOM.
YEAH. THAT'S WHY I'M STILL GROUNDED, TOAD. DUH.
THIS IS GROSS.
THE GROSSEST.

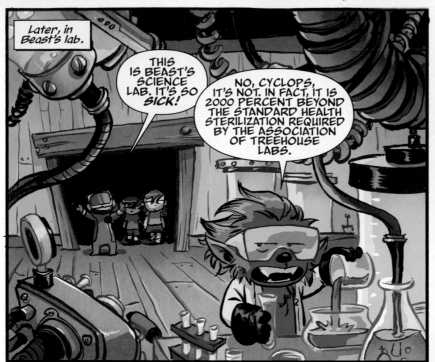

*Later, in Beast's lab.*

THIS IS BEAST'S SCIENCE LAB. IT'S SO *SICK!*

NO, CYCLOPS, IT'S NOT. IN FACT, IT IS 2000 PERCENT BEYOND THE STANDARD HEALTH STERILIZATION REQUIRED BY THE ASSOCIATION OF TREEHOUSE LABS.

INTERESTING. ALL I HEARD WAS *NERD, NERD, NERDY NERDS.*

NOW TELL THEM WHAT YOU'RE COOKING UP.

I CONCOCTED THIS SERUM TO REPLICATE A MUTATION BASED ON A SYNTHETIC X-GENE I FUSED WITH ZACHARY AND ZOE'S DNA I SAMPLED FROM STRANDS OF THEIR HAIR.

FIRST, EEW. STEALING OUR HAIR IS PRETTY CREEPY.

SECOND... *AWESOME!* HOW LONG UNTIL WE...

BOOF

...MUTATE?

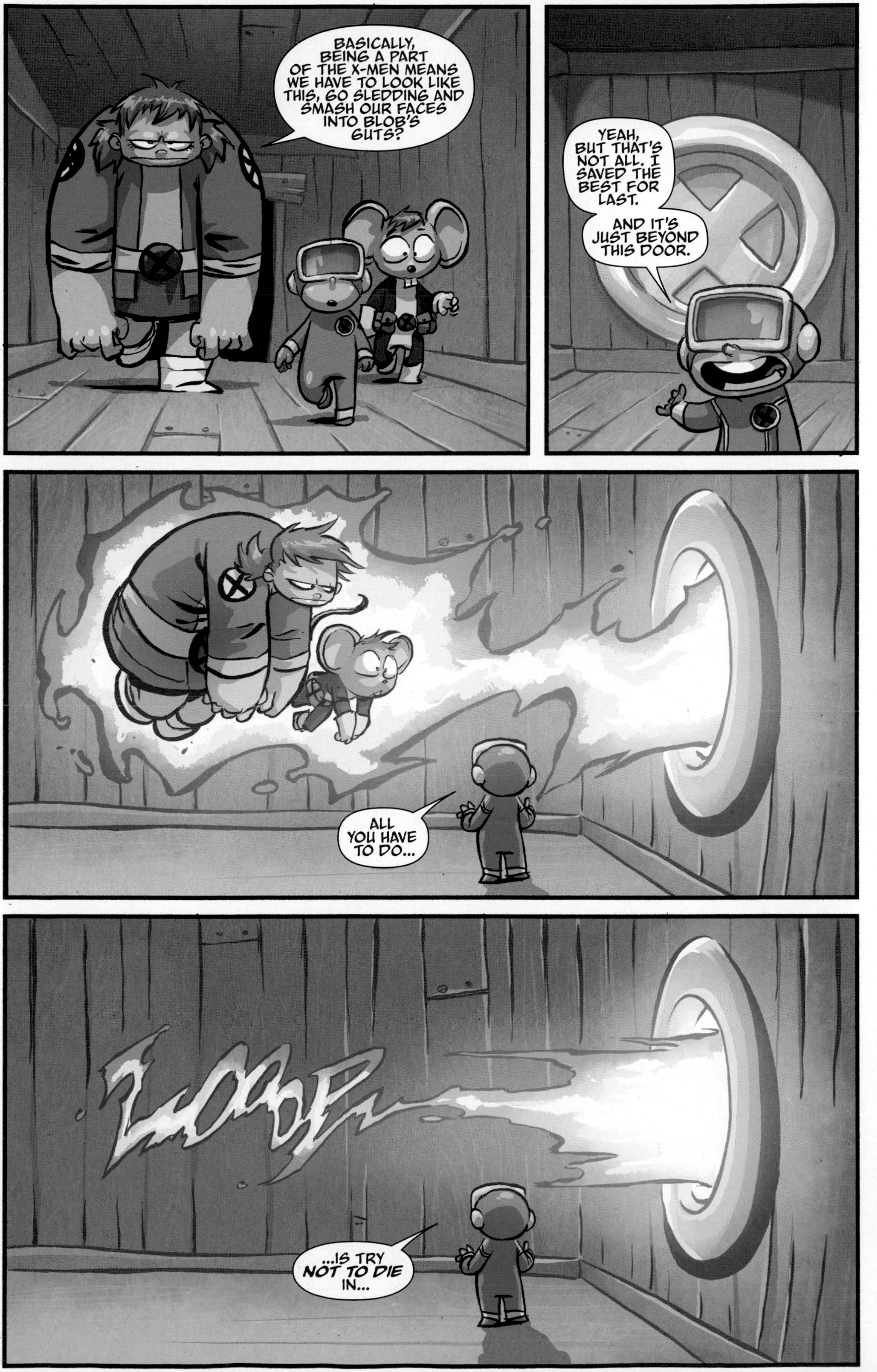
BASICALLY, BEING A PART OF THE X-MEN MEANS WE HAVE TO LOOK LIKE THIS, GO SLEDDING AND SMASH OUR FACES INTO BLOB'S GUTS?
YEAH, BUT THAT'S NOT ALL. I SAVED THE BEST FOR LAST.
AND IT'S JUST BEYOND THIS DOOR.
ALL YOU HAVE TO DO...
ZOOP
...IS TRY NOT TO DIE IN...

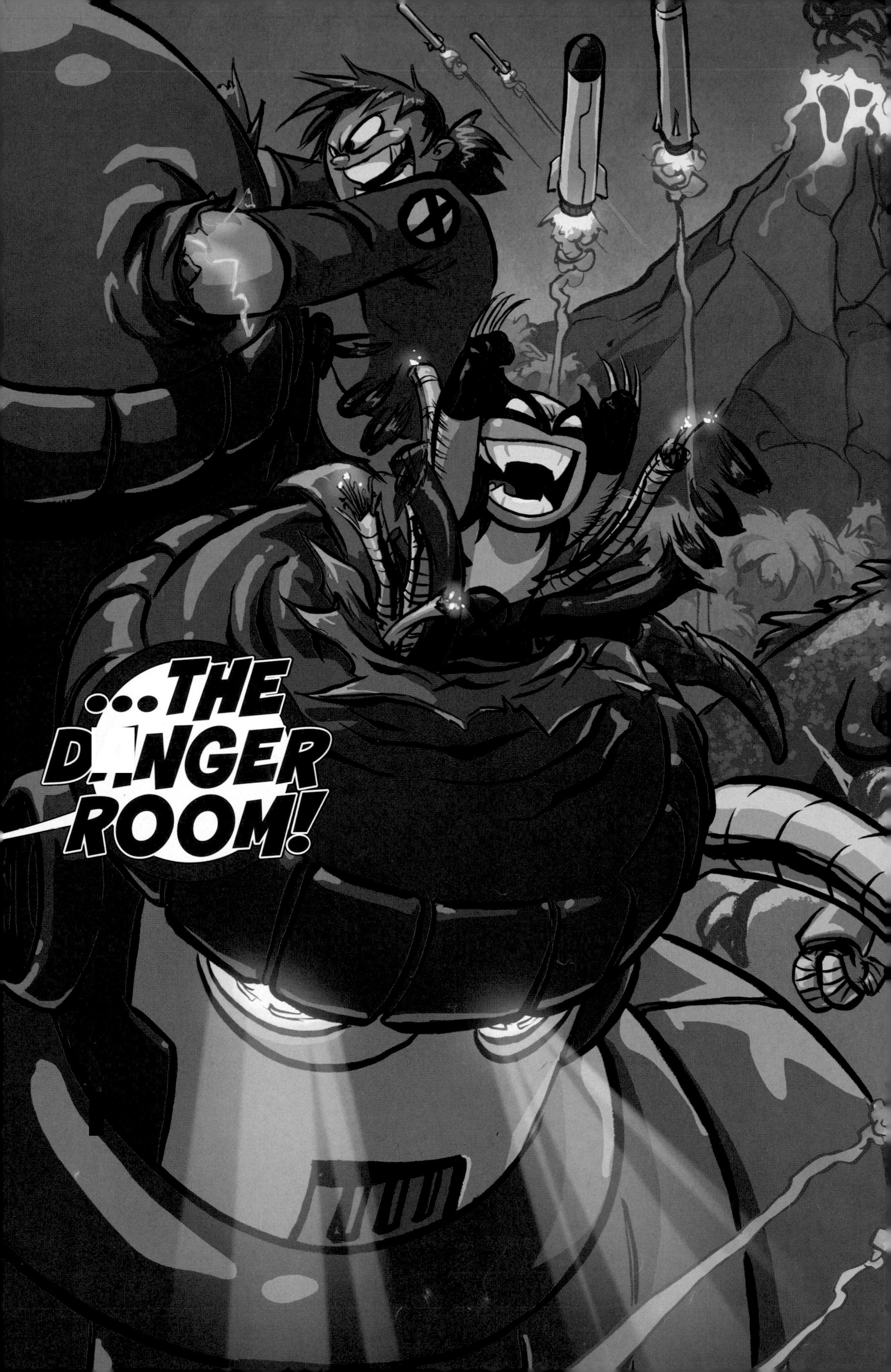
...THE D NGER ROOM!

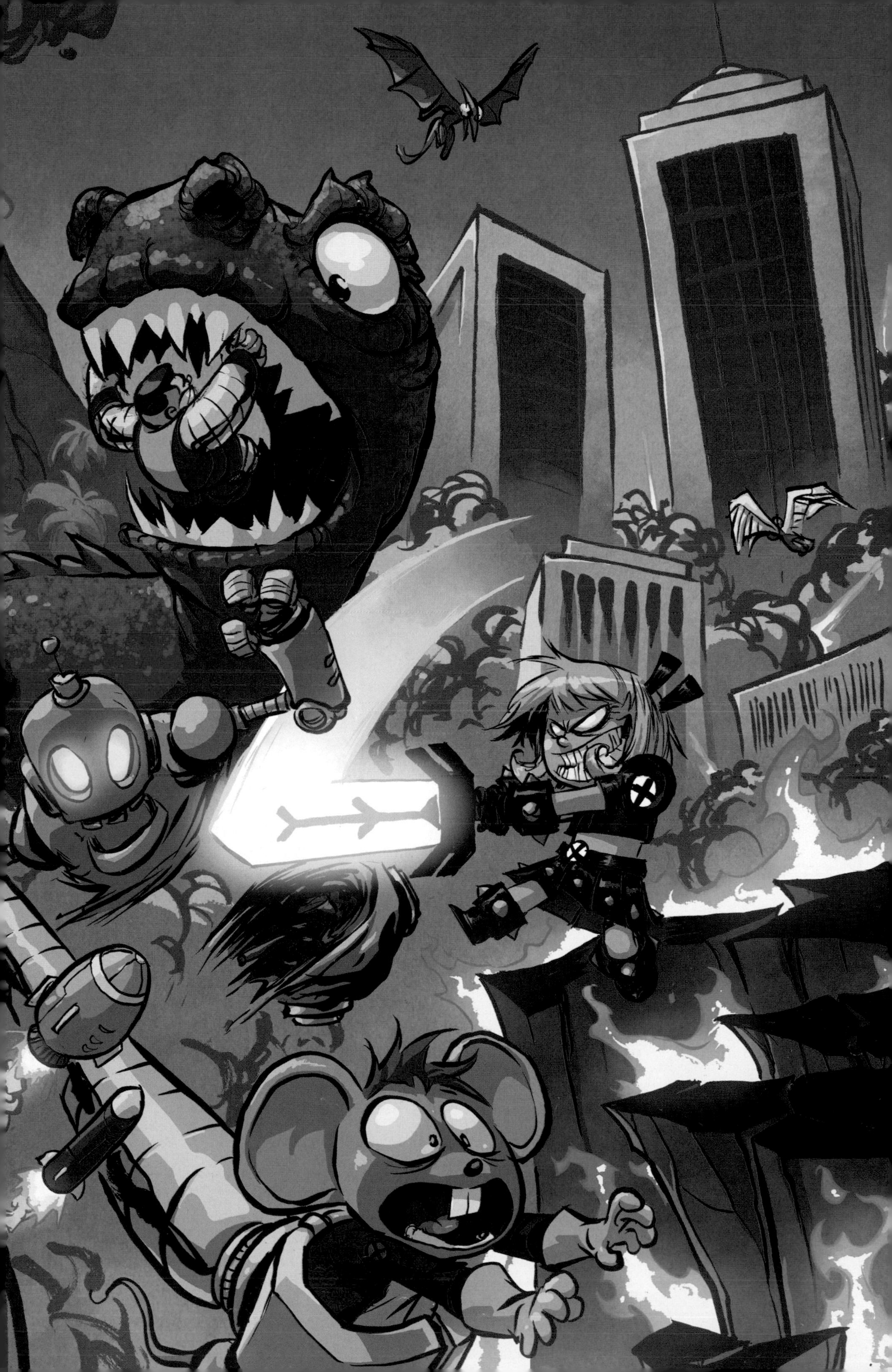

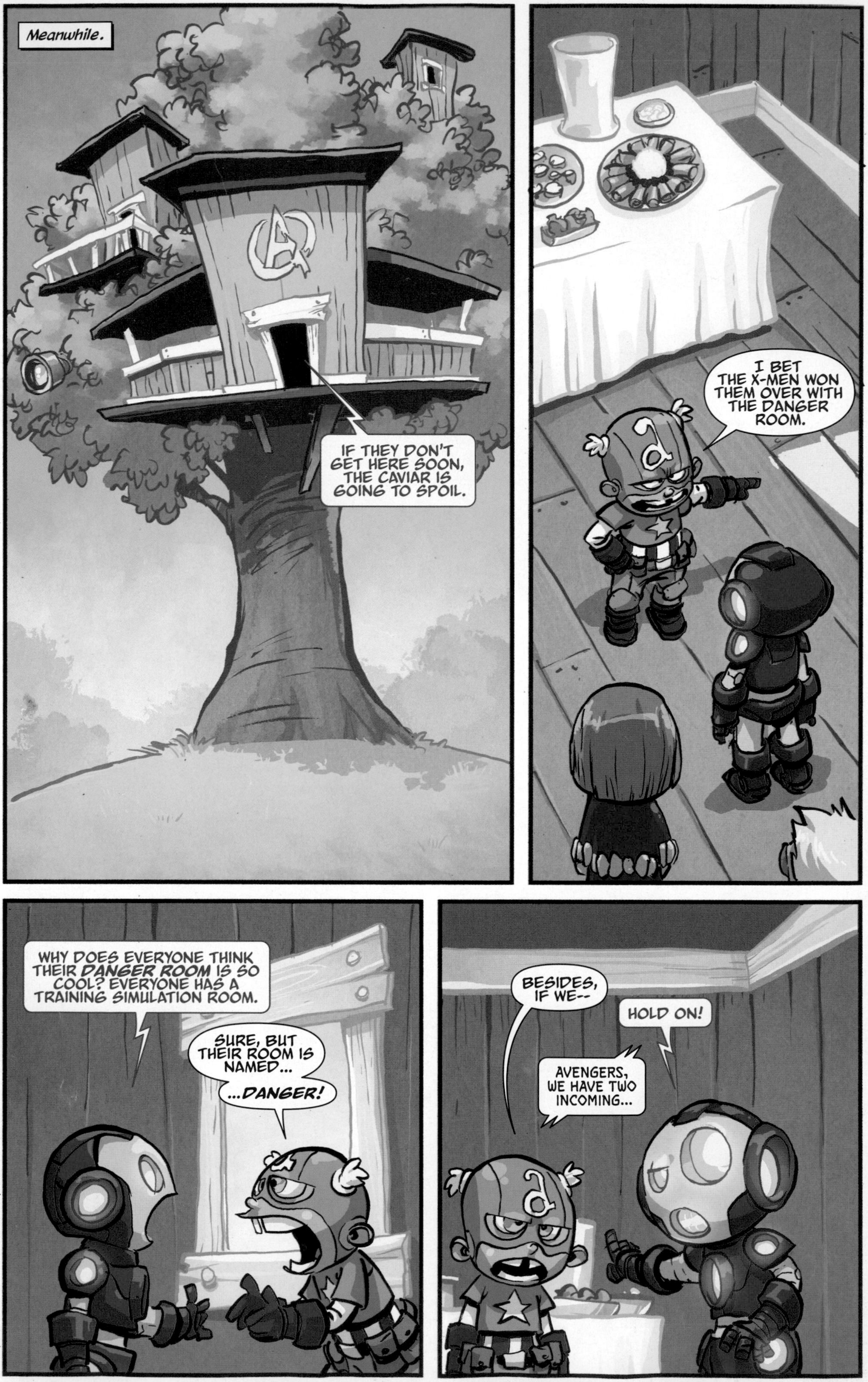

Meanwhile.
IF THEY DON'T GET HERE SOON, THE CAVIAR IS GOING TO SPOIL.
I BET THE X-MEN WON THEM OVER WITH THE DANGER ROOM.
WHY DOES EVERYONE THINK THEIR DANGER ROOM IS SO COOL? EVERYONE HAS A TRAINING SIMULATION ROOM.
SURE, BUT THEIR ROOM IS NAMED...
...DANGER!
BESIDES, IF WE--
HOLD ON!
AVENGERS, WE HAVE TWO INCOMING...

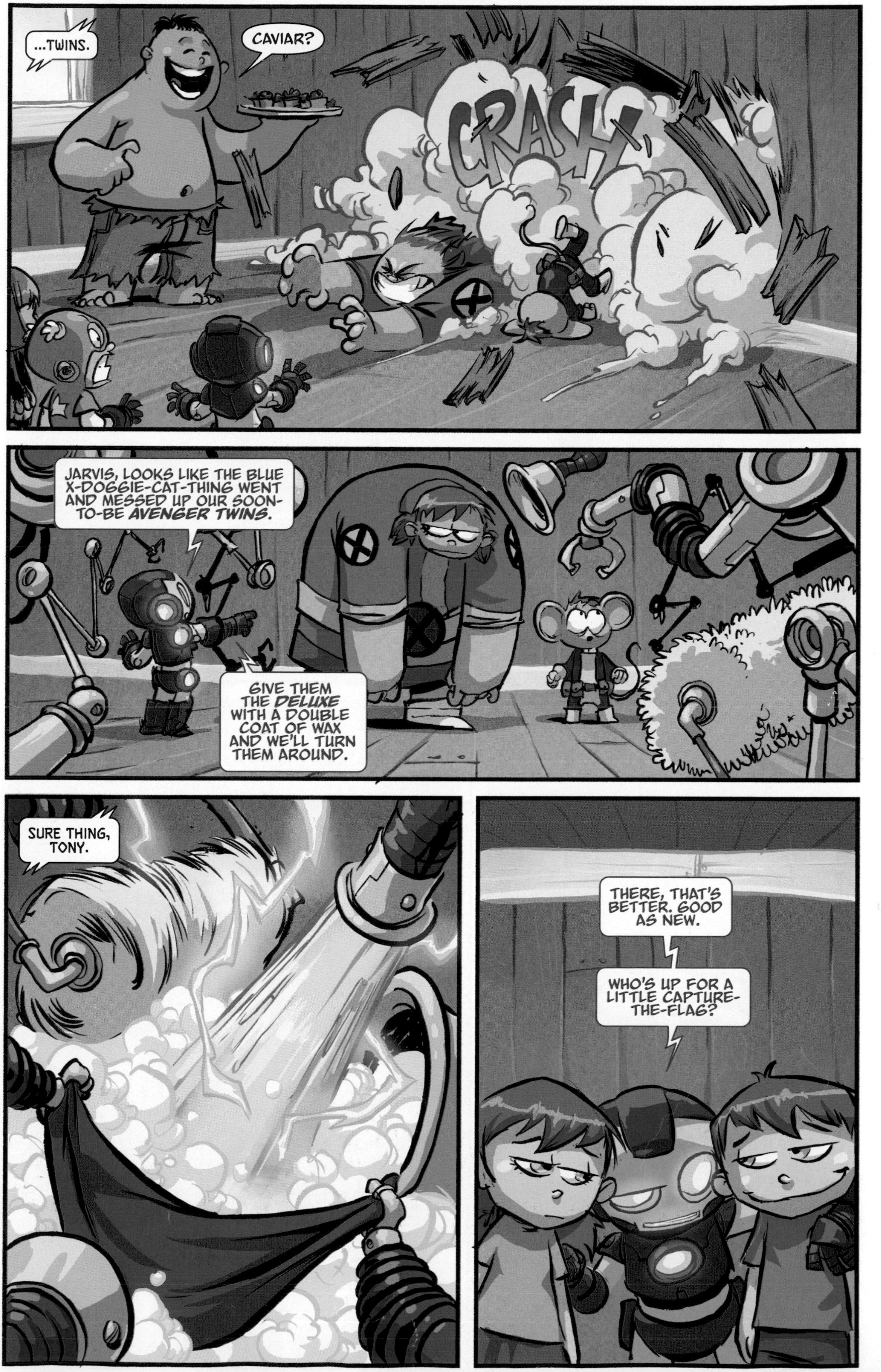

...TWINS.
CAVIAR?
CRASH
JARVIS, LOOKS LIKE THE BLUE X-DOGGIE-CAT-THING WENT AND MESSED UP OUR SOON-TO-BE *AVENGER TWINS*.
GIVE THEM THE *DELUXE* WITH A DOUBLE COAT OF WAX AND WE'LL TURN THEM AROUND.
SURE THING, TONY.
THERE, THAT'S BETTER. GOOD AS NEW.
WHO'S UP FOR A LITTLE CAPTURE-THE-FLAG?

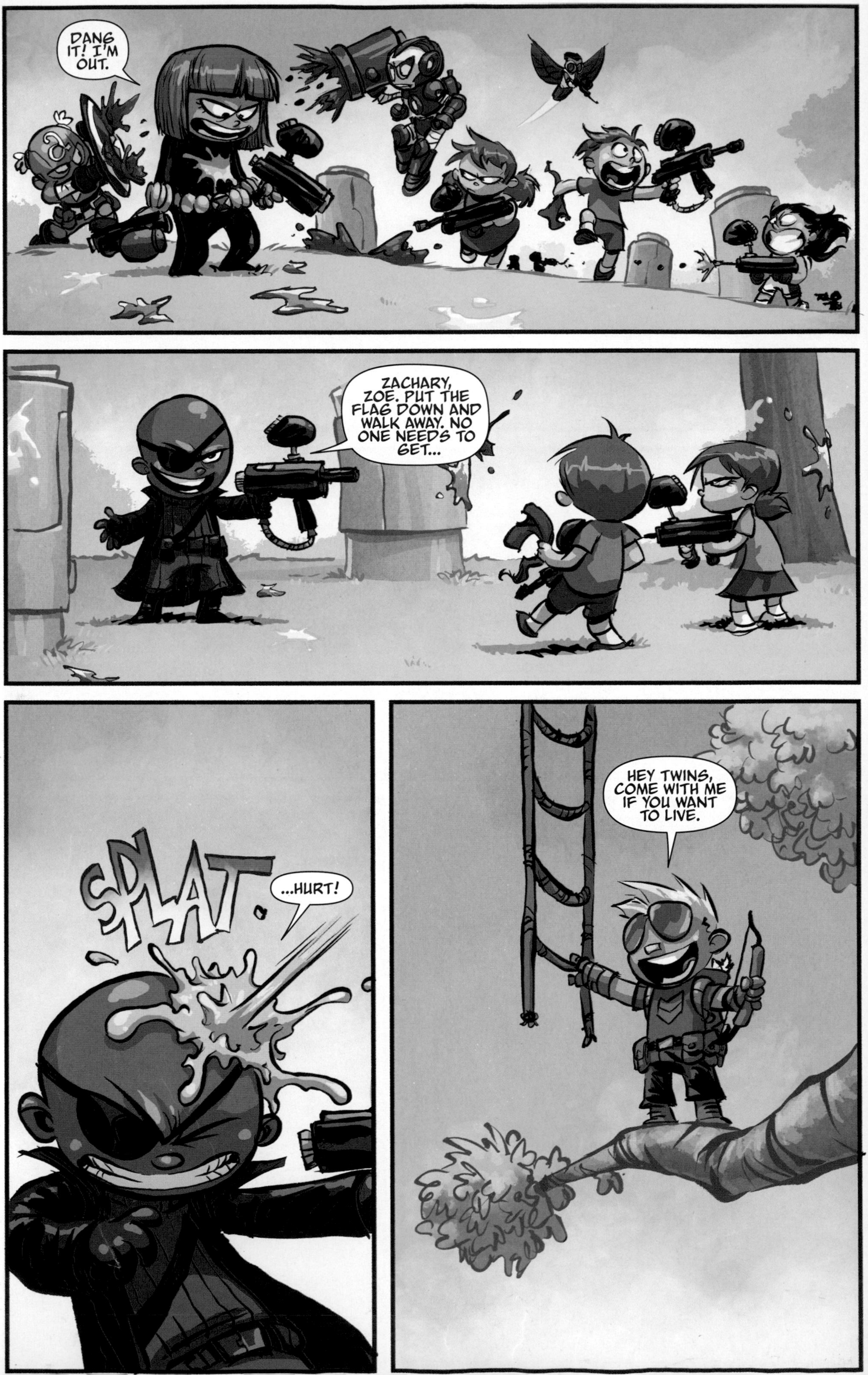
DANG IT! I'M OUT.
ZACHARY, ZOE. PUT THE FLAG DOWN AND WALK AWAY. NO ONE NEEDS TO GET...
SPLAT
...HURT!
HEY TWINS, COME WITH ME IF YOU WANT TO LIVE.

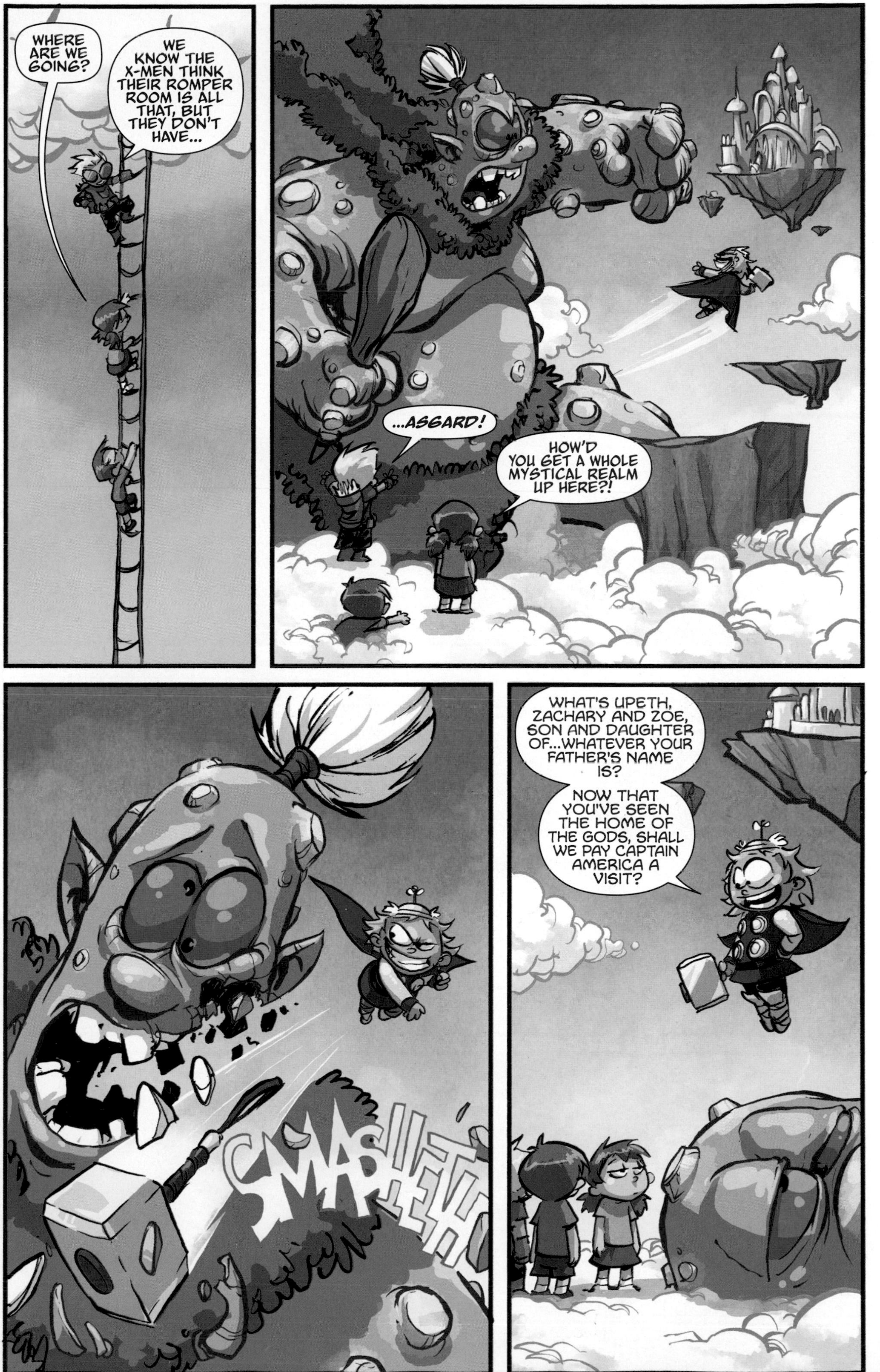

WHERE ARE WE GOING?
WE KNOW THE X-MEN THINK THEIR ROMPER ROOM IS ALL THAT, BUT THEY DON'T HAVE...
...ASGARD!
HOW'D YOU GET A WHOLE MYSTICAL REALM UP HERE?!
SMASH
WHAT'S UPETH, ZACHARY AND ZOE, SON AND DAUGHTER OF...WHATEVER YOUR FATHER'S NAME IS?
NOW THAT YOU'VE SEEN THE HOME OF THE GODS, SHALL WE PAY CAPTAIN AMERICA A VISIT?

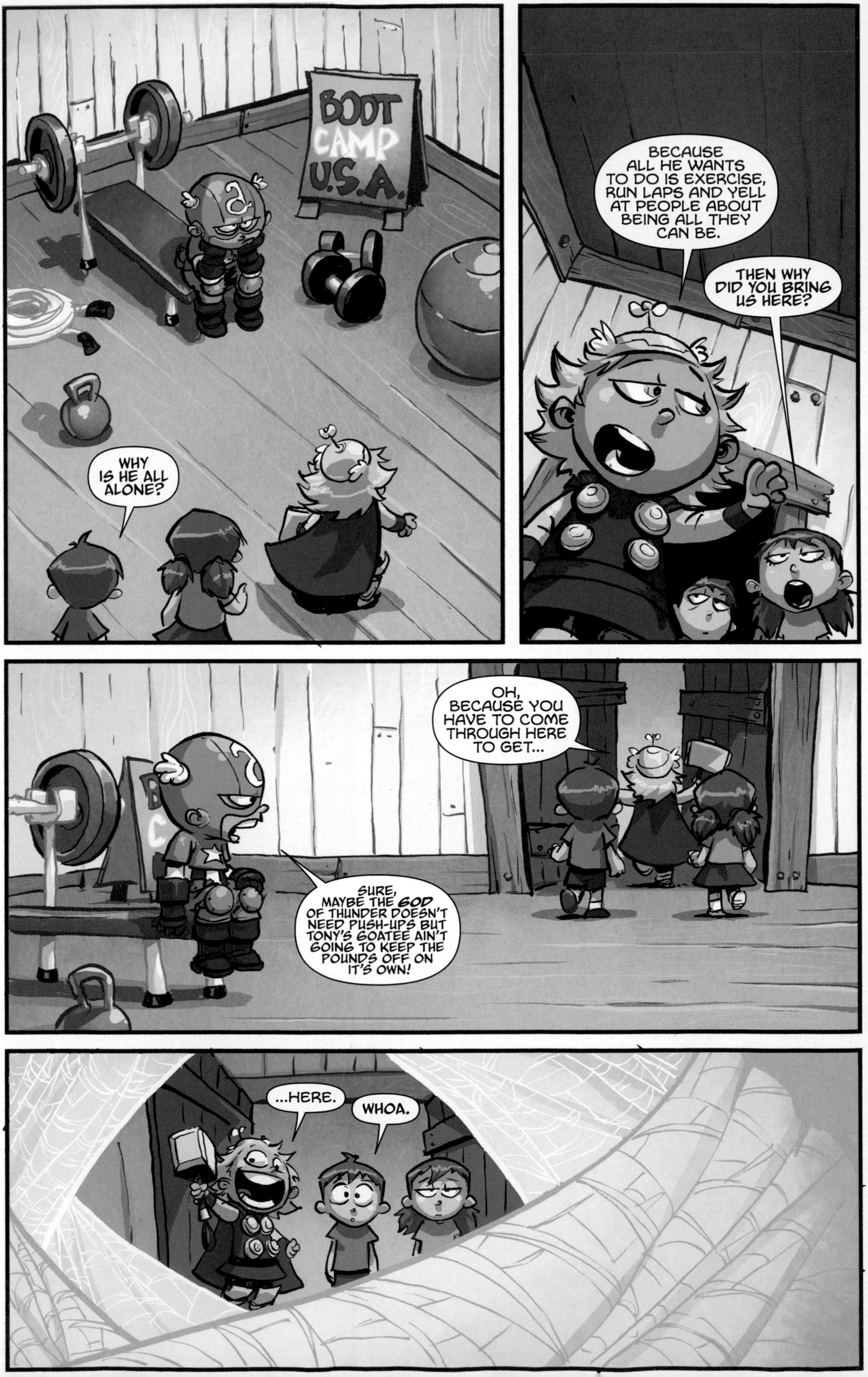
BOOT CAMP U.S.A.
WHY IS HE ALL ALONE?
BECAUSE ALL HE WANTS TO DO IS EXERCISE, RUN LAPS AND YELL AT PEOPLE ABOUT BEING ALL THEY CAN BE.
THEN WHY DID YOU BRING US HERE?
SURE, MAYBE THE *GOD* OF THUNDER DOESN'T NEED PUSH-UPS BUT TONY'S GOATEE AIN'T GOING TO KEEP THE POUNDS OFF ON IT'S OWN!
OH, BECAUSE YOU HAVE TO COME THROUGH HERE TO GET...
...HERE.
WHOA.

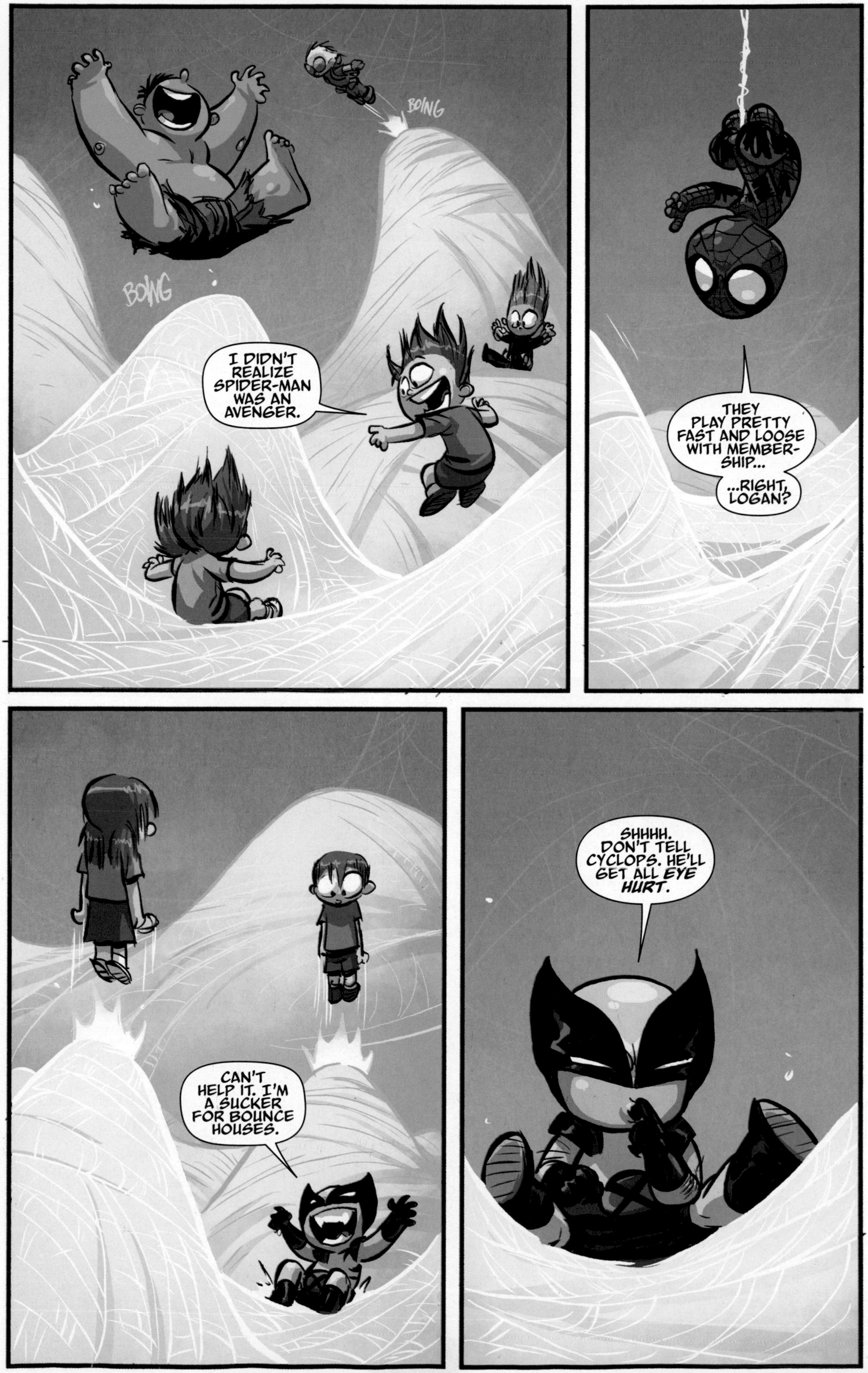
BOING
BOING
I DIDN'T REALIZE SPIDER-MAN WAS AN AVENGER.
THEY PLAY PRETTY FAST AND LOOSE WITH MEMBER-SHIP...
...RIGHT, LOGAN?
CAN'T HELP IT. I'M A SUCKER FOR BOUNCE HOUSES.
SHHHH. DON'T TELL CYCLOPS. HE'LL GET ALL *EYE HURT*.

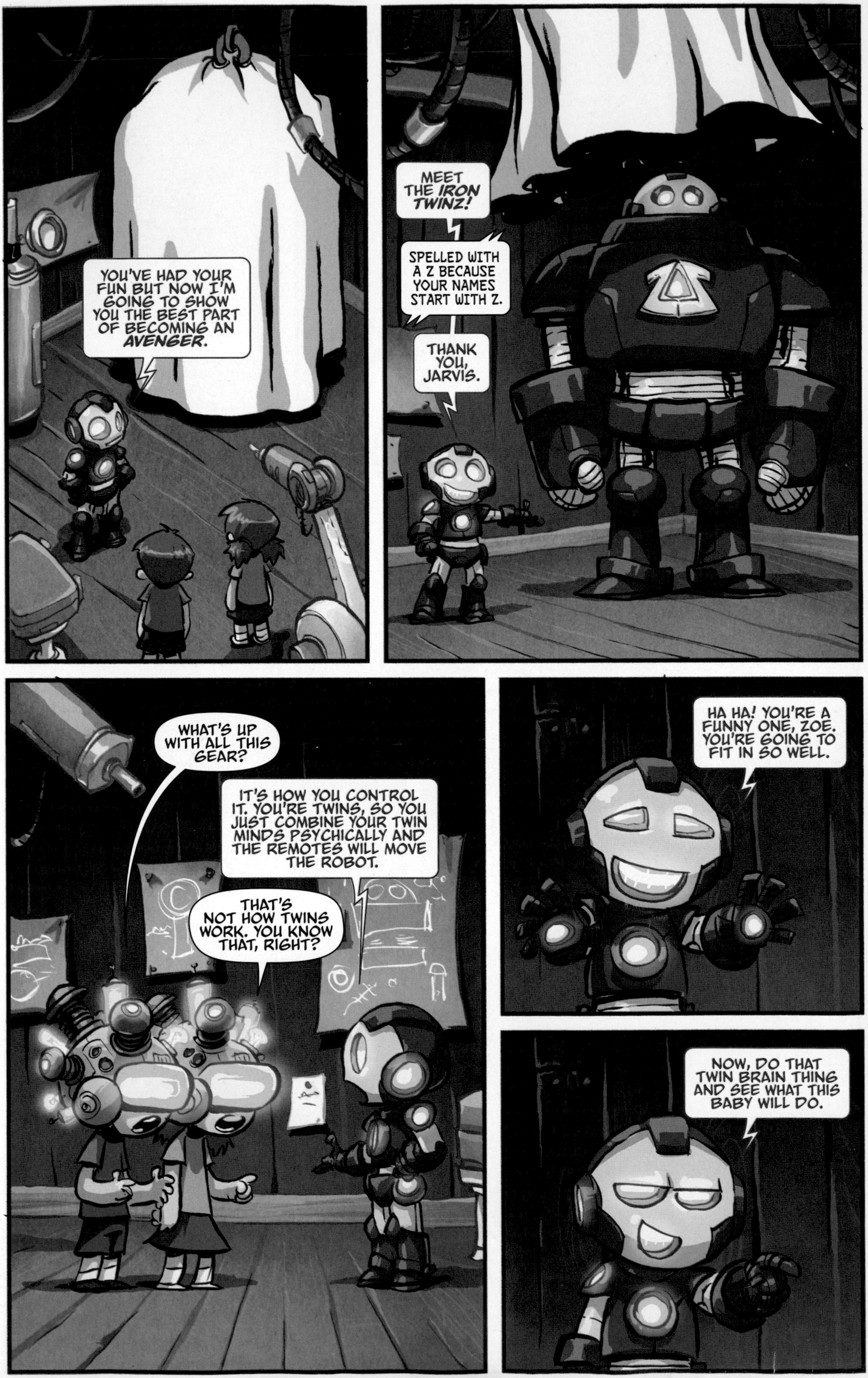
YOU'VE HAD YOUR FUN BUT NOW I'M GOING TO SHOW YOU THE BEST PART OF BECOMING AN *AVENGER*.
MEET THE *IRON TWINZ!*
SPELLED WITH A Z BECAUSE YOUR NAMES START WITH Z.
THANK YOU, JARVIS.
WHAT'S UP WITH ALL THIS GEAR?
IT'S HOW YOU CONTROL IT. YOU'RE TWINS, SO YOU JUST COMBINE YOUR TWIN MINDS PSYCHICALLY AND THE REMOTES WILL MOVE THE ROBOT.
THAT'S NOT HOW TWINS WORK. YOU KNOW THAT, RIGHT?
HA HA! YOU'RE A FUNNY ONE, ZOE. YOU'RE GOING TO FIT IN SO WELL.
NOW, DO THAT TWIN BRAIN THING AND SEE WHAT THIS BABY WILL DO.

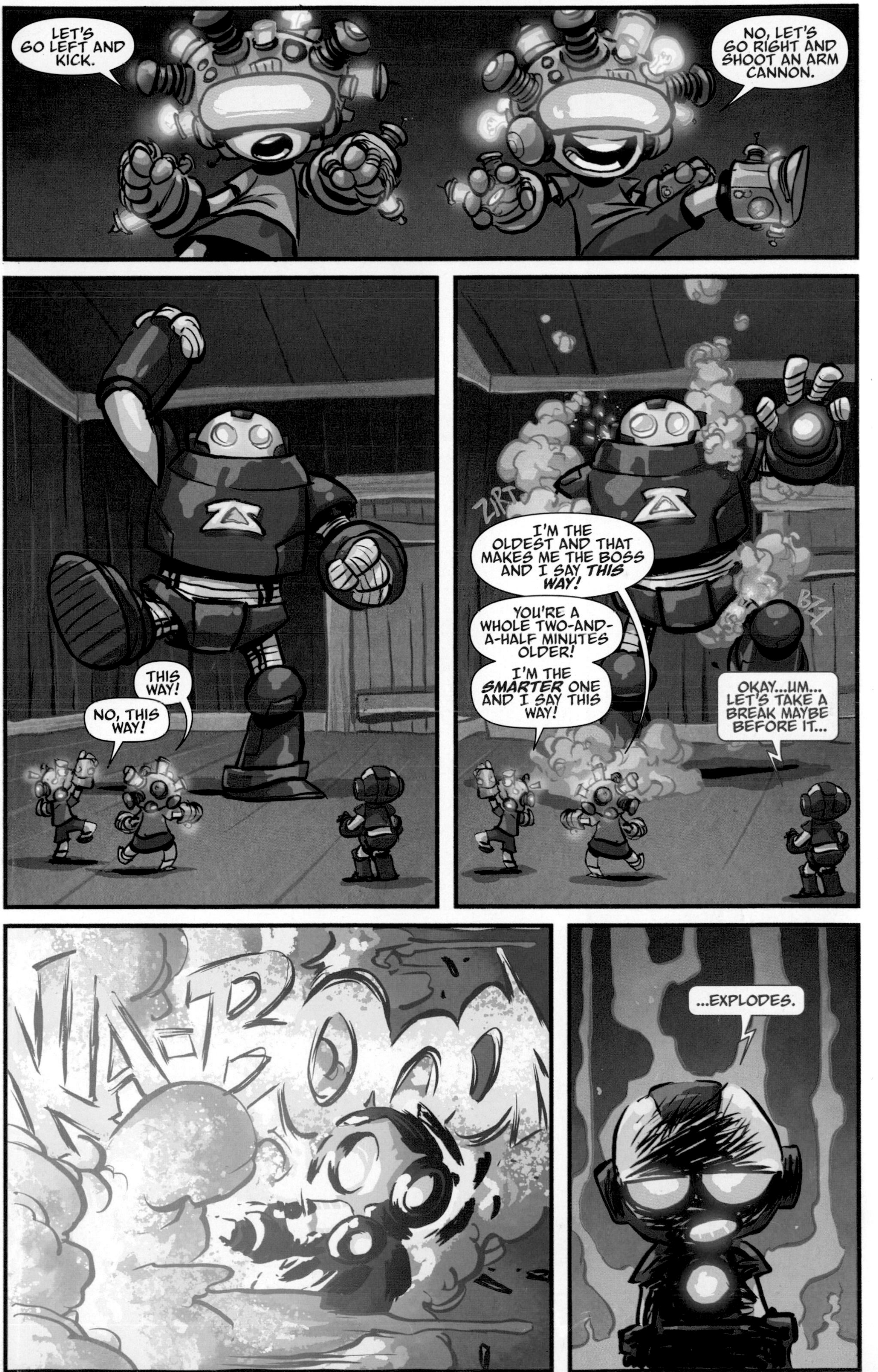
LET'S GO LEFT AND KICK.
NO, LET'S GO RIGHT AND SHOOT AN ARM CANNON.
THIS WAY!
NO, THIS WAY!
ZIRT
I'M THE OLDEST AND THAT MAKES ME THE BOSS AND I SAY *THIS WAY!*
YOU'RE A WHOLE TWO-AND-A-HALF MINUTES OLDER!
I'M THE *SMARTER* ONE AND I SAY THIS WAY!
BZZ
OKAY...UM... LET'S TAKE A BREAK MAYBE BEFORE IT...
...EXPLODES.

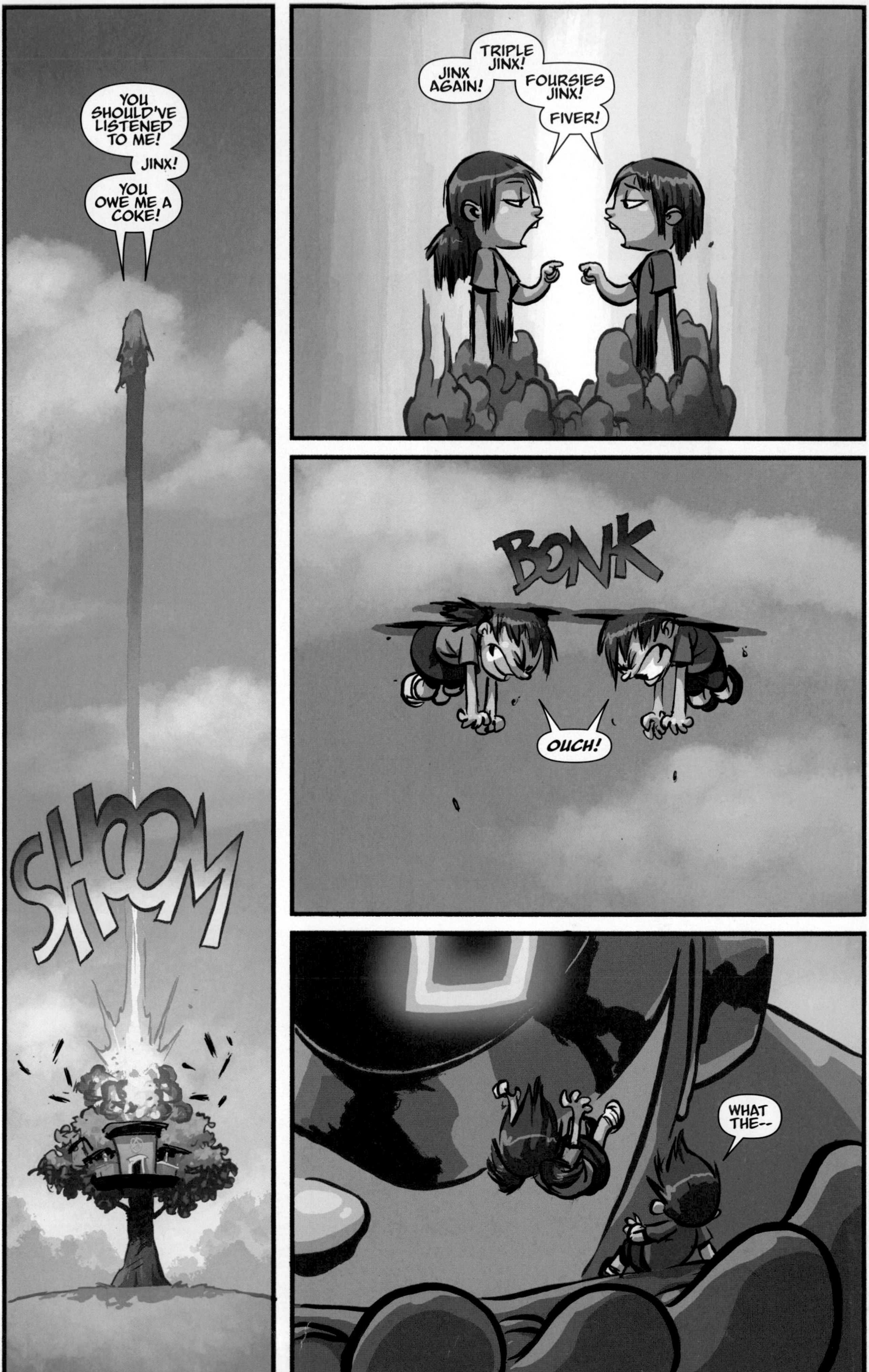
YOU SHOULD'VE LISTENED TO ME!
JINX!
YOU OWE ME A COKE!
SHOOM
JINX AGAIN!
TRIPLE JINX!
FOURSIES JINX!
FIVER!
BONK
OUCH!
WHAT THE--

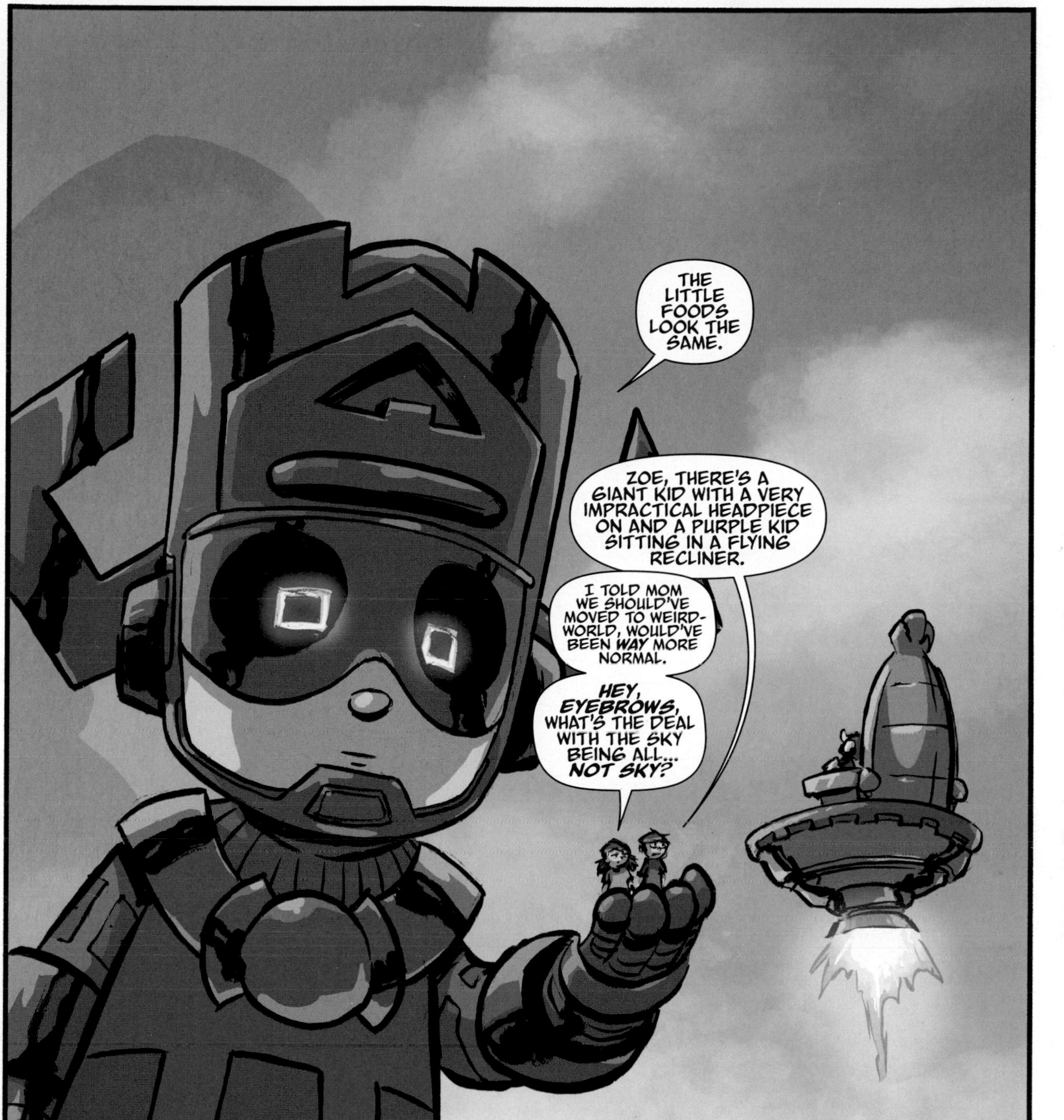
THE LITTLE FOODS LOOK THE SAME.
ZOE, THERE'S A GIANT KID WITH A VERY IMPRACTICAL HEADPIECE ON AND A PURPLE KID SITTING IN A FLYING RECLINER.
I TOLD MOM WE SHOULD'VE MOVED TO WEIRD-WORLD, WOULD'VE BEEN WAY MORE NORMAL.
HEY, EYEBROWS, WHAT'S THE DEAL WITH THE SKY BEING ALL... NOT SKY?
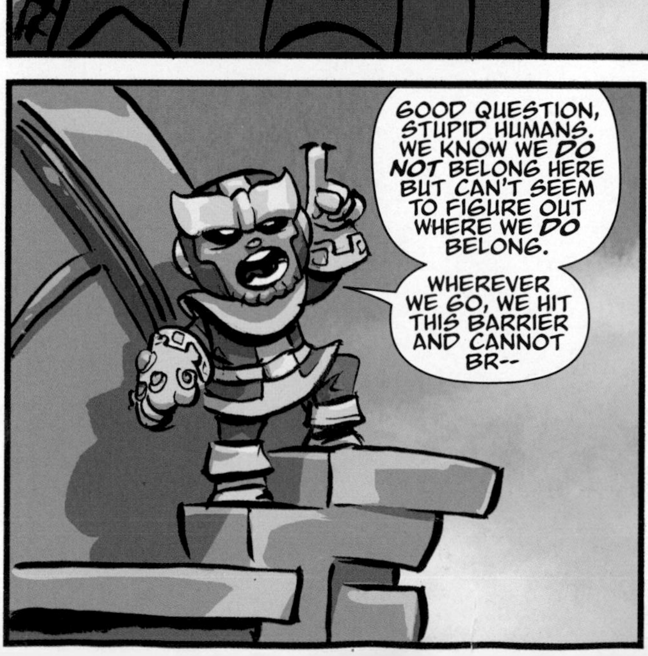
GOOD QUESTION, STUPID HUMANS. WE KNOW WE DO NOT BELONG HERE BUT CAN'T SEEM TO FIGURE OUT WHERE WE DO BELONG.
WHEREVER WE GO, WE HIT THIS BARRIER AND CANNOT BR--
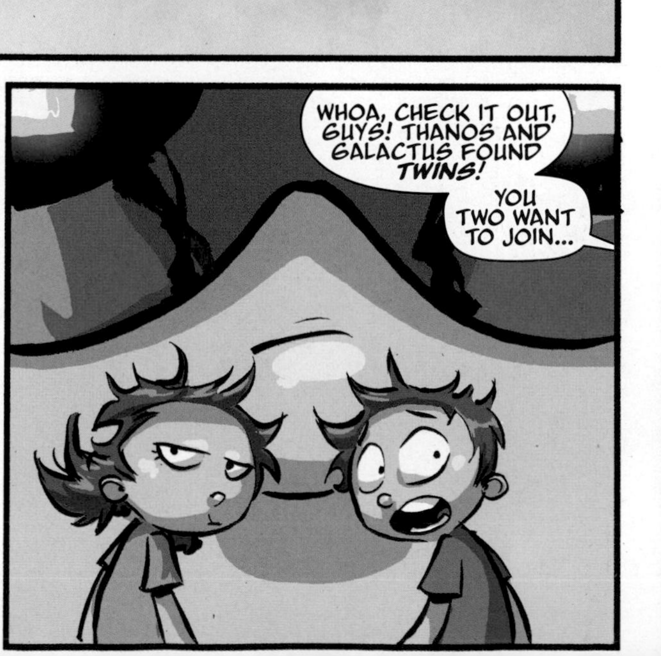
WHOA, CHECK IT OUT, GUYS! THANOS AND GALACTUS FOUND TWINS!
YOU TWO WANT TO JOIN...

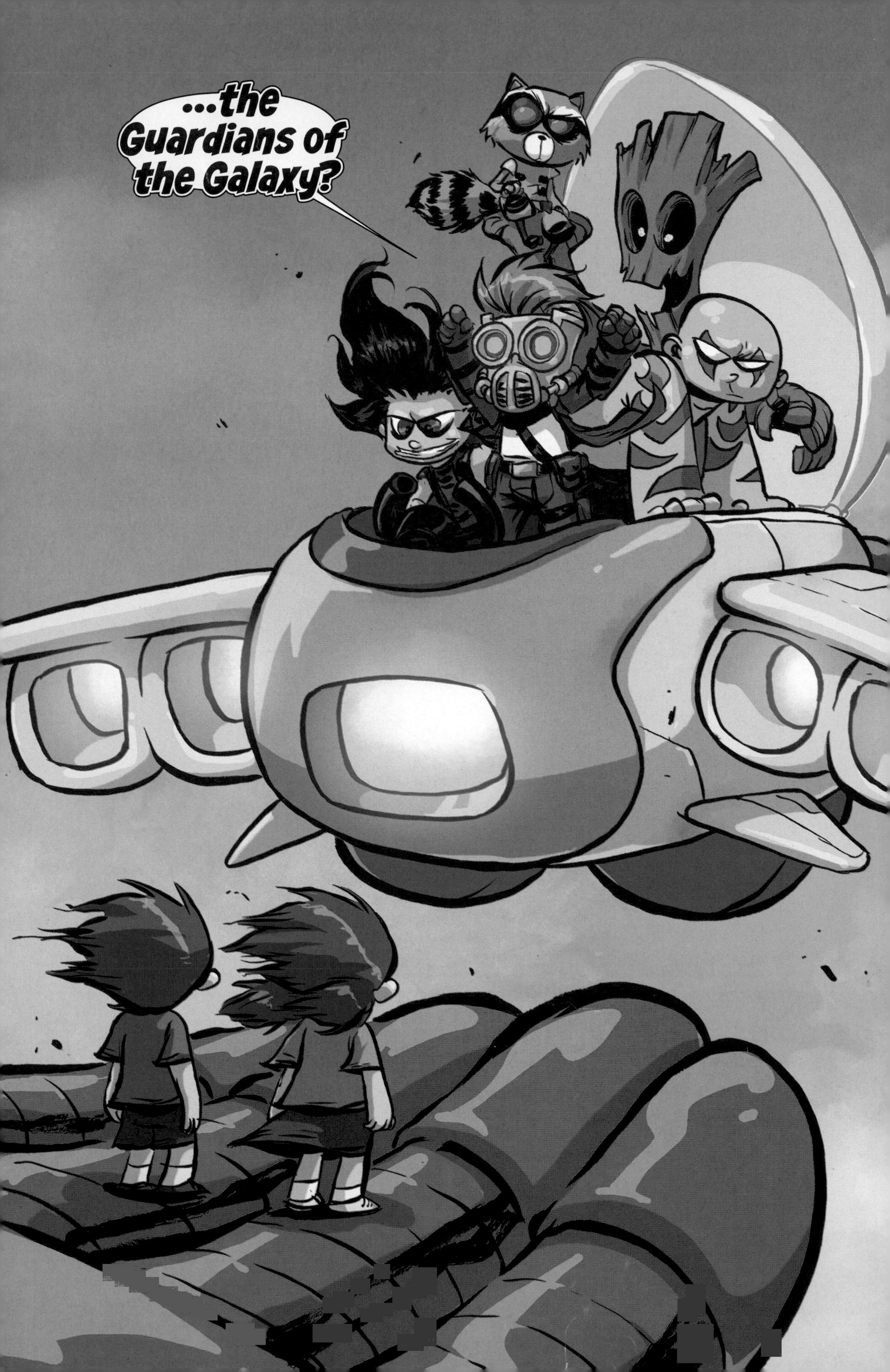
...the Guardians of the Galaxy?

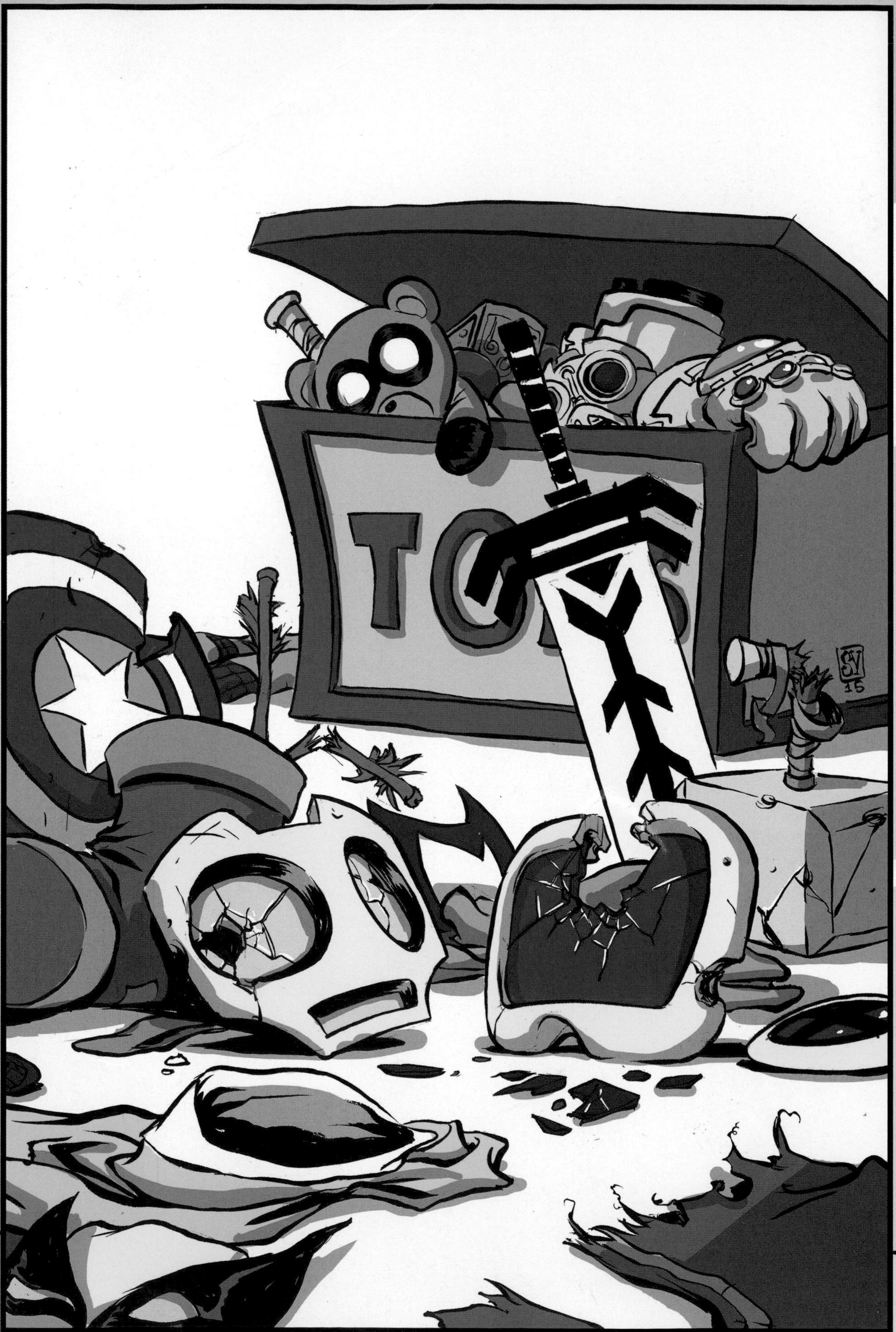
SY
15

GIANT-SIZE LITTLE MARVEL: AVX #4

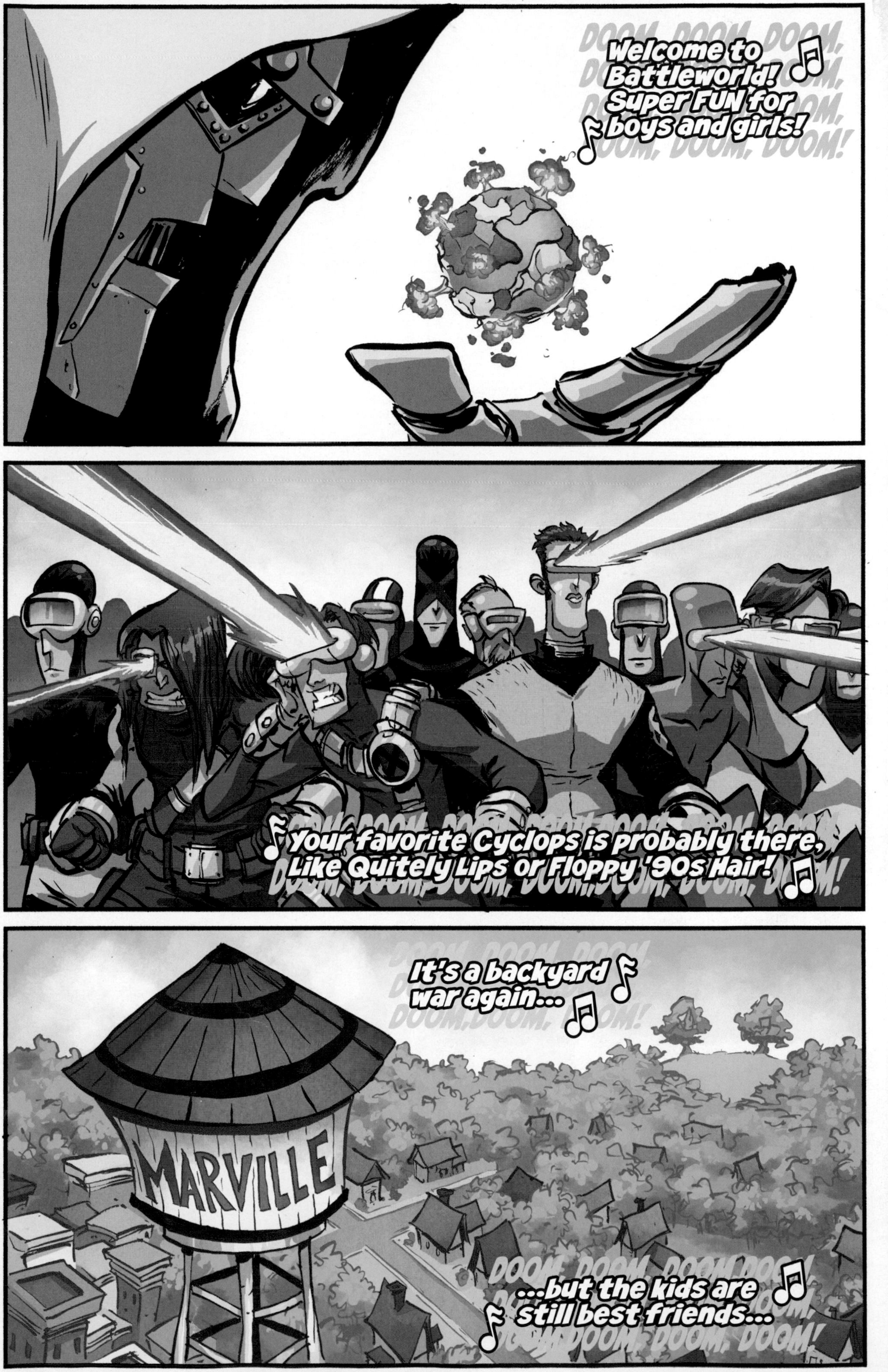
DOOM, DOOM, DOOM, DOOM, DOOM, DOOM, DOOM, DOOM, DOOM!
Welcome to Battleworld! Super FUN for boys and girls!
Your favorite Cyclops is probably there, Like Quitely Lips or Floppy '90s Hair!
It's a backyard war again...
MARVILLE
...but the kids are still best friends...

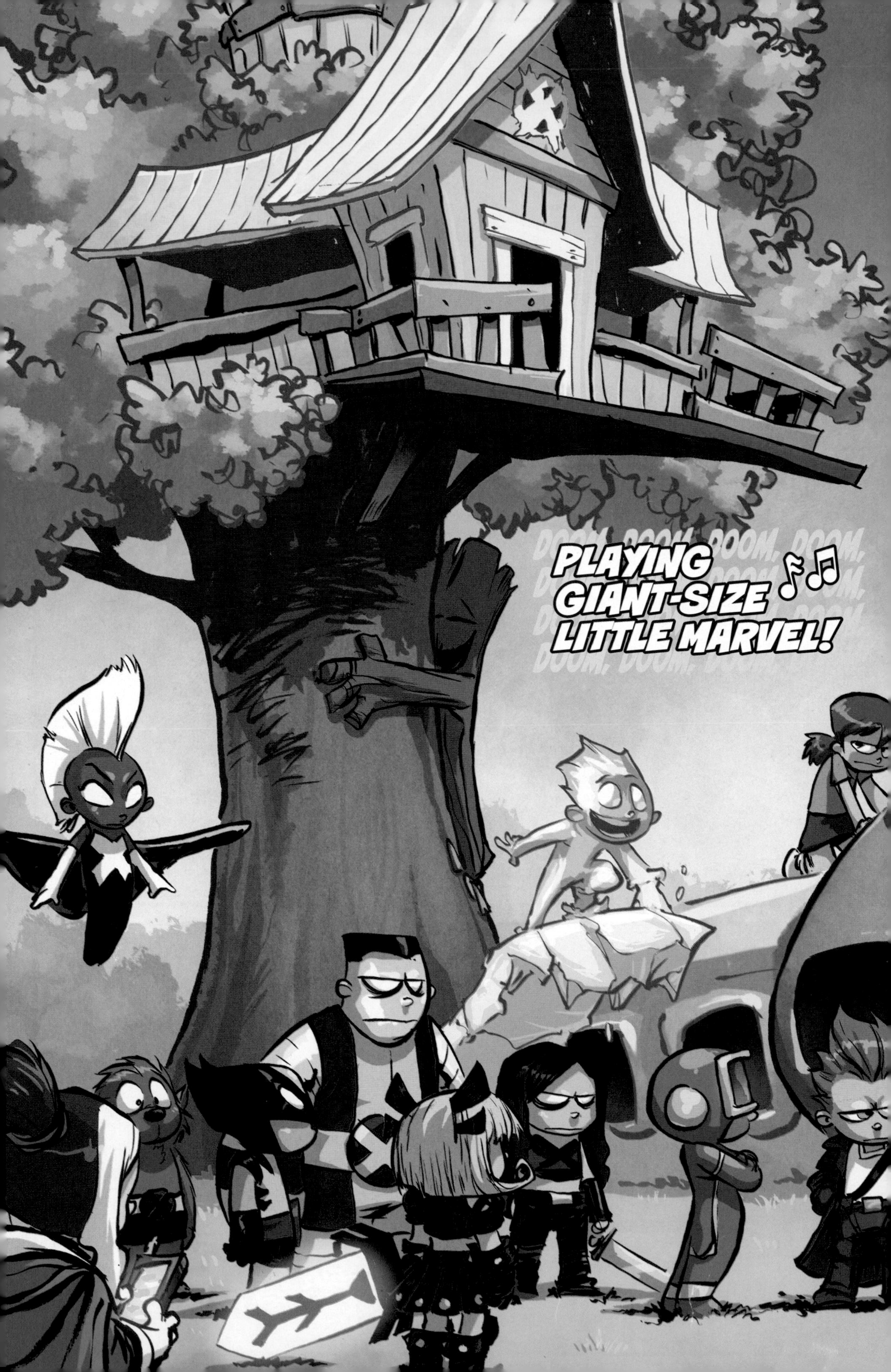
PLAYING GIANT-SIZE LITTLE MARVEL!

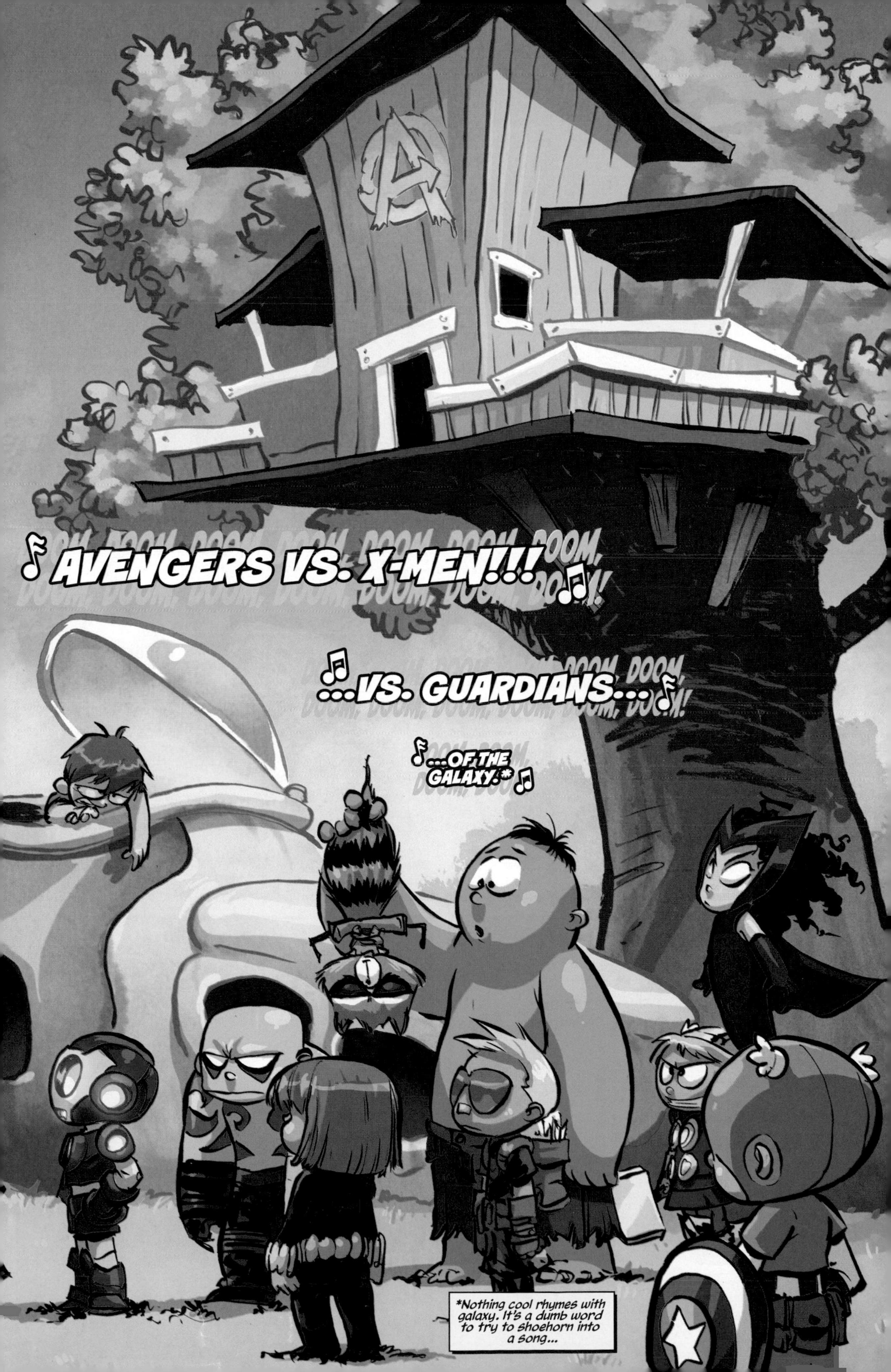
AVENGERS VS. X-MEN!!!
...VS. GUARDIANS...
...OF THE GALAXY.*
*Nothing cool rhymes with galaxy. It's a dumb word to try to shoehorn into a song...

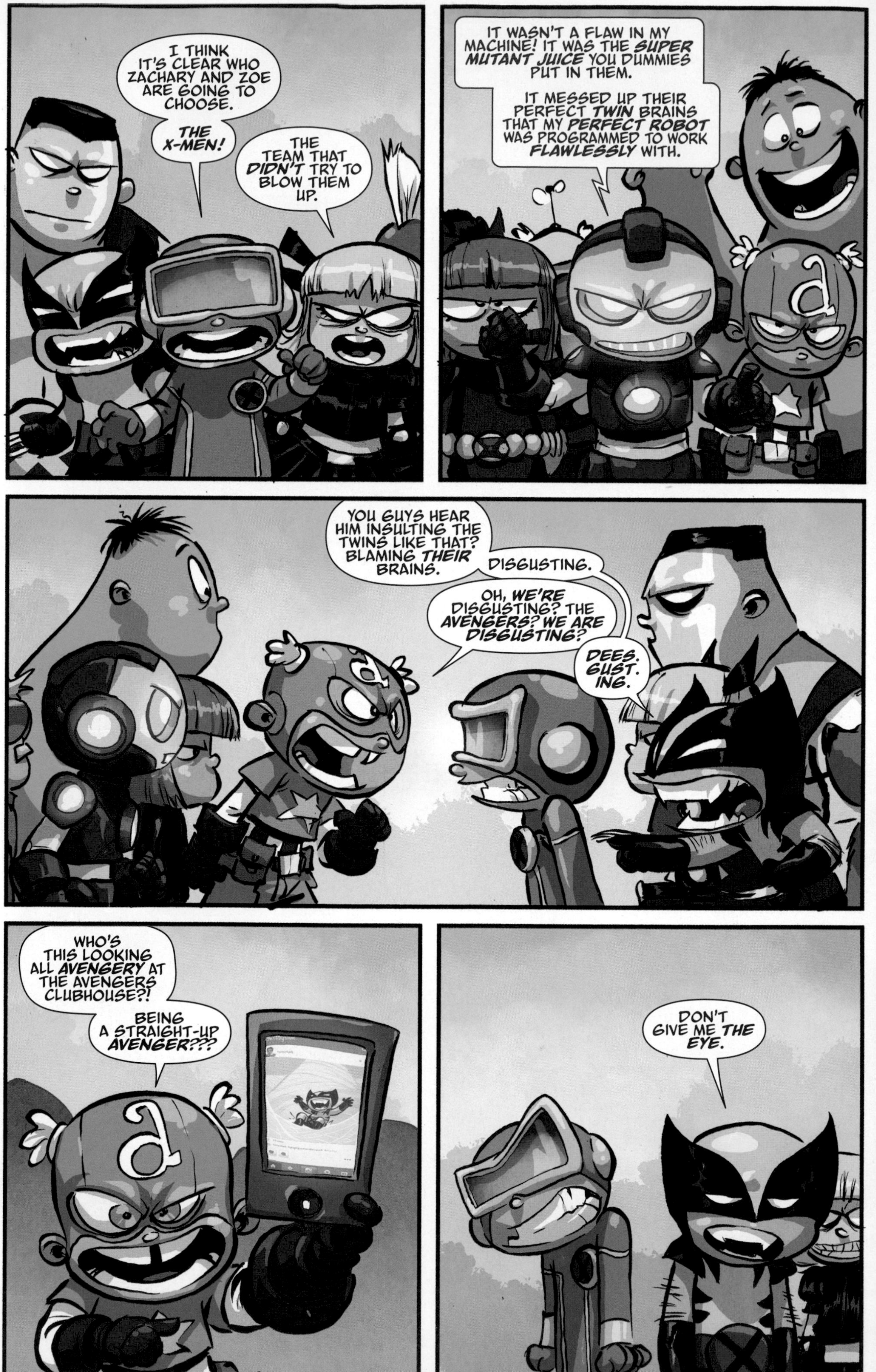
I THINK IT'S CLEAR WHO ZACHARY AND ZOE ARE GOING TO CHOOSE.
THE X-MEN!
THE TEAM THAT DIDN'T TRY TO BLOW THEM UP.
IT WASN'T A FLAW IN MY MACHINE! IT WAS THE SUPER MUTANT JUICE YOU DUMMIES PUT IN THEM.
IT MESSED UP THEIR PERFECT TWIN BRAINS THAT MY PERFECT ROBOT WAS PROGRAMMED TO WORK FLAWLESSLY WITH.
YOU GUYS HEAR HIM INSULTING THE TWINS LIKE THAT? BLAMING THEIR BRAINS.
DISGUSTING.
OH, WE'RE DISGUSTING? THE AVENGERS? WE ARE DISGUSTING?
DEES. GUST. ING.
WHO'S THIS LOOKING ALL AVENGERY AT THE AVENGERS CLUBHOUSE?!
BEING A STRAIGHT-UP AVENGER???
DON'T GIVE ME THE EYE.

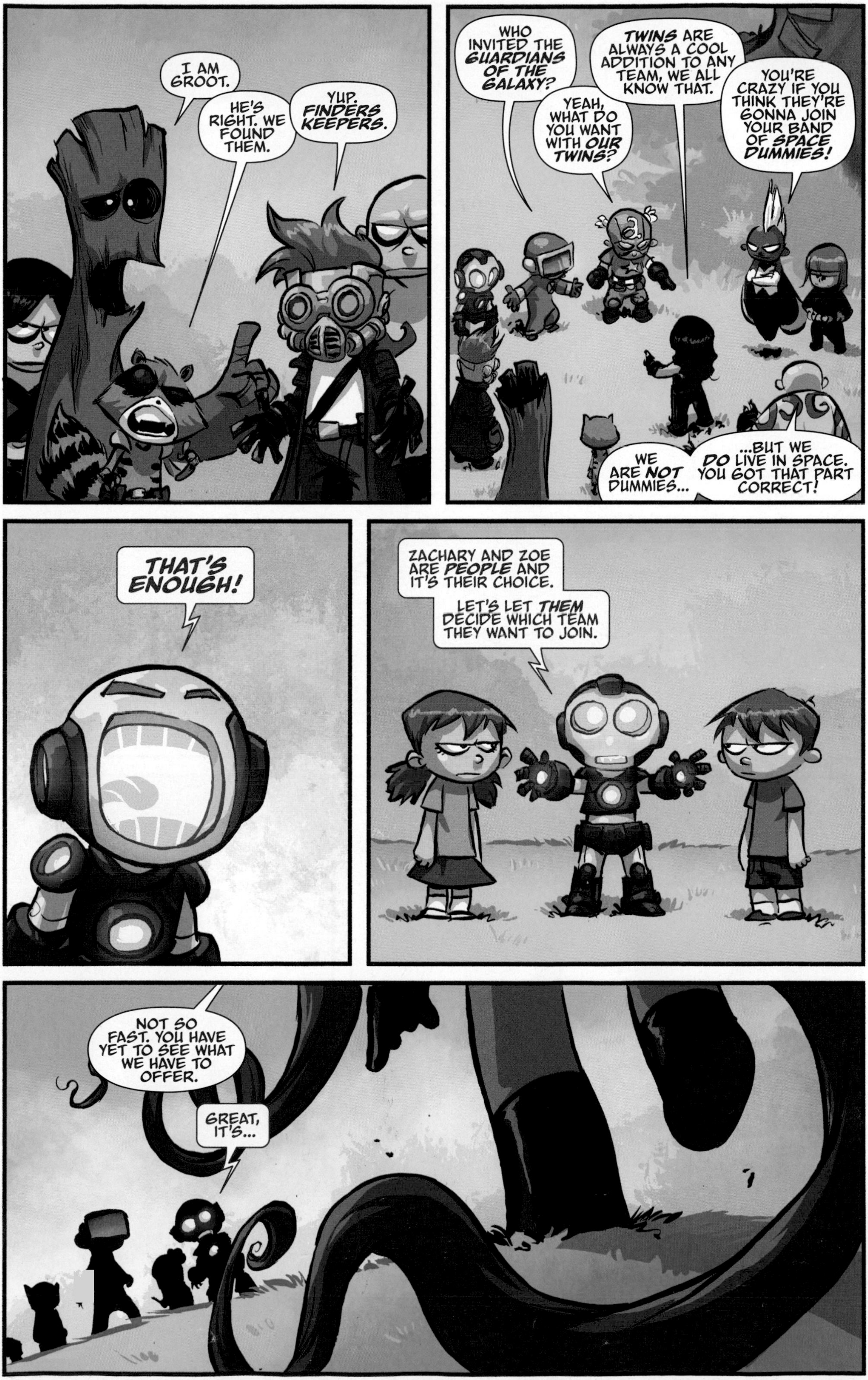
I AM GROOT.
HE'S RIGHT. WE FOUND THEM.
YUP. FINDERS KEEPERS.
WHO INVITED THE GUARDIANS OF THE GALAXY?
YEAH, WHAT DO YOU WANT WITH OUR TWINS?
TWINS ARE ALWAYS A COOL ADDITION TO ANY TEAM, WE ALL KNOW THAT.
YOU'RE CRAZY IF YOU THINK THEY'RE GONNA JOIN YOUR BAND OF SPACE DUMMIES!
WE ARE NOT DUMMIES...
...BUT WE DO LIVE IN SPACE. YOU GOT THAT PART CORRECT!
THAT'S ENOUGH!
ZACHARY AND ZOE ARE PEOPLE AND IT'S THEIR CHOICE.
LET'S LET THEM DECIDE WHICH TEAM THEY WANT TO JOIN.
NOT SO FAST. YOU HAVE YET TO SEE WHAT WE HAVE TO OFFER.
GREAT, IT'S...

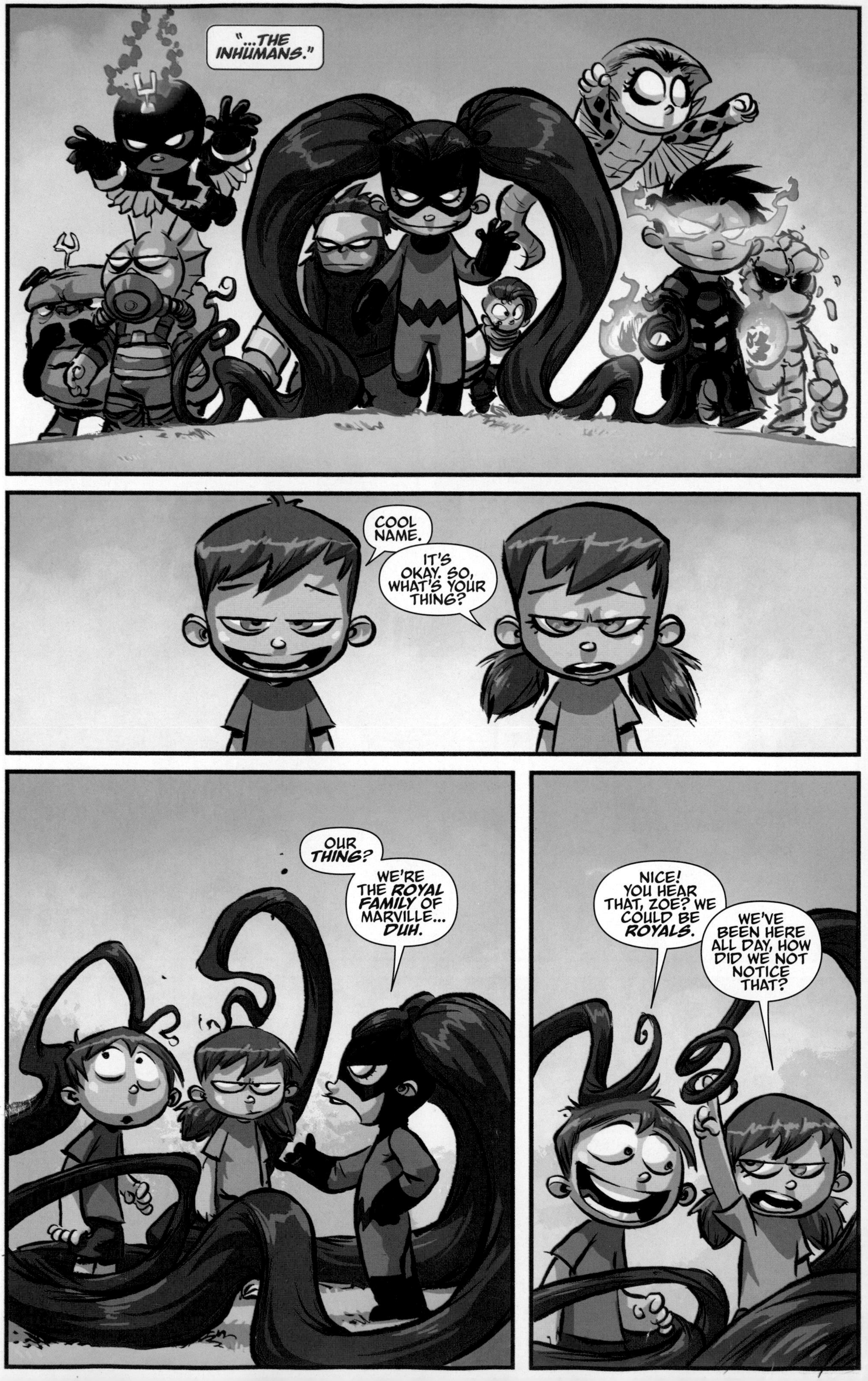
"...THE INHÜMANS."
COOL NAME.
IT'S OKAY. SO, WHAT'S YOUR THING?
OUR THING?
WE'RE THE ROYAL FAMILY OF MARVILLE... DUH.
NICE! YOU HEAR THAT, ZOE? WE COULD BE ROYALS.
WE'VE BEEN HERE ALL DAY, HOW DID WE NOT NOTICE THAT?

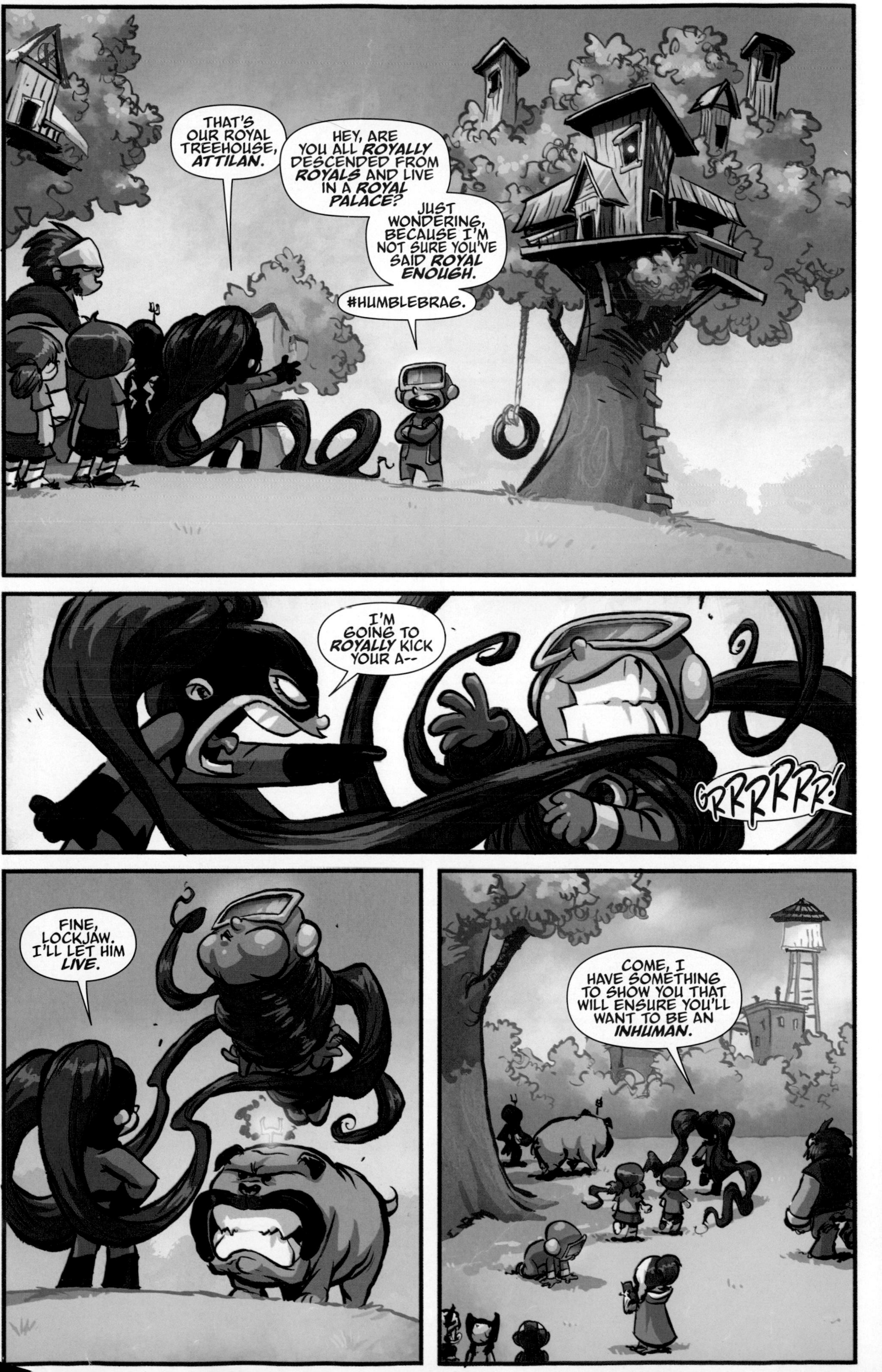
THAT'S OUR ROYAL TREEHOUSE, ATTILAN.
HEY, ARE YOU ALL ROYALLY DESCENDED FROM ROYALS AND LIVE IN A ROYAL PALACE?
JUST WONDERING, BECAUSE I'M NOT SURE YOU'VE SAID ROYAL ENOUGH.
#HUMBLEBRAG.
I'M GOING TO ROYALLY KICK YOUR A--
GRRRRRR!
FINE, LOCKJAW. I'LL LET HIM LIVE.
COME, I HAVE SOMETHING TO SHOW YOU THAT WILL ENSURE YOU'LL WANT TO BE AN INHUMAN.

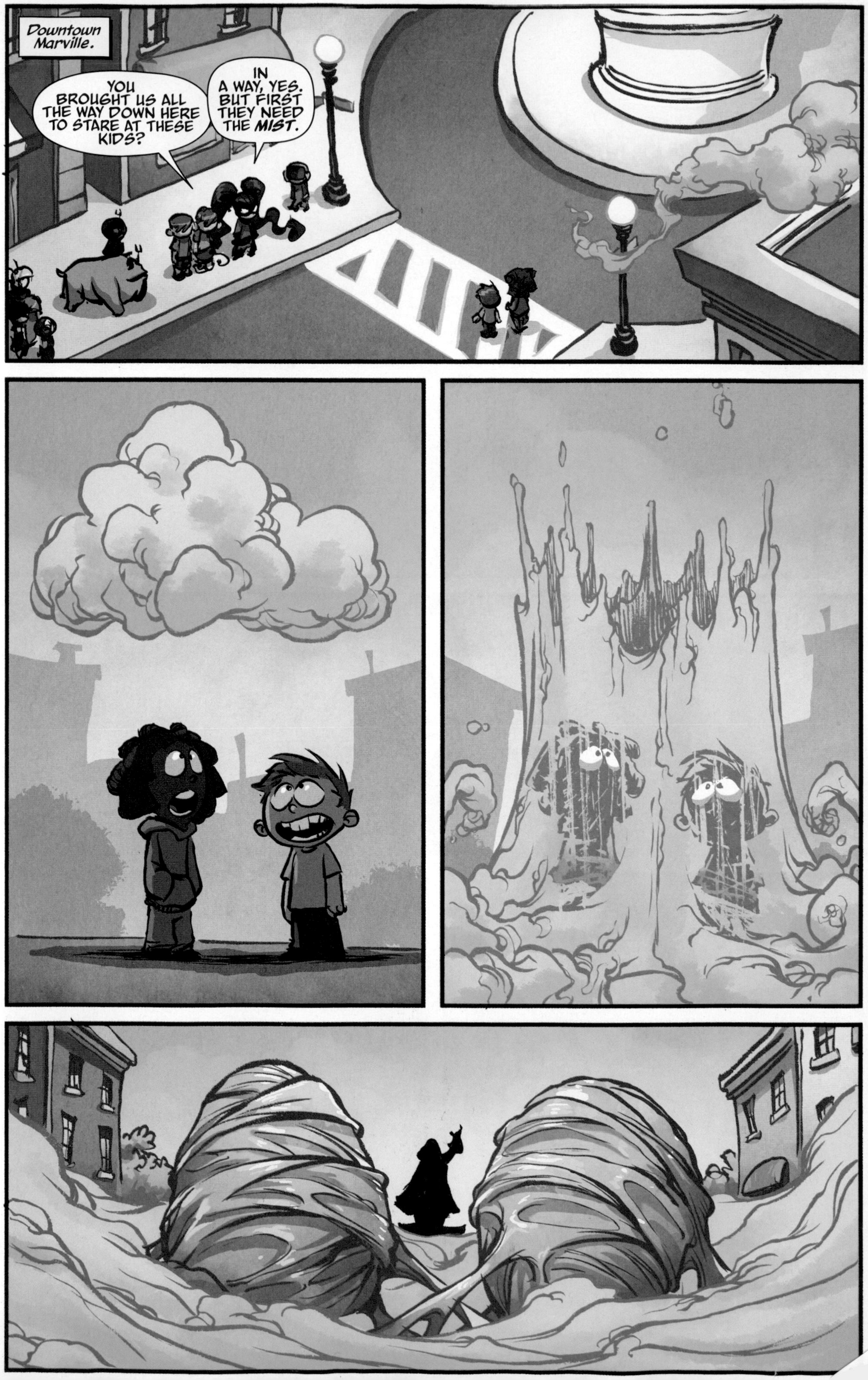
Downtown Marville.
YOU BROUGHT US ALL THE WAY DOWN HERE TO STARE AT THESE KIDS?
IN A WAY, YES. BUT FIRST THEY NEED THE *MIST*.

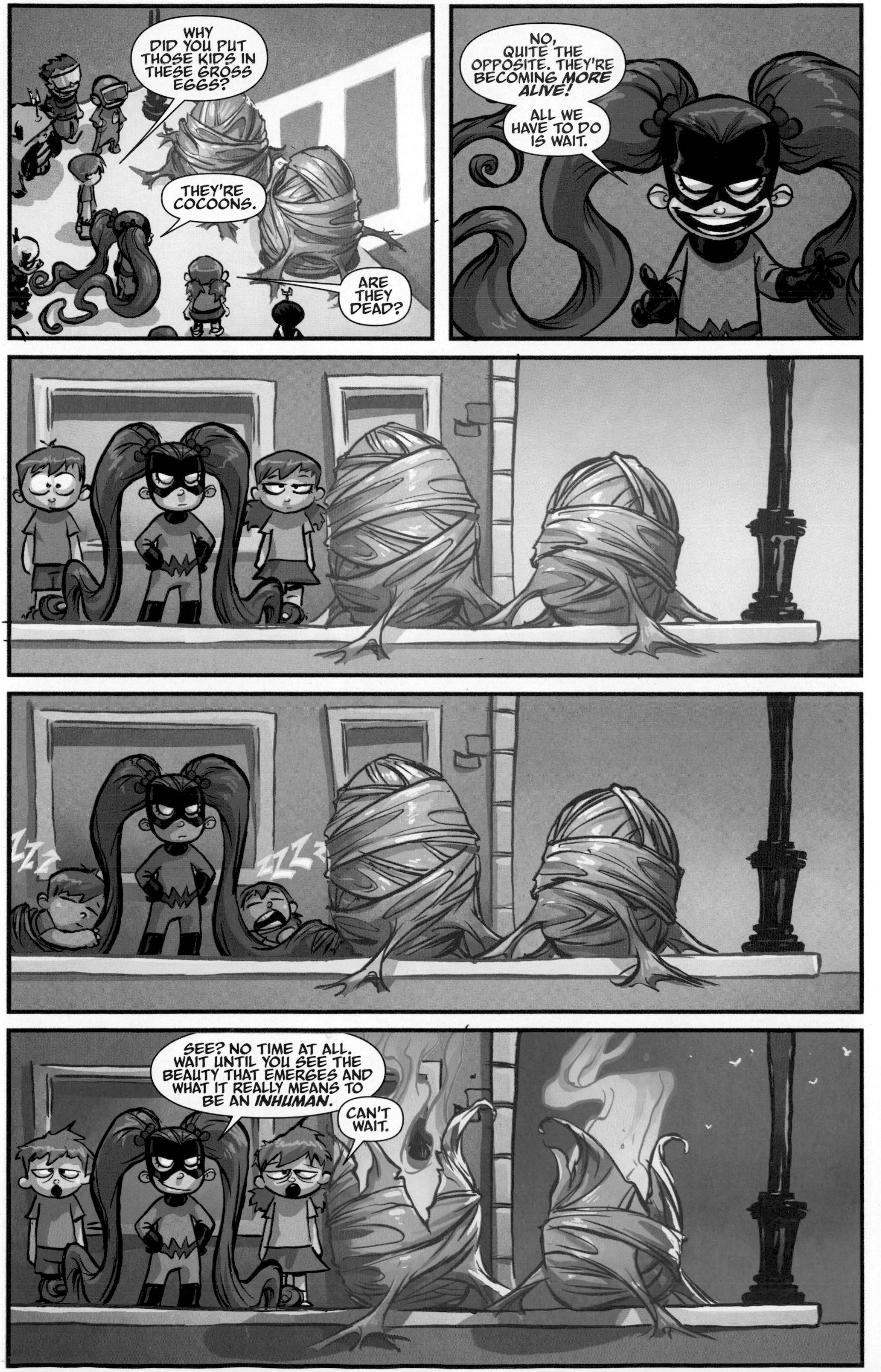
WHY DID YOU PUT THOSE KIDS IN THESE GROSS EGGS?
THEY'RE COCOONS.
ARE THEY DEAD?
NO, QUITE THE OPPOSITE. THEY'RE BECOMING MORE ALIVE!
ALL WE HAVE TO DO IS WAIT.
ZZZ
ZZZ
SEE? NO TIME AT ALL. WAIT UNTIL YOU SEE THE BEAUTY THAT EMERGES AND WHAT IT REALLY MEANS TO BE AN INHUMAN.
CAN'T WAIT.

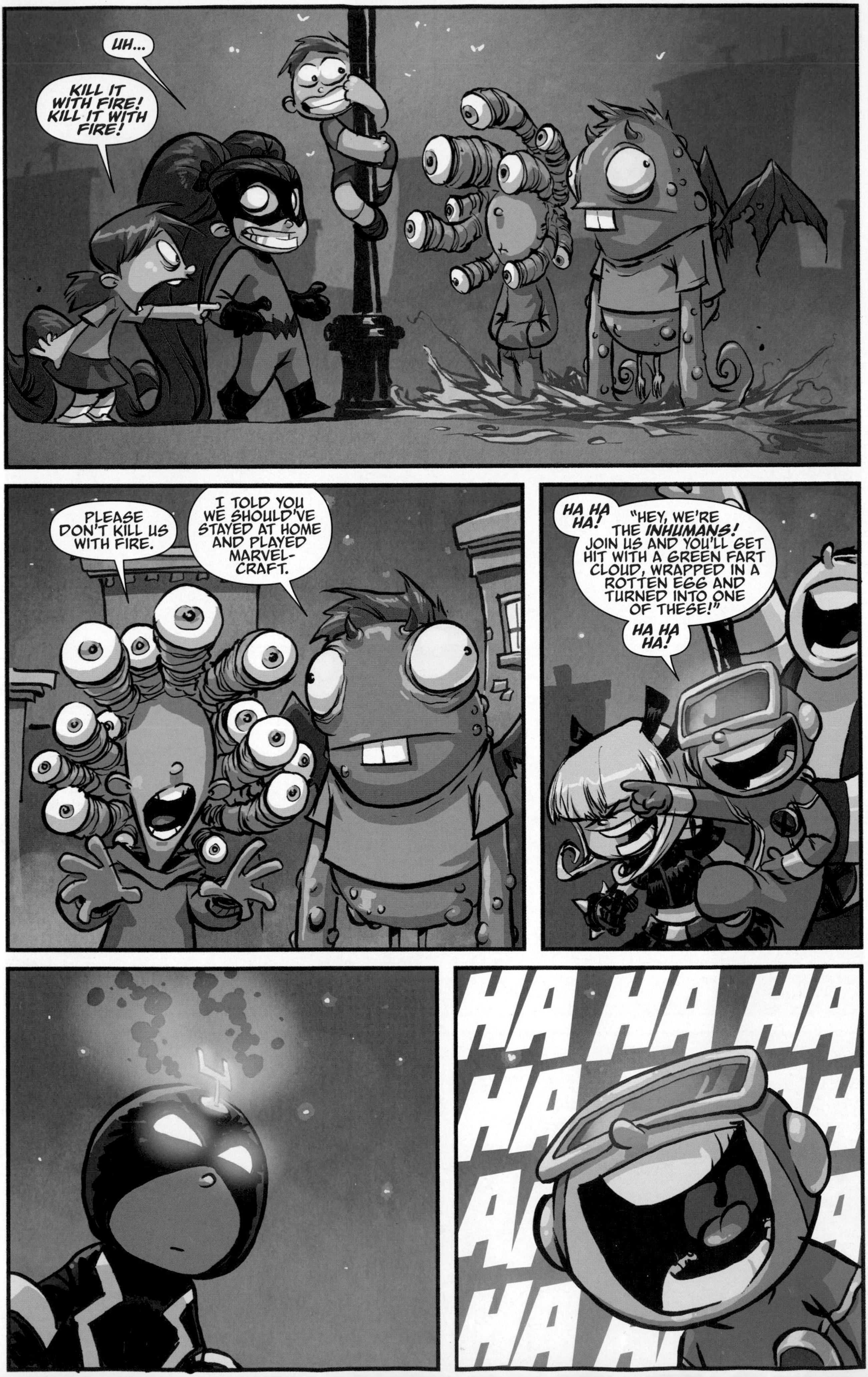

UH...
KILL IT WITH FIRE! KILL IT WITH FIRE!
PLEASE DON'T KILL US WITH FIRE.
I TOLD YOU WE SHOULD'VE STAYED AT HOME AND PLAYED MARVEL-CRAFT.
HA HA HA!
"HEY, WE'RE THE INHUMANS! JOIN US AND YOU'LL GET HIT WITH A GREEN FART CLOUD, WRAPPED IN A ROTTEN EGG AND TURNED INTO ONE OF THESE!"
HA HA HA!
HA HA HA HA HA HA

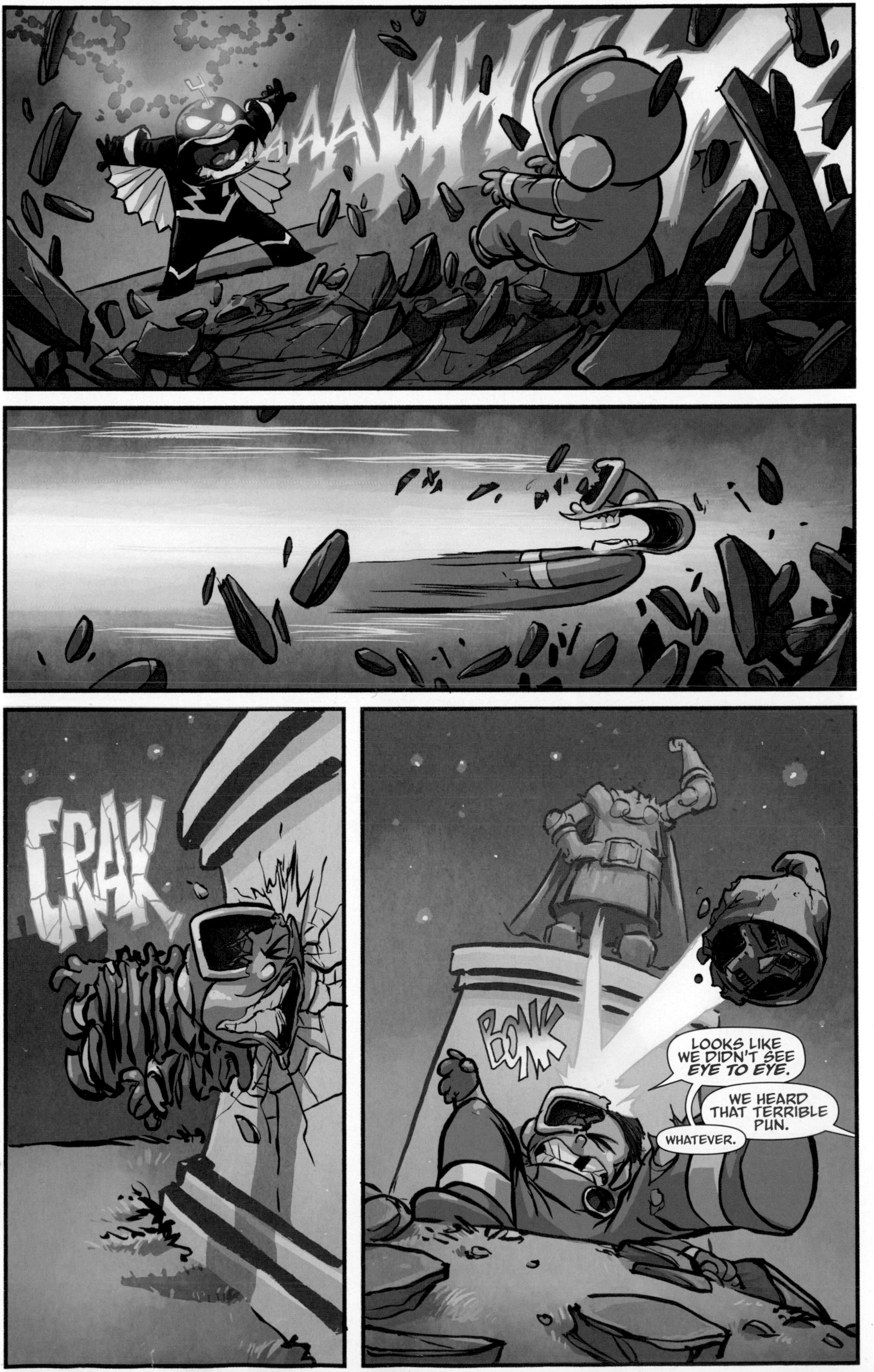
CRAK
BONK
LOOKS LIKE WE DIDN'T SEE EYE TO EYE.
WE HEARD THAT TERRIBLE PUN.
WHATEVER.

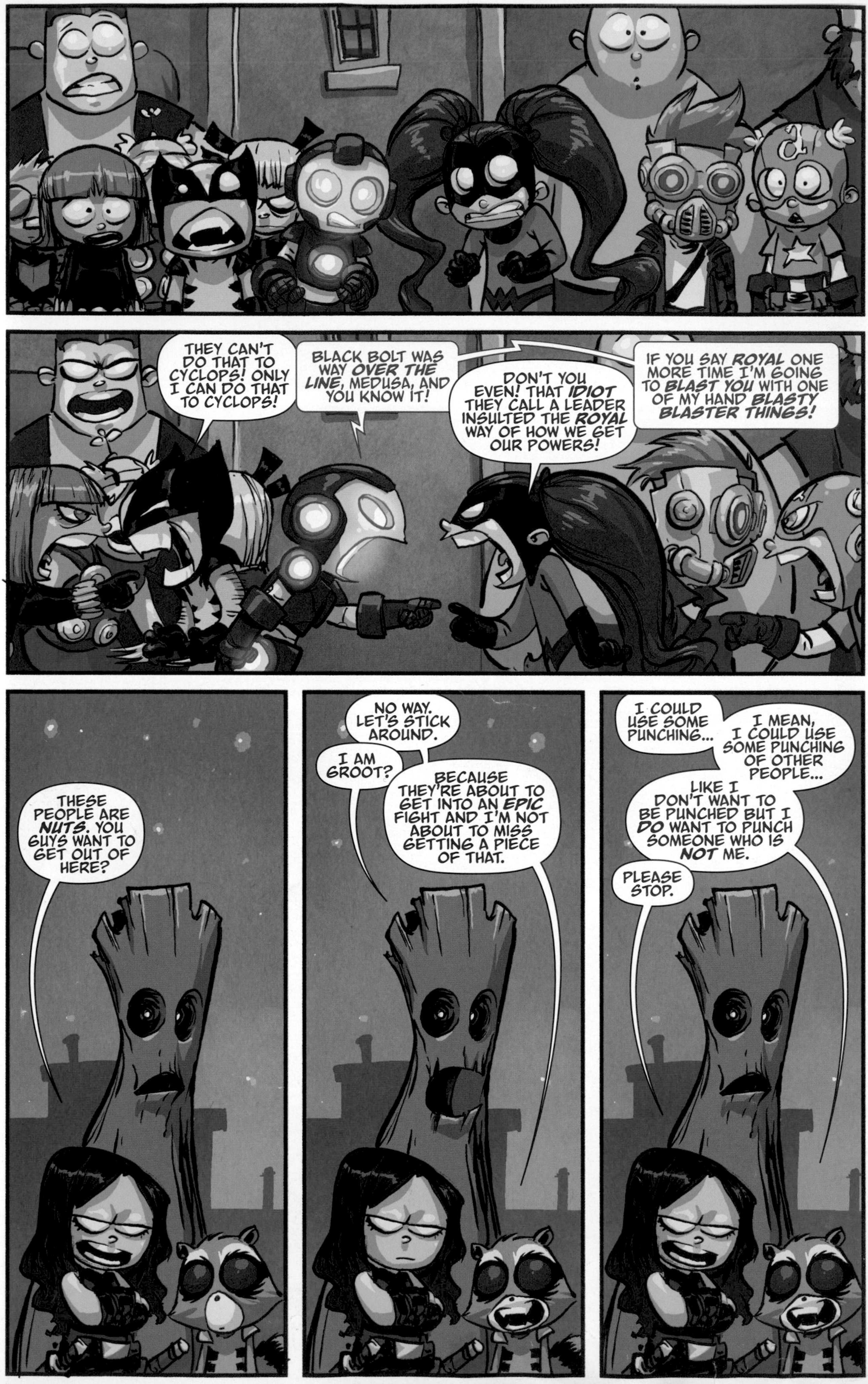
THEY CAN'T DO THAT TO CYCLOPS! ONLY I CAN DO THAT TO CYCLOPS!
BLACK BOLT WAS WAY OVER THE LINE, MEDUSA, AND YOU KNOW IT!
DON'T YOU EVEN! THAT IDIOT THEY CALL A LEADER INSULTED THE ROYAL WAY OF HOW WE GET OUR POWERS!
IF YOU SAY ROYAL ONE MORE TIME I'M GOING TO BLAST YOU WITH ONE OF MY HAND BLASTY BLASTER THINGS!
THESE PEOPLE ARE NUTS. YOU GUYS WANT TO GET OUT OF HERE?
NO WAY. LET'S STICK AROUND.
I AM GROOT?
BECAUSE THEY'RE ABOUT TO GET INTO AN EPIC FIGHT AND I'M NOT ABOUT TO MISS GETTING A PIECE OF THAT.
I COULD USE SOME PUNCHING...
I MEAN, I COULD USE SOME PUNCHING OF OTHER PEOPLE...
LIKE I DON'T WANT TO BE PUNCHED BUT I DO WANT TO PUNCH SOMEONE WHO IS NOT ME.
PLEASE STOP.

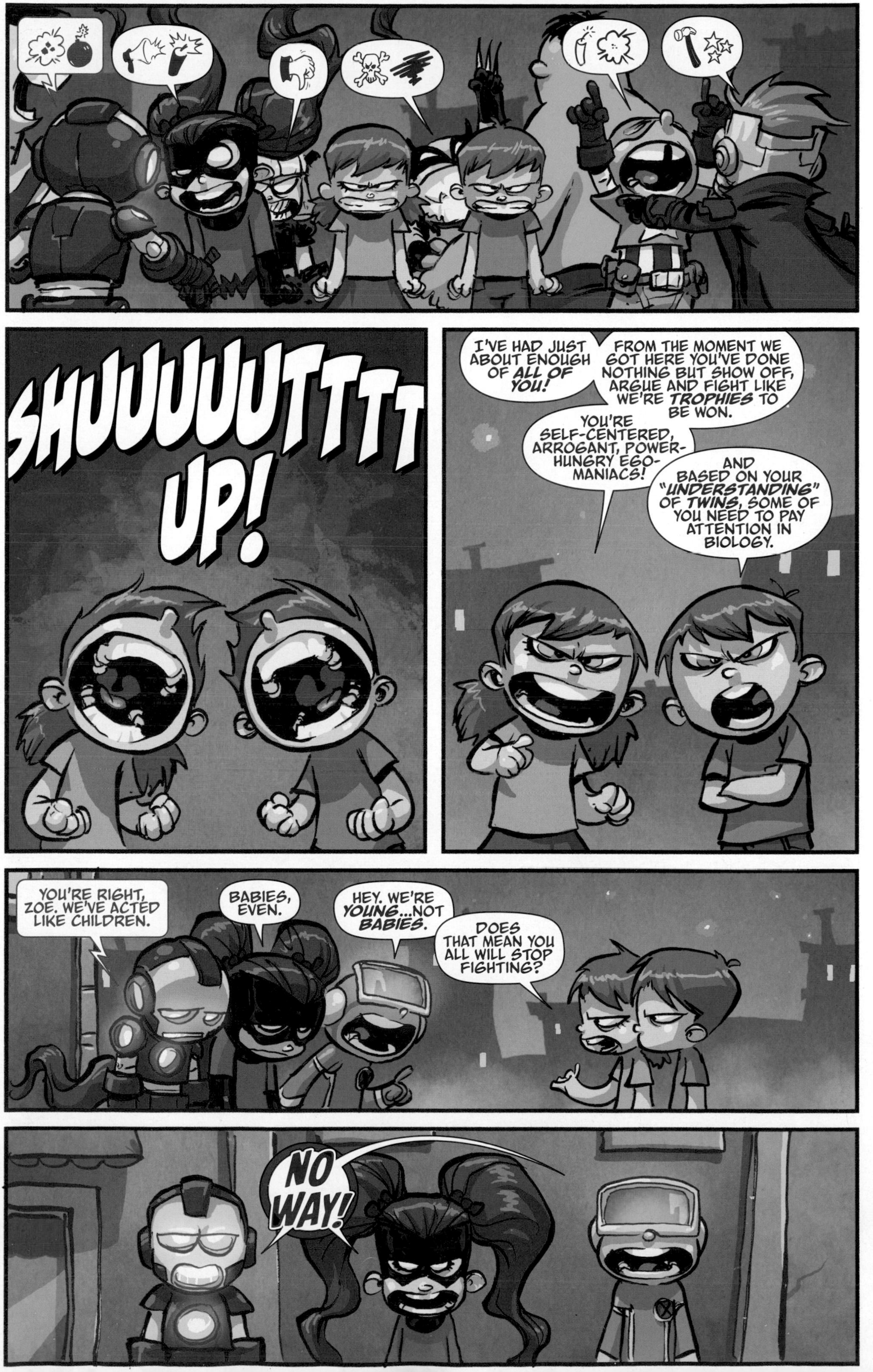
SHUUUUUTTTT UP!
I'VE HAD JUST ABOUT ENOUGH OF ALL OF YOU!
FROM THE MOMENT WE GOT HERE YOU'VE DONE NOTHING BUT SHOW OFF, ARGUE AND FIGHT LIKE WE'RE TROPHIES TO BE WON.
YOU'RE SELF-CENTERED, ARROGANT, POWER-HUNGRY EGO-MANIACS!
AND BASED ON YOUR "UNDERSTANDING" OF TWINS, SOME OF YOU NEED TO PAY ATTENTION IN BIOLOGY.
YOU'RE RIGHT, ZOE. WE'VE ACTED LIKE CHILDREN.
BABIES, EVEN.
HEY. WE'RE YOUNG...NOT BABIES.
DOES THAT MEAN YOU ALL WILL STOP FIGHTING?
NO WAY!

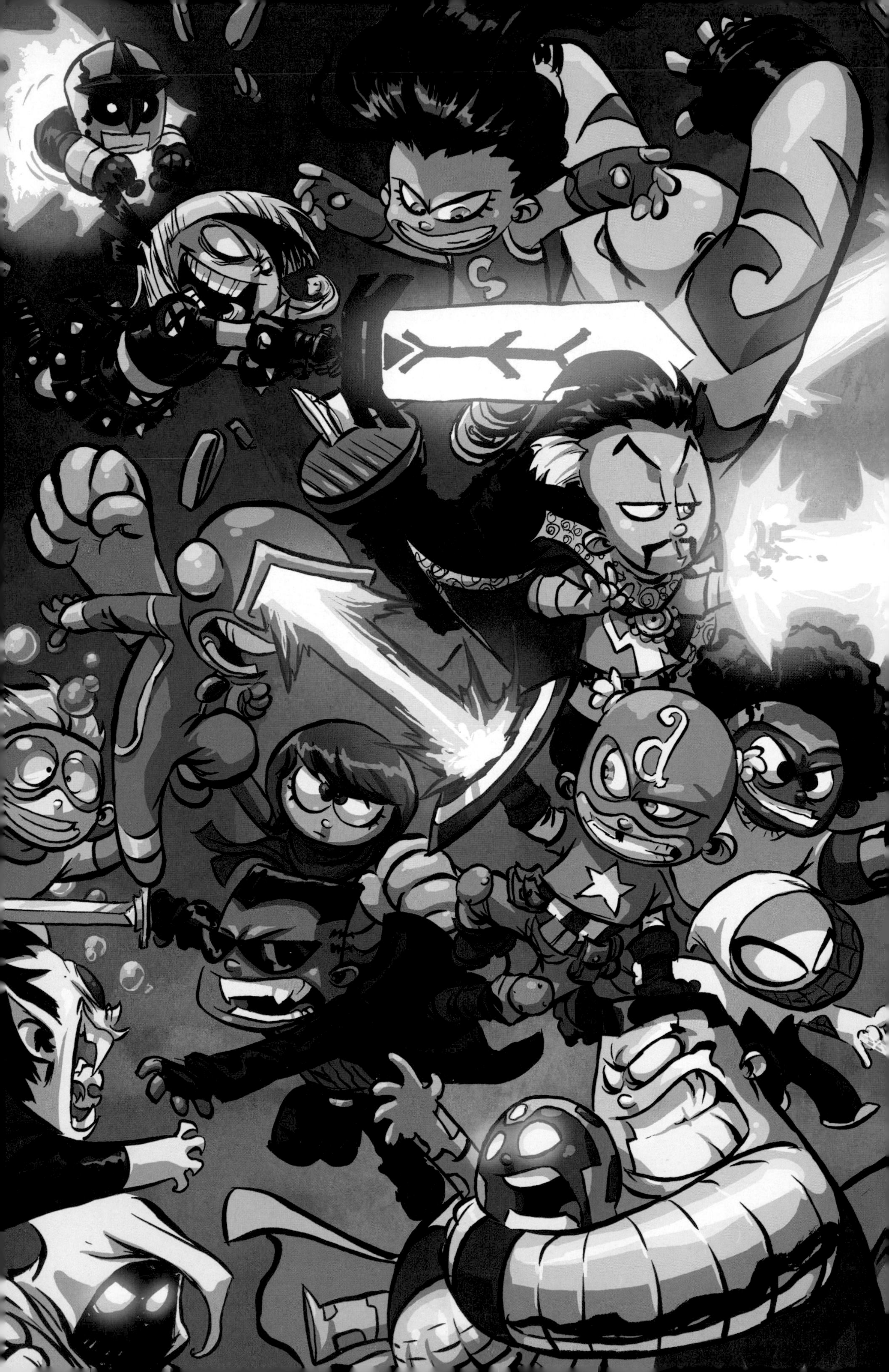

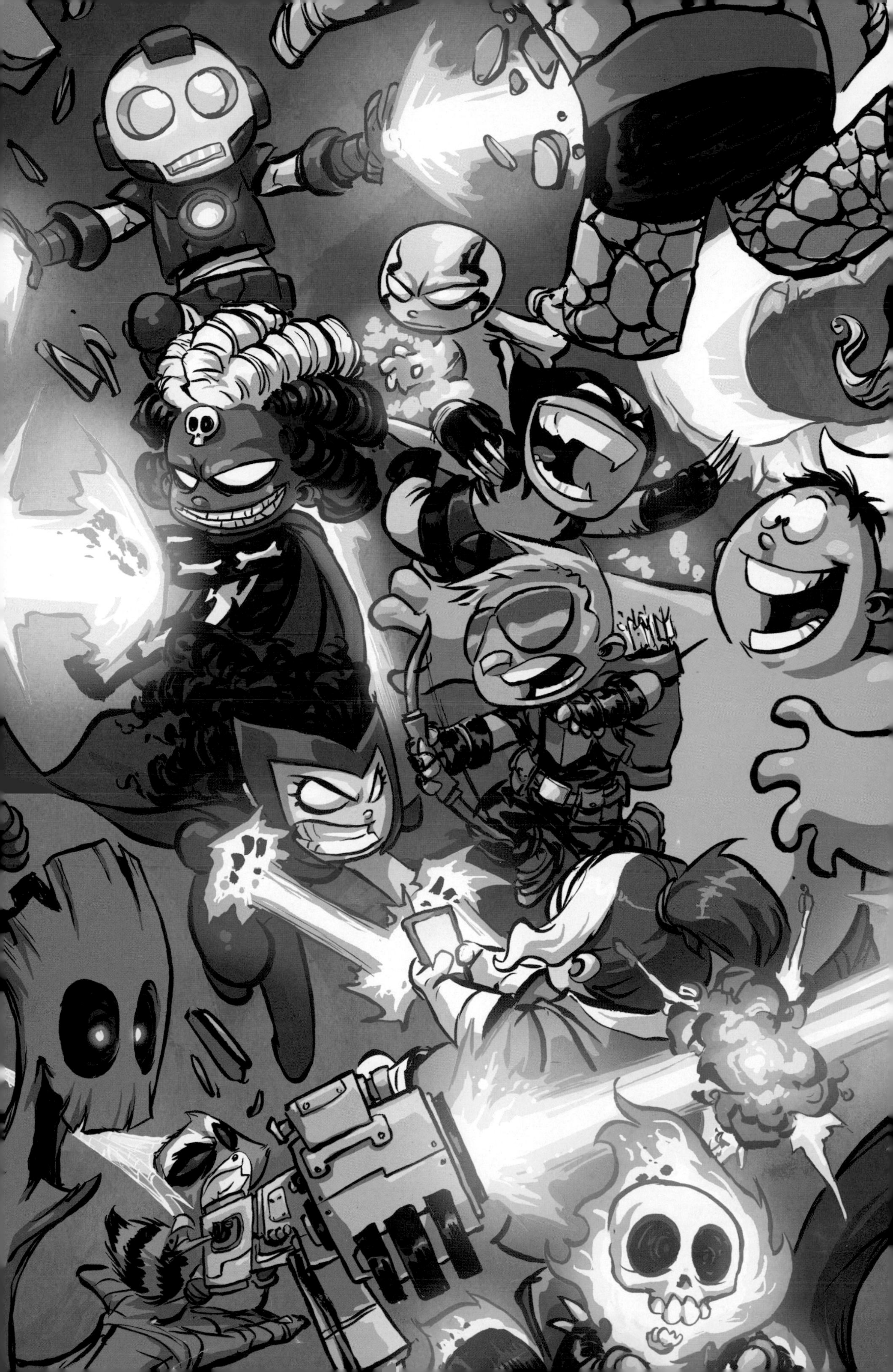

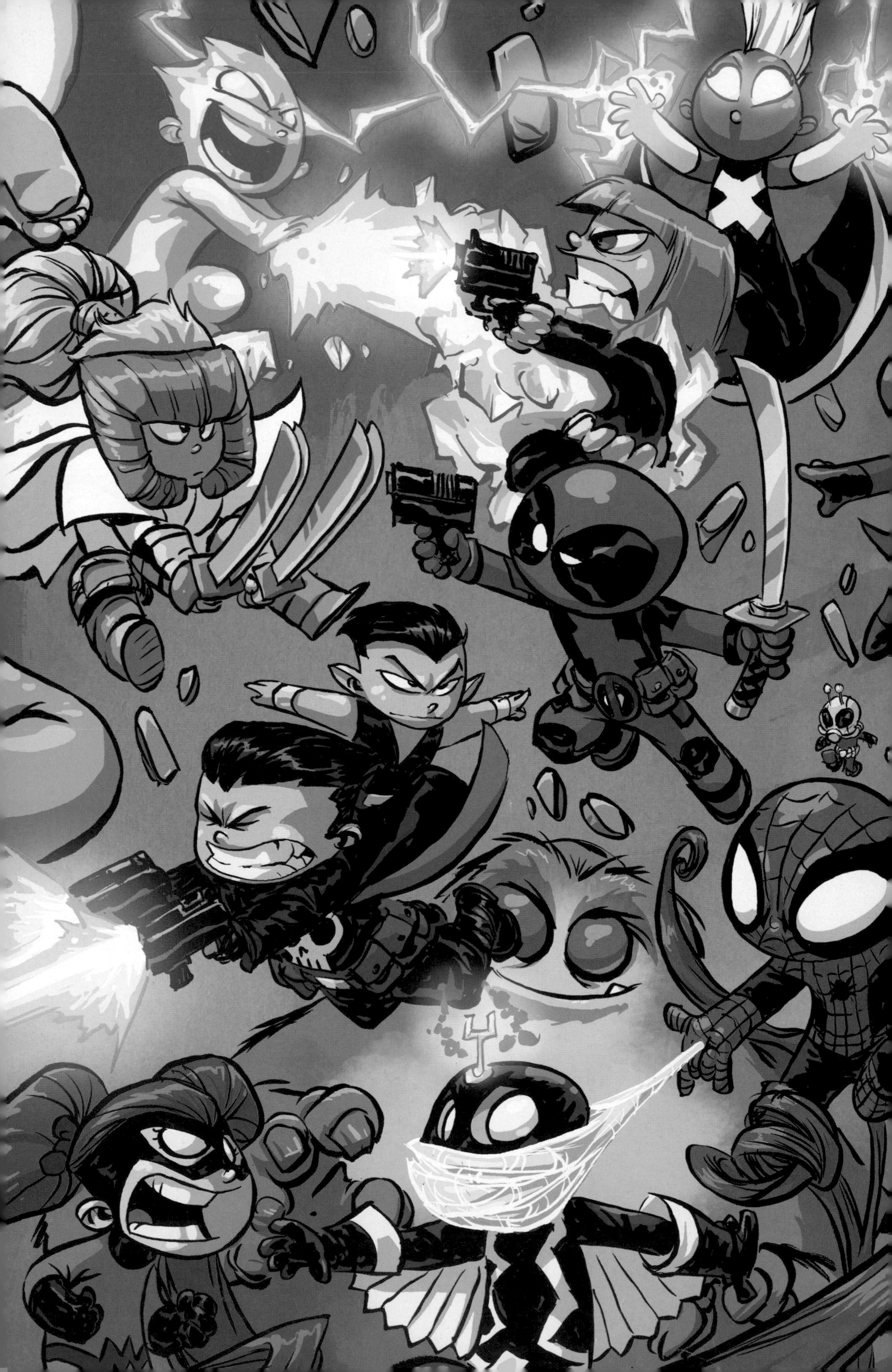

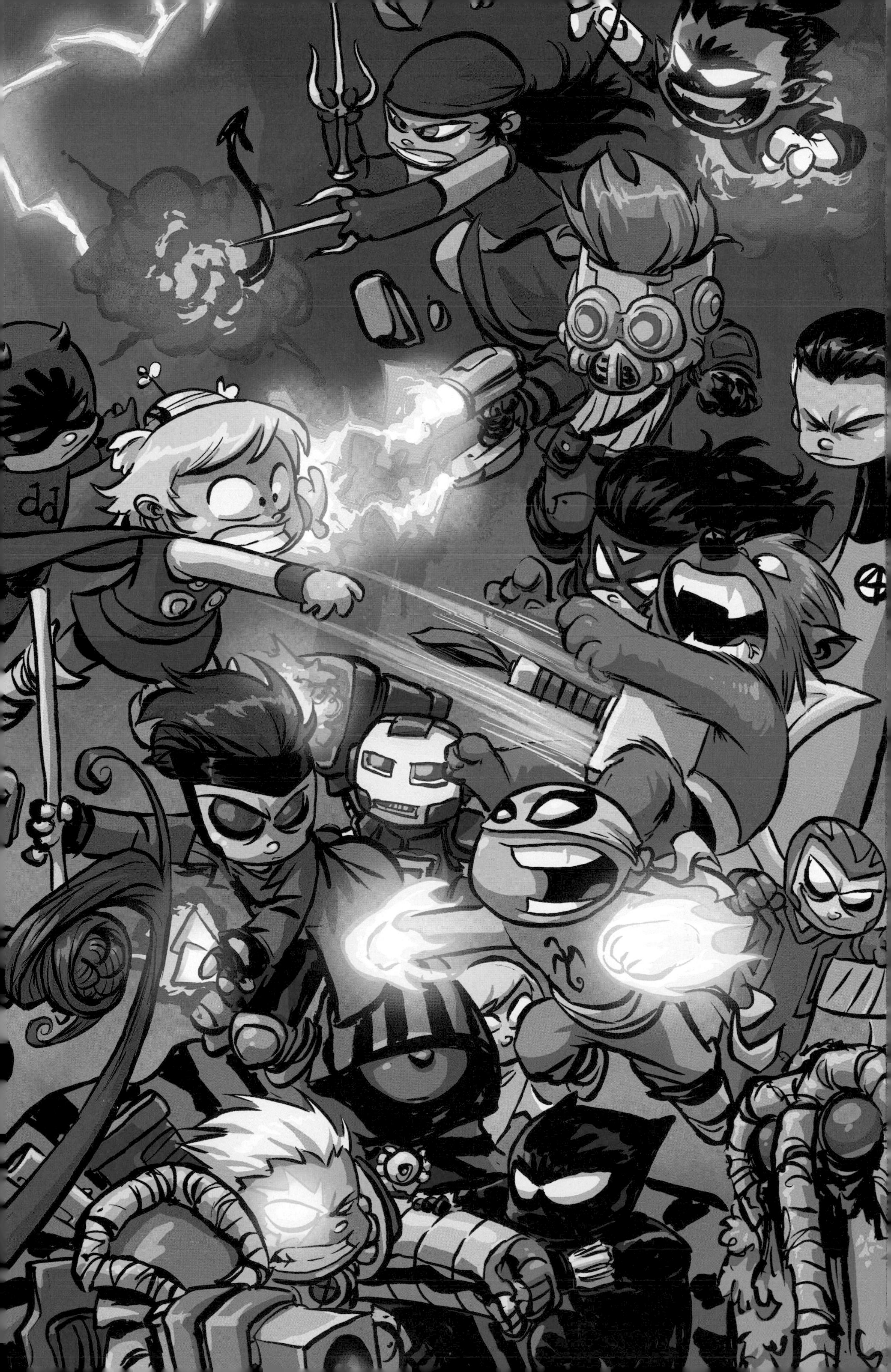

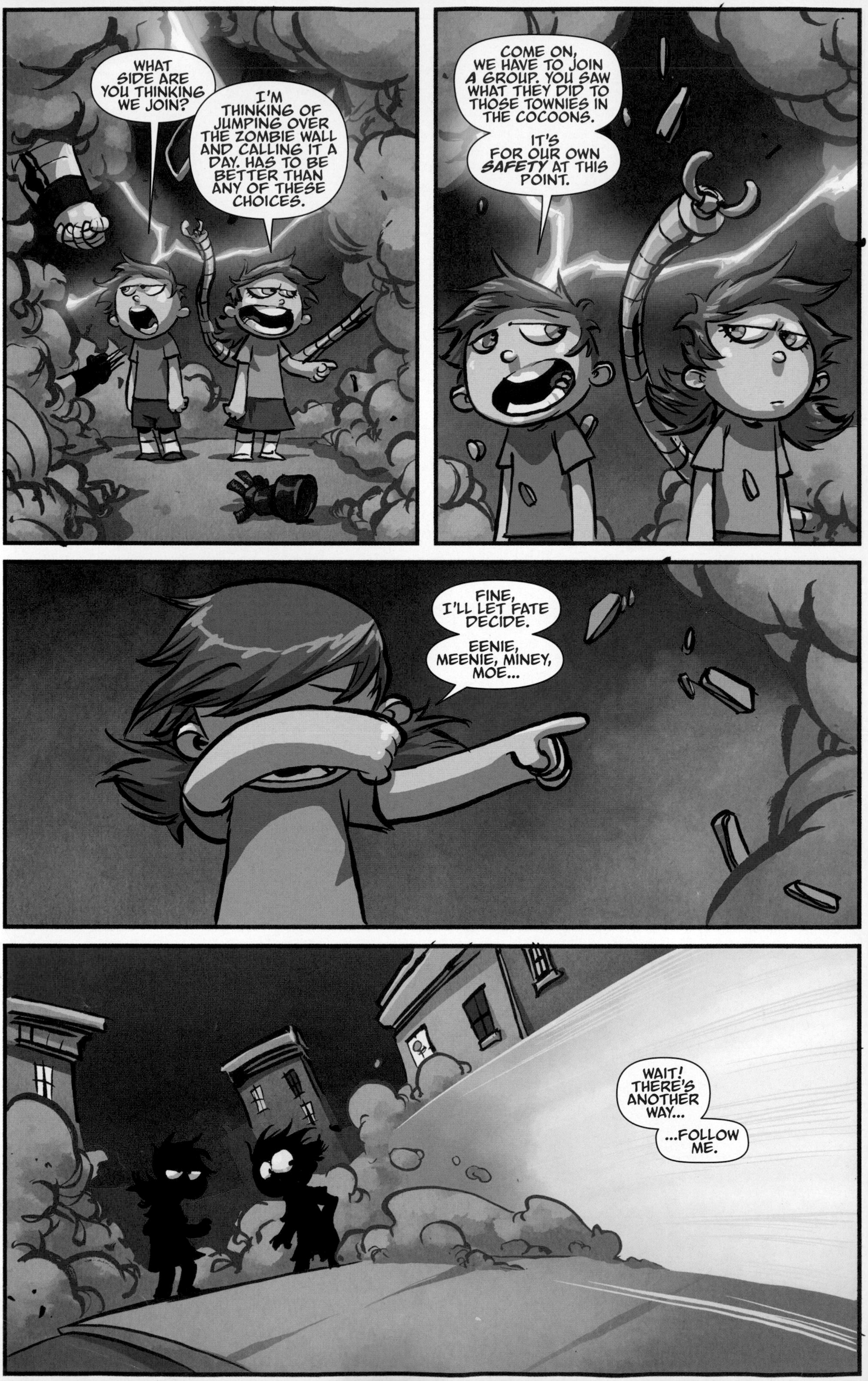
WHAT SIDE ARE YOU THINKING WE JOIN?
I'M THINKING OF JUMPING OVER THE ZOMBIE WALL AND CALLING IT A DAY. HAS TO BE BETTER THAN ANY OF THESE CHOICES.
COME ON, WE HAVE TO JOIN A GROUP. YOU SAW WHAT THEY DID TO THOSE TOWNIES IN THE COCOONS.
IT'S FOR OUR OWN SAFETY AT THIS POINT.
FINE, I'LL LET FATE DECIDE.
EENIE, MEENIE, MINEY, MOE...
WAIT! THERE'S ANOTHER WAY...
...FOLLOW ME.

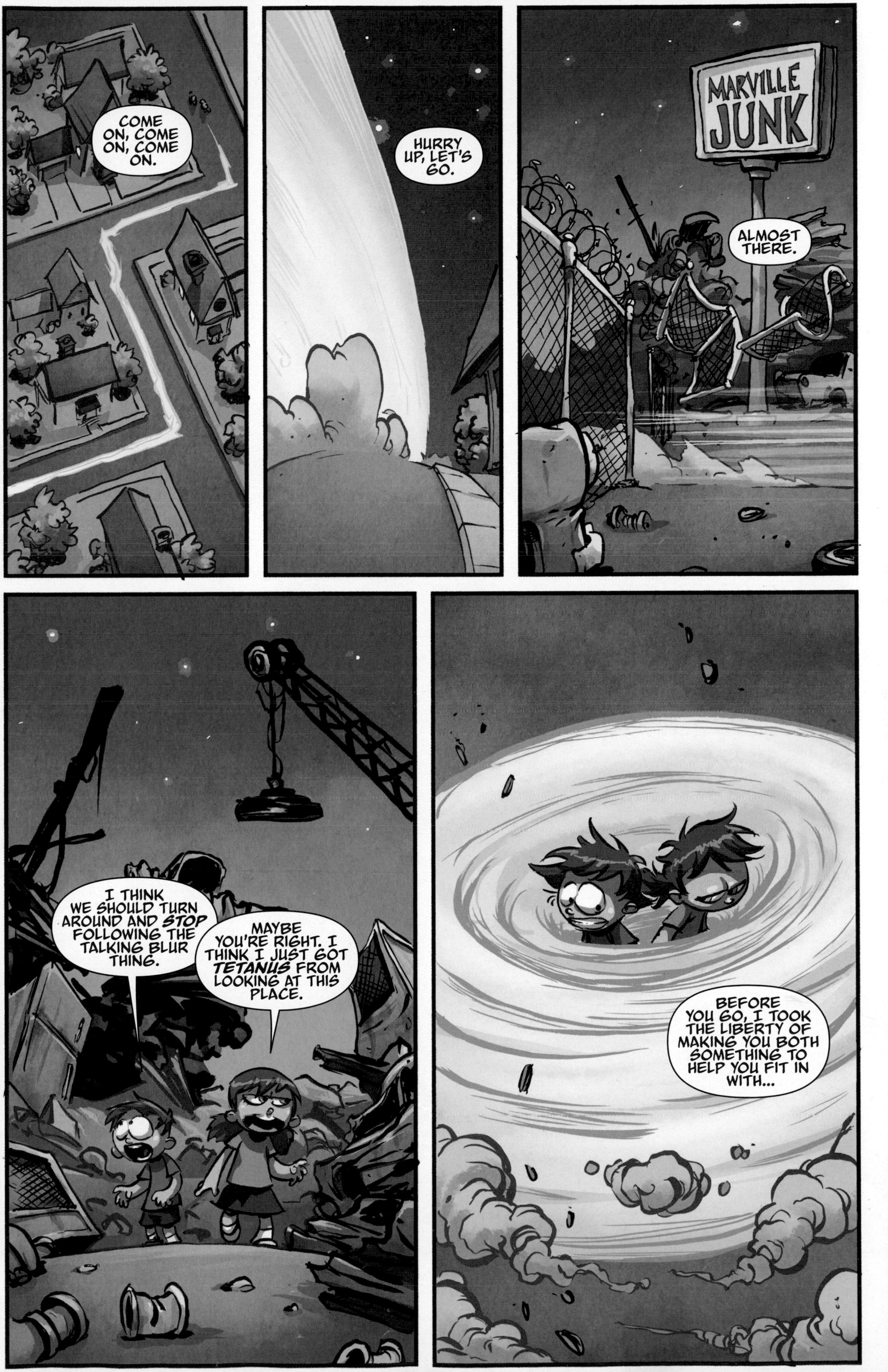
COME ON, COME ON, COME ON.
HURRY UP, LET'S GO.
MARVILLE JUNK
ALMOST THERE.
I THINK WE SHOULD TURN AROUND AND *STOP* FOLLOWING THE TALKING BLUR THING.
MAYBE YOU'RE RIGHT. I THINK I JUST GOT *TETANUS* FROM LOOKING AT THIS PLACE.
BEFORE YOU GO, I TOOK THE LIBERTY OF MAKING YOU BOTH SOMETHING TO HELP YOU FIT IN WITH...

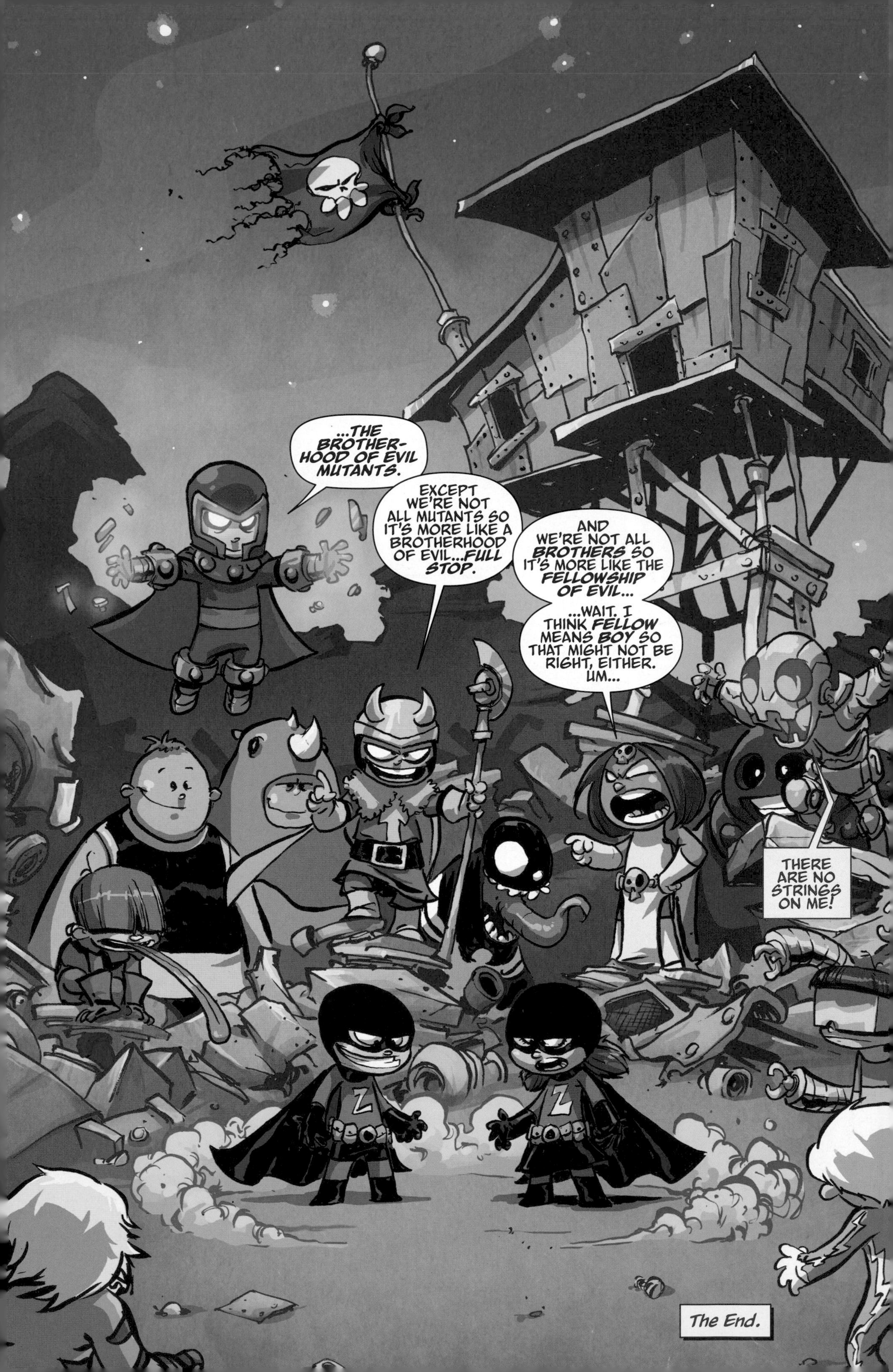
...THE BROTHER-HOOD OF EVIL MUTANTS.
EXCEPT WE'RE NOT ALL MUTANTS SO IT'S MORE LIKE A BROTHERHOOD OF EVIL...FULL STOP.
AND WE'RE NOT ALL BROTHERS SO IT'S MORE LIKE THE FELLOWSHIP OF EVIL...
...WAIT. I THINK FELLOW MEANS BOY SO THAT MIGHT NOT BE RIGHT, EITHER. UM...
THERE ARE NO STRINGS ON ME!
The End.

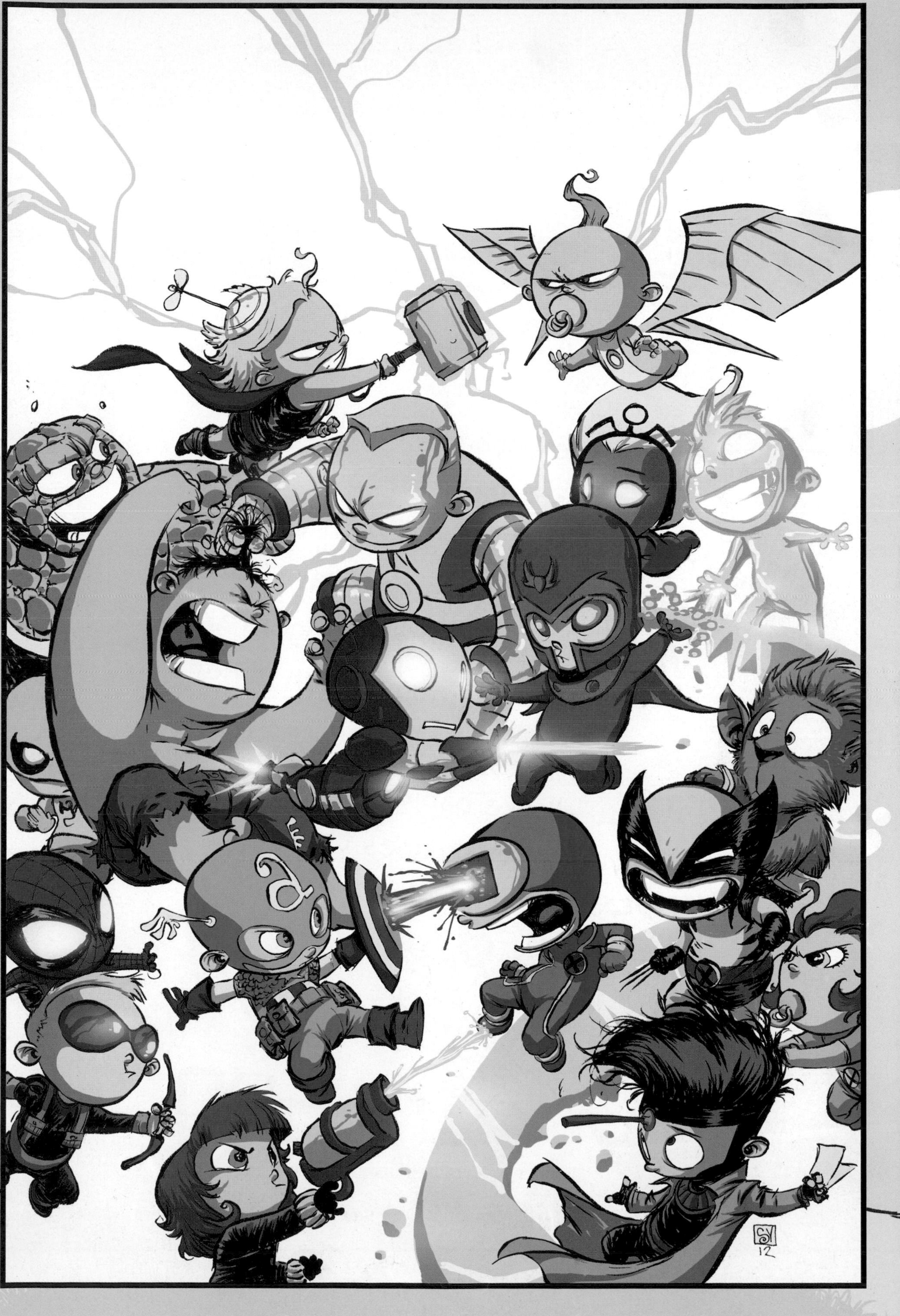

A-BABIES VS. X-BABIES #1

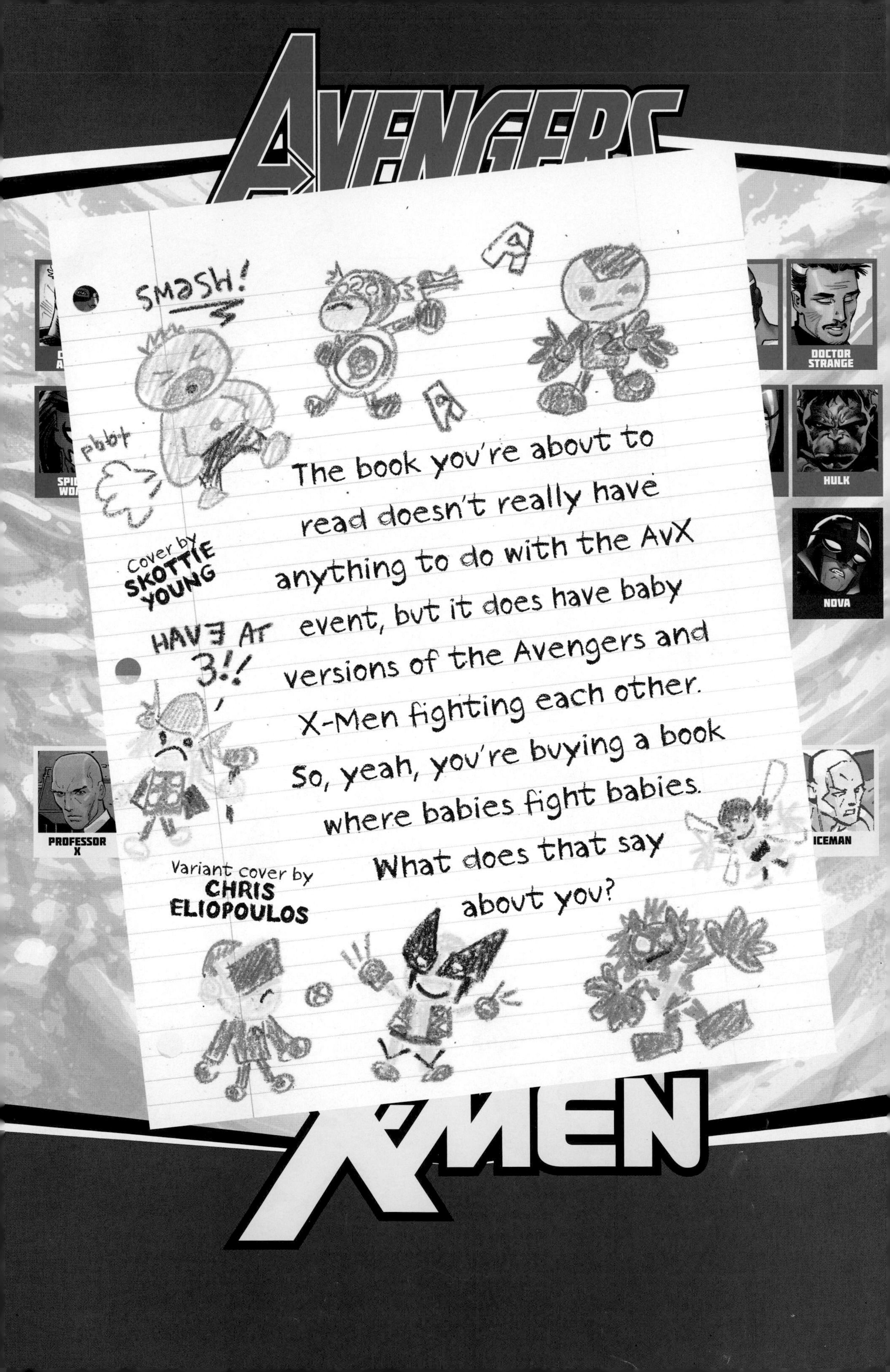
AVENGERS
DOCTOR STRANGE
HULK
NOVA
PROFESSOR X
ICEMAN
SMASH!
pbbt
Cover by SKOTTIE YOUNG
HAVE AT 3!!
Variant cover by CHRIS ELIOPOULOS
The book you're about to read doesn't really have anything to do with the AvX event, but it does have baby versions of the Avengers and X-Men fighting each other. So, yeah, you're buying a book where babies fight babies. What does that say about you?
X-MEN

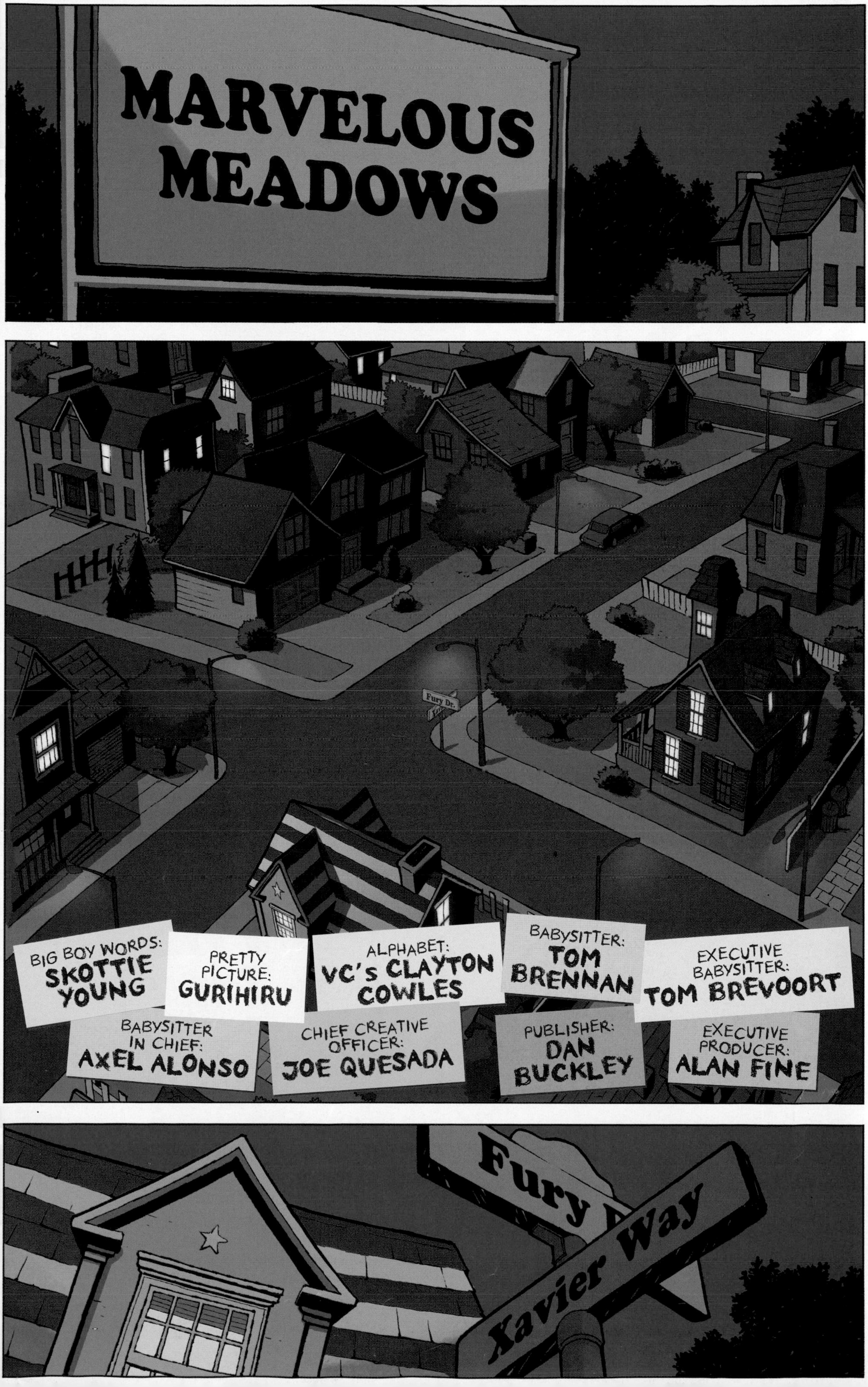
MARVELOUS MEADOWS
Fury Dr.
BIG BOY WORDS: SKOTTIE YOUNG
PRETTY PICTURE: GURIHIRU
ALPHABET: VC's CLAYTON COWLES
BABYSITTER: TOM BRENNAN
EXECUTIVE BABYSITTER: TOM BREVOORT
BABYSITTER IN CHIEF: AXEL ALONSO
CHIEF CREATIVE OFFICER: JOE QUESADA
PUBLISHER: DAN BUCKLEY
EXECUTIVE PRODUCER: ALAN FINE
Fury
Xavier Way

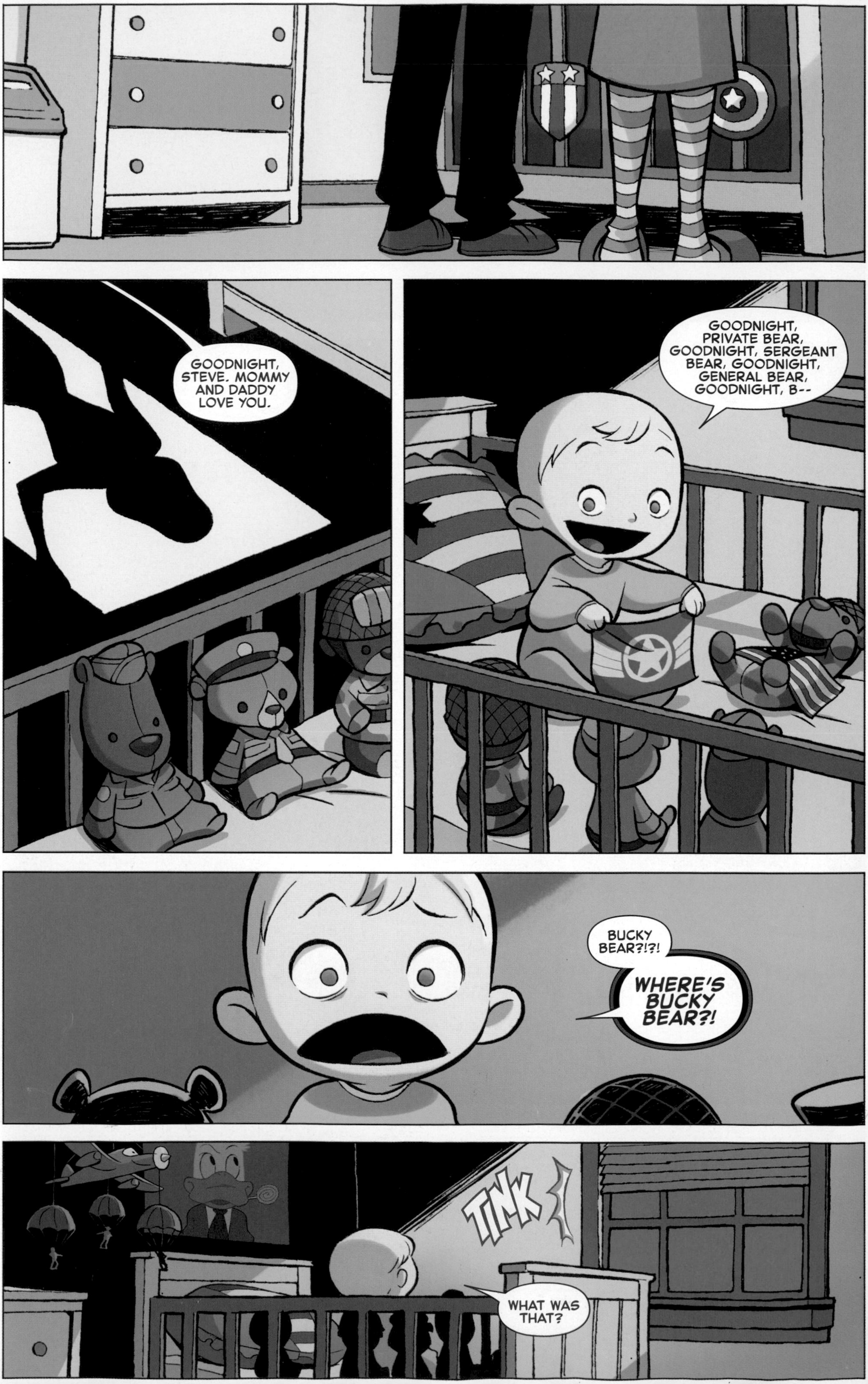
GOODNIGHT, STEVE. MOMMY AND DADDY LOVE YOU.
GOODNIGHT, PRIVATE BEAR, GOODNIGHT, SERGEANT BEAR, GOODNIGHT, GENERAL BEAR, GOODNIGHT, B--
BUCKY BEAR?!?!
WHERE'S BUCKY BEAR?!
TINK
WHAT WAS THAT?

BUCKY BEAR!!!

I'M SORRY, MEN. I DON'T KNOW HOW THIS HAPPENED, BUT WE WON'T LEAVE A MAN BEHIND.

I JUST NEED TO ASSESS THE SITUATION AND PUT TOGETHER A STRADEGY--

HEY?!?!

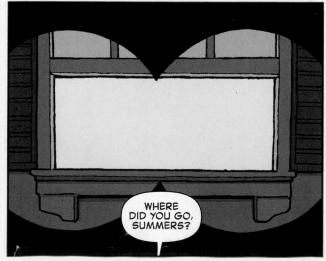

WHERE DID YOU GO, SUMMERS?

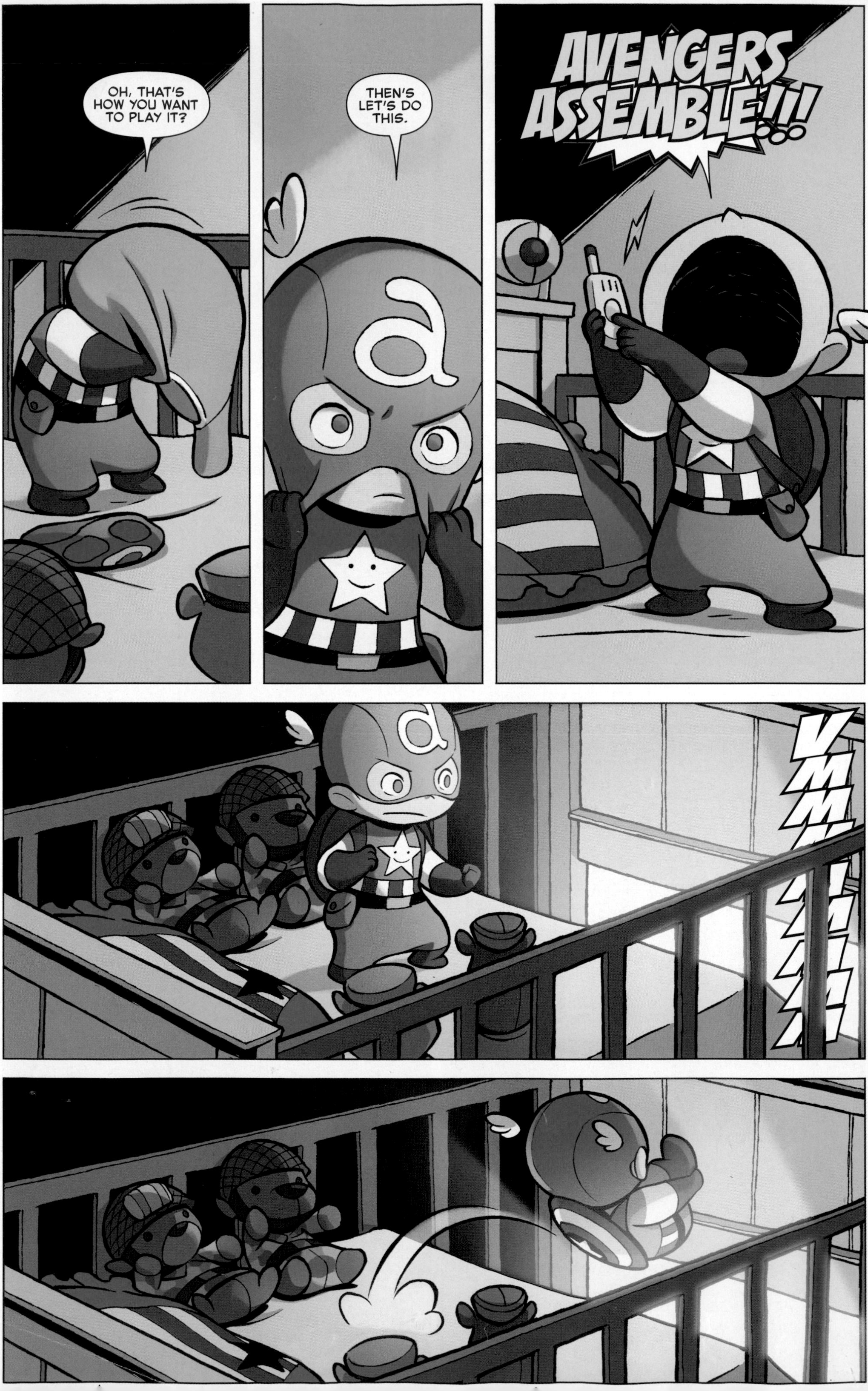
OH, THAT'S HOW YOU WANT TO PLAY IT?
THEN'S LET'S DO THIS.
AVENGERS ASSEMBLE!!!
VMMMMMMMM!

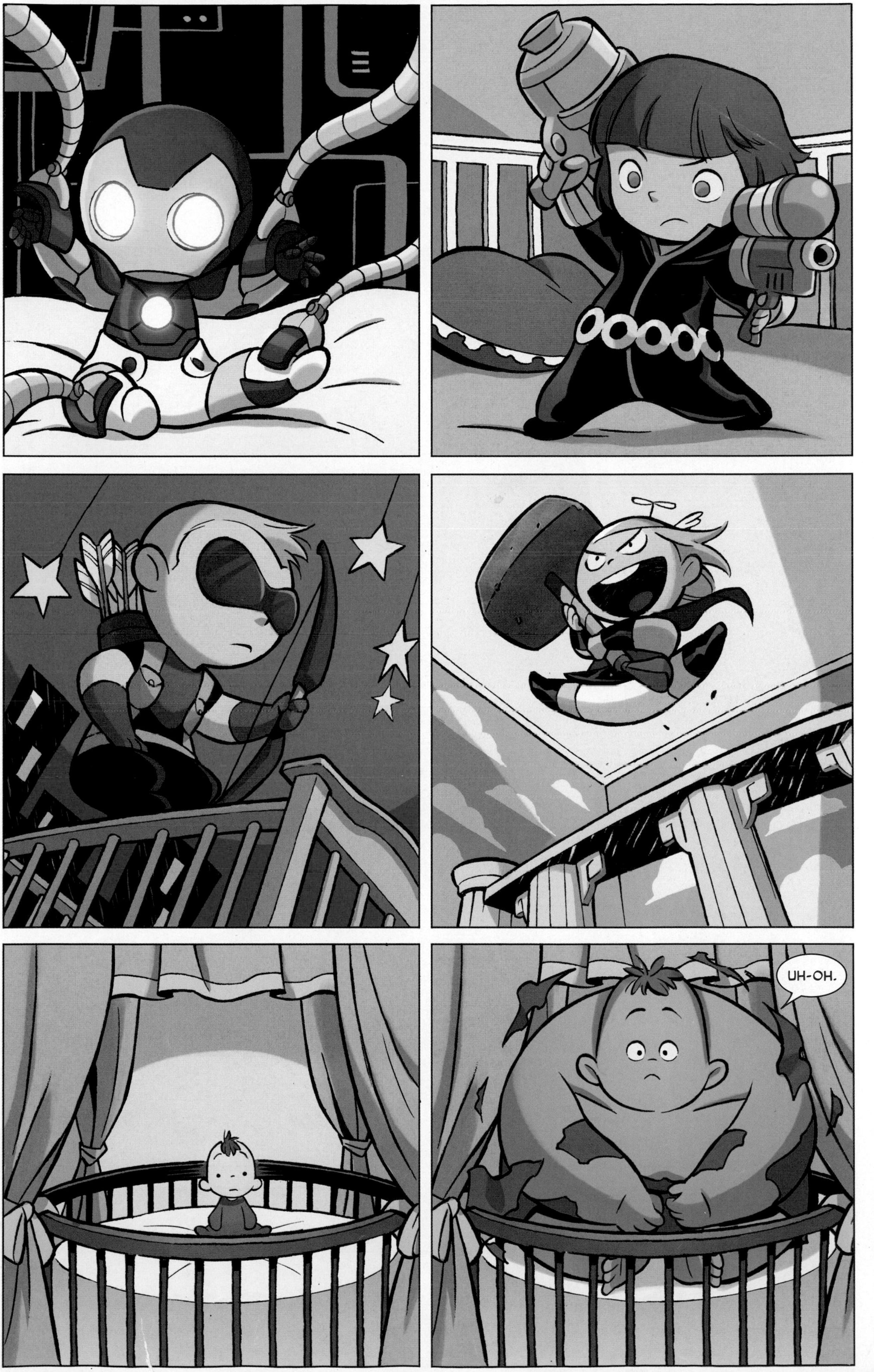
UH-OH.

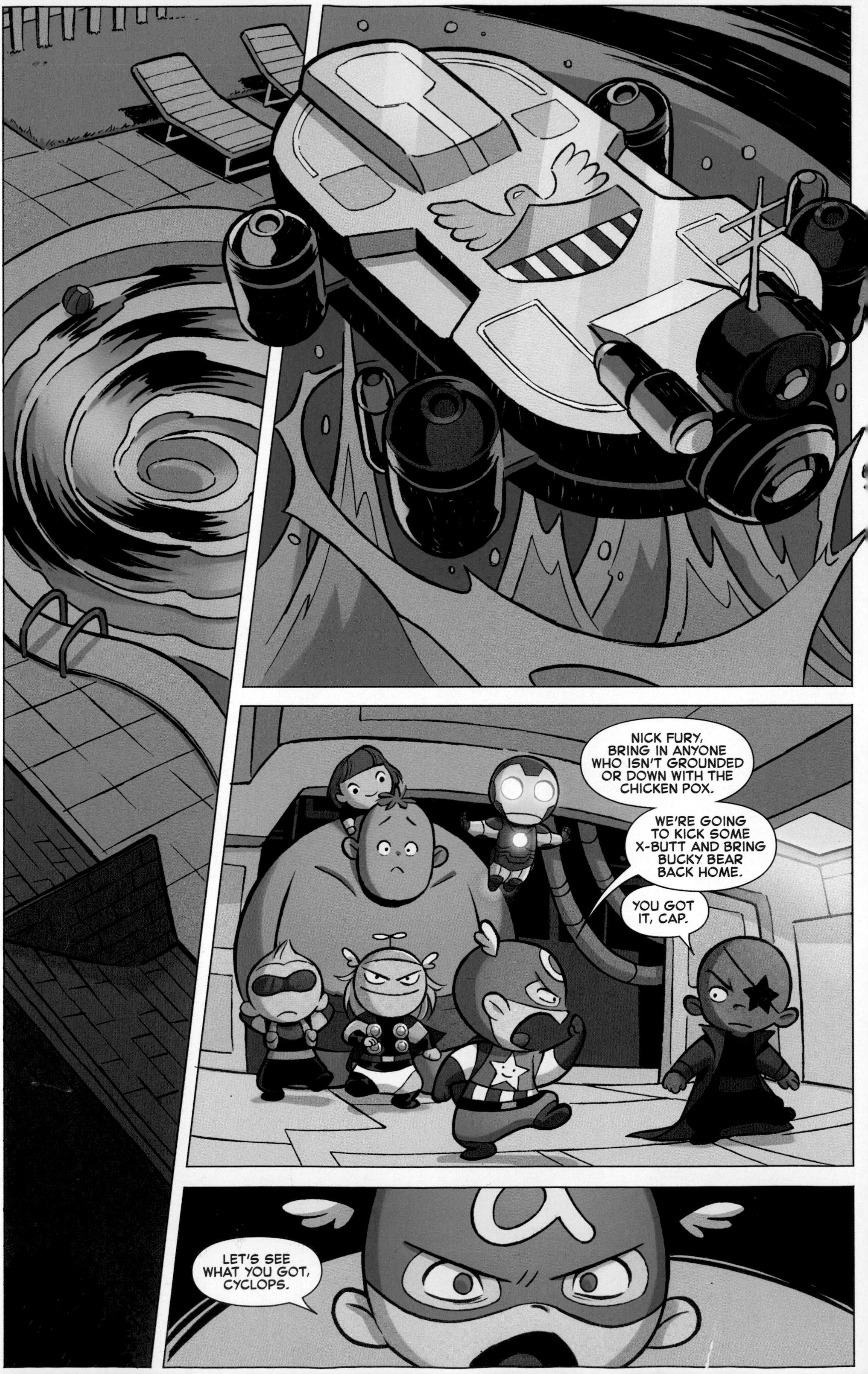
NICK FURY, BRING IN ANYONE WHO ISN'T GROUNDED OR DOWN WITH THE CHICKEN POX.
WE'RE GOING TO KICK SOME X-BUTT AND BRING BUCKY BEAR BACK HOME.
YOU GOT IT, CAP.
LET'S SEE WHAT YOU GOT, CYCLOPS.

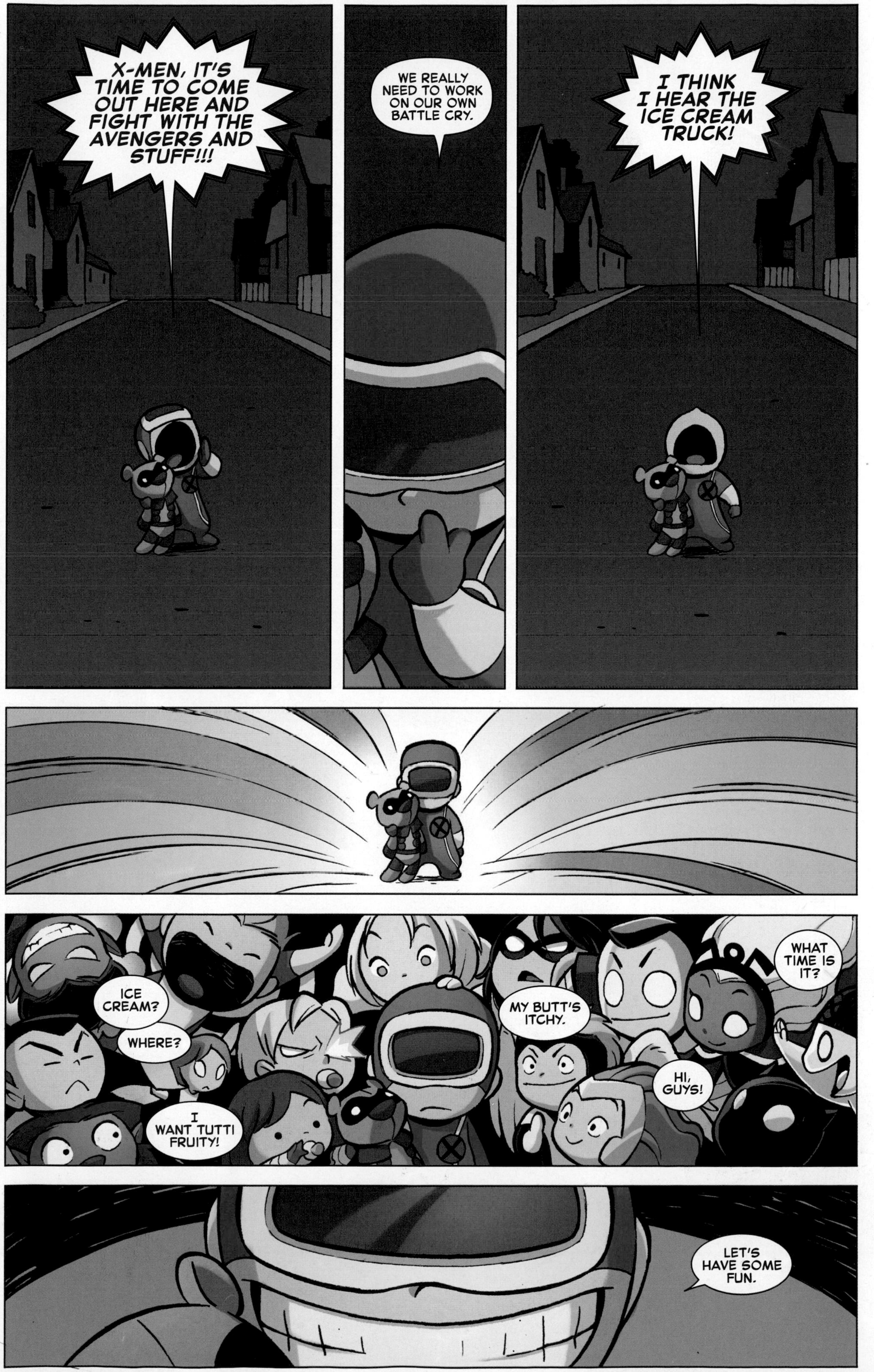
X-MEN, IT'S TIME TO COME OUT HERE AND FIGHT WITH THE AVENGERS AND STUFF!!!
WE REALLY NEED TO WORK ON OUR OWN BATTLE CRY.
I THINK I HEAR THE ICE CREAM TRUCK!
ICE CREAM?
WHERE?
I WANT TUTTI FRUITY!
MY BUTT'S ITCHY.
HI, GUYS!
WHAT TIME IS IT?
LET'S HAVE SOME FUN.

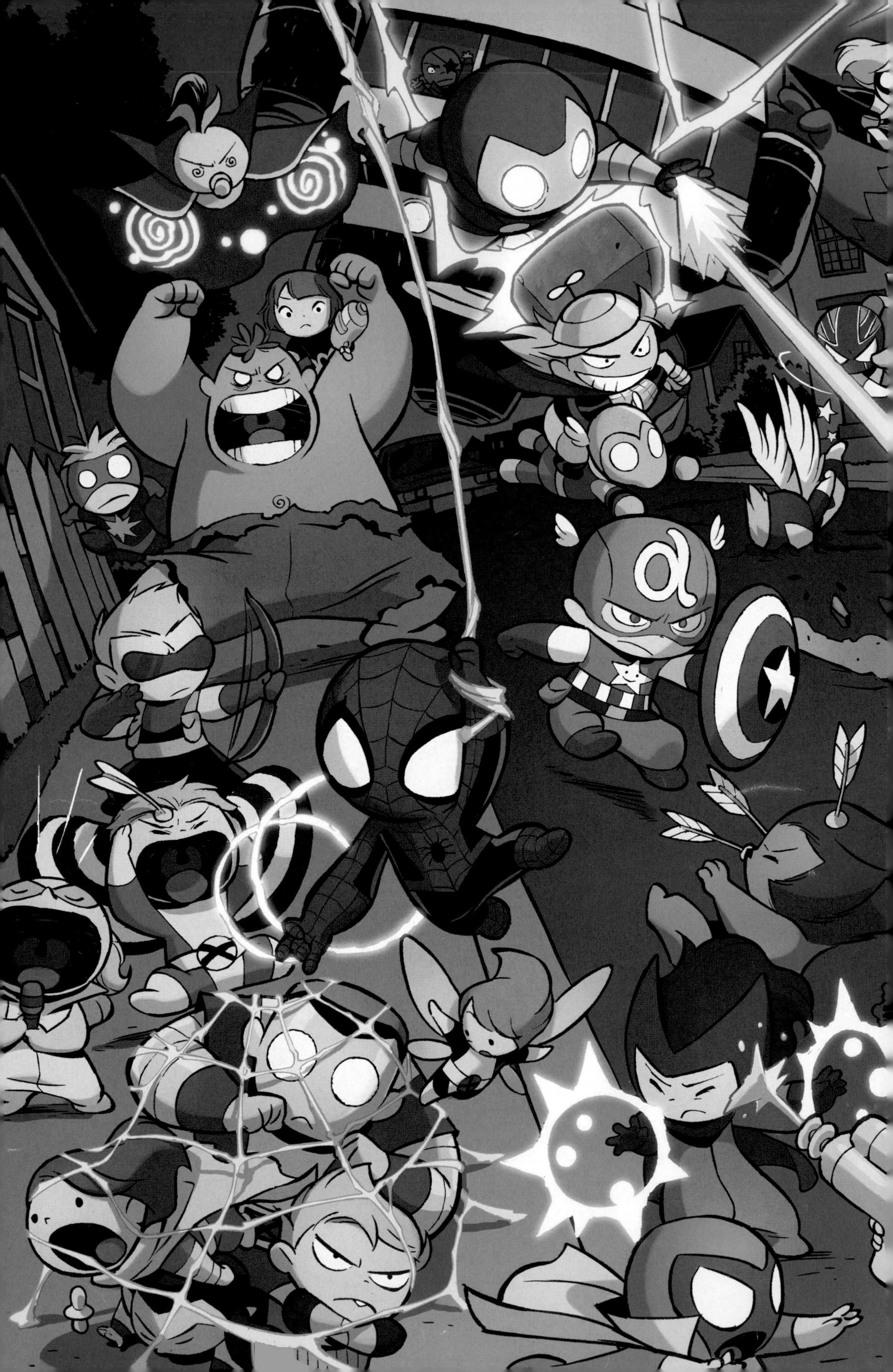

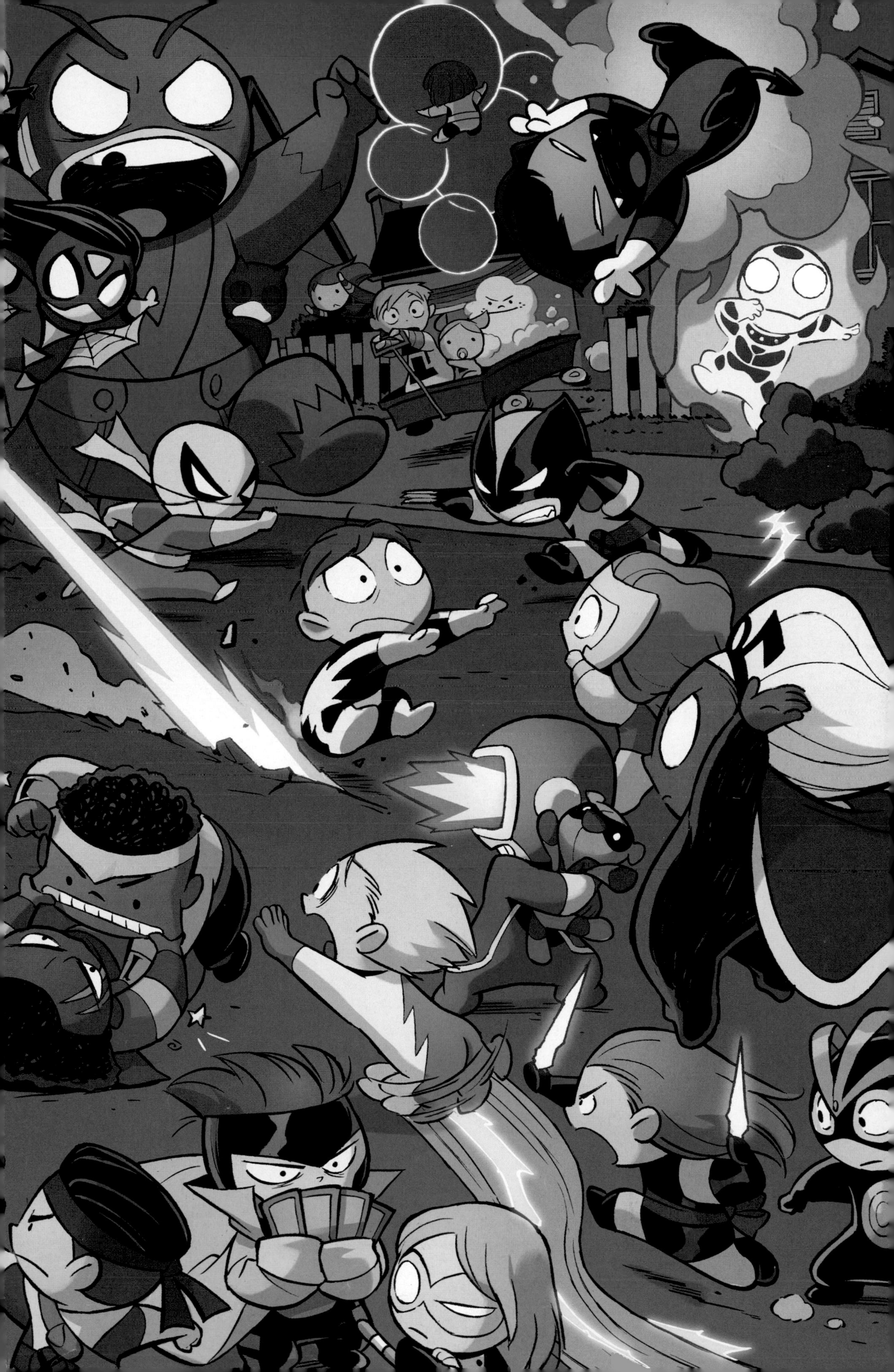

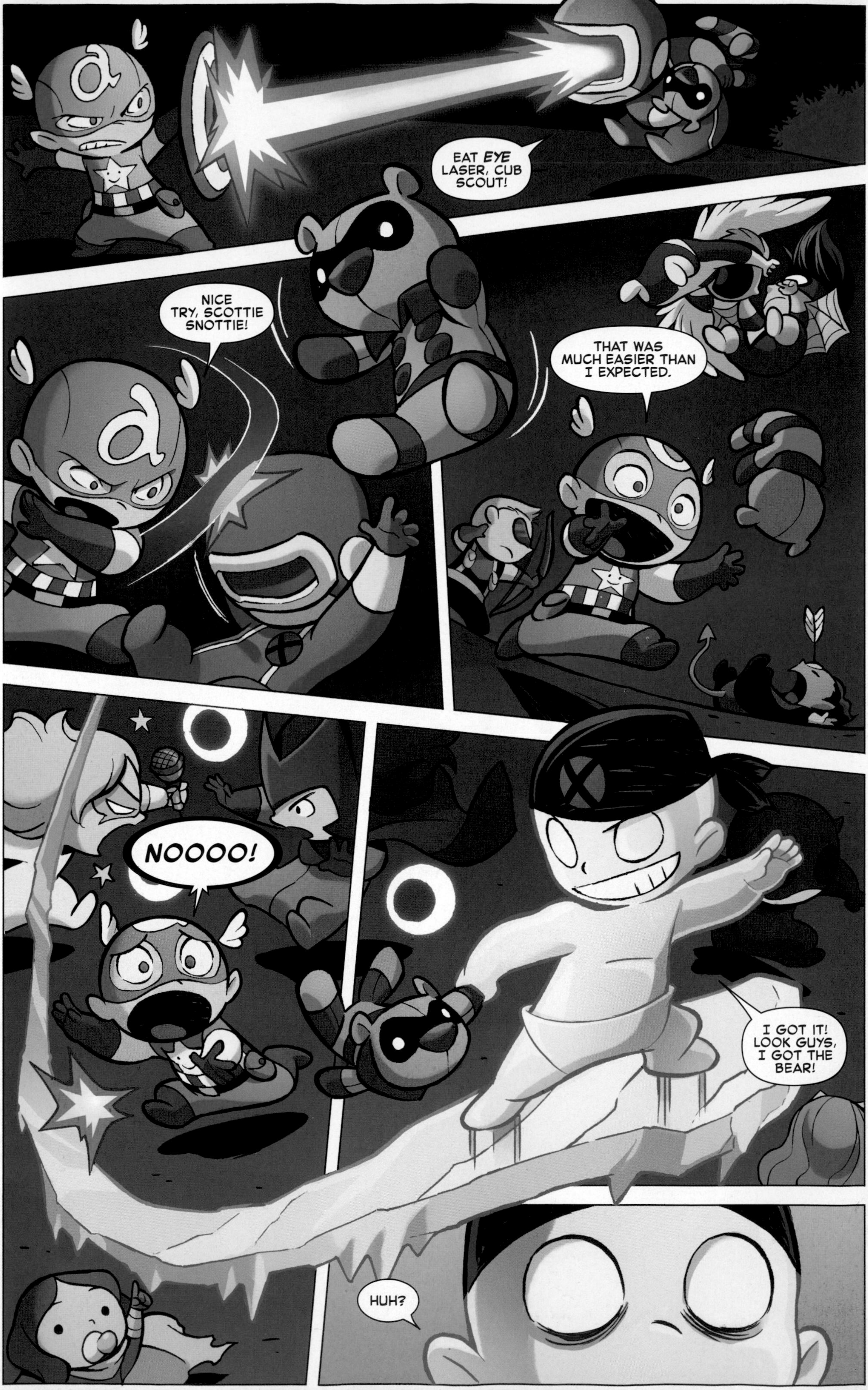
EAT EYE LASER, CUB SCOUT!
NICE TRY, SCOTTIE SNOTTIE!
THAT WAS MUCH EASIER THAN I EXPECTED.
NOOOO!
I GOT IT! LOOK GUYS, I GOT THE BEAR!
HUH?

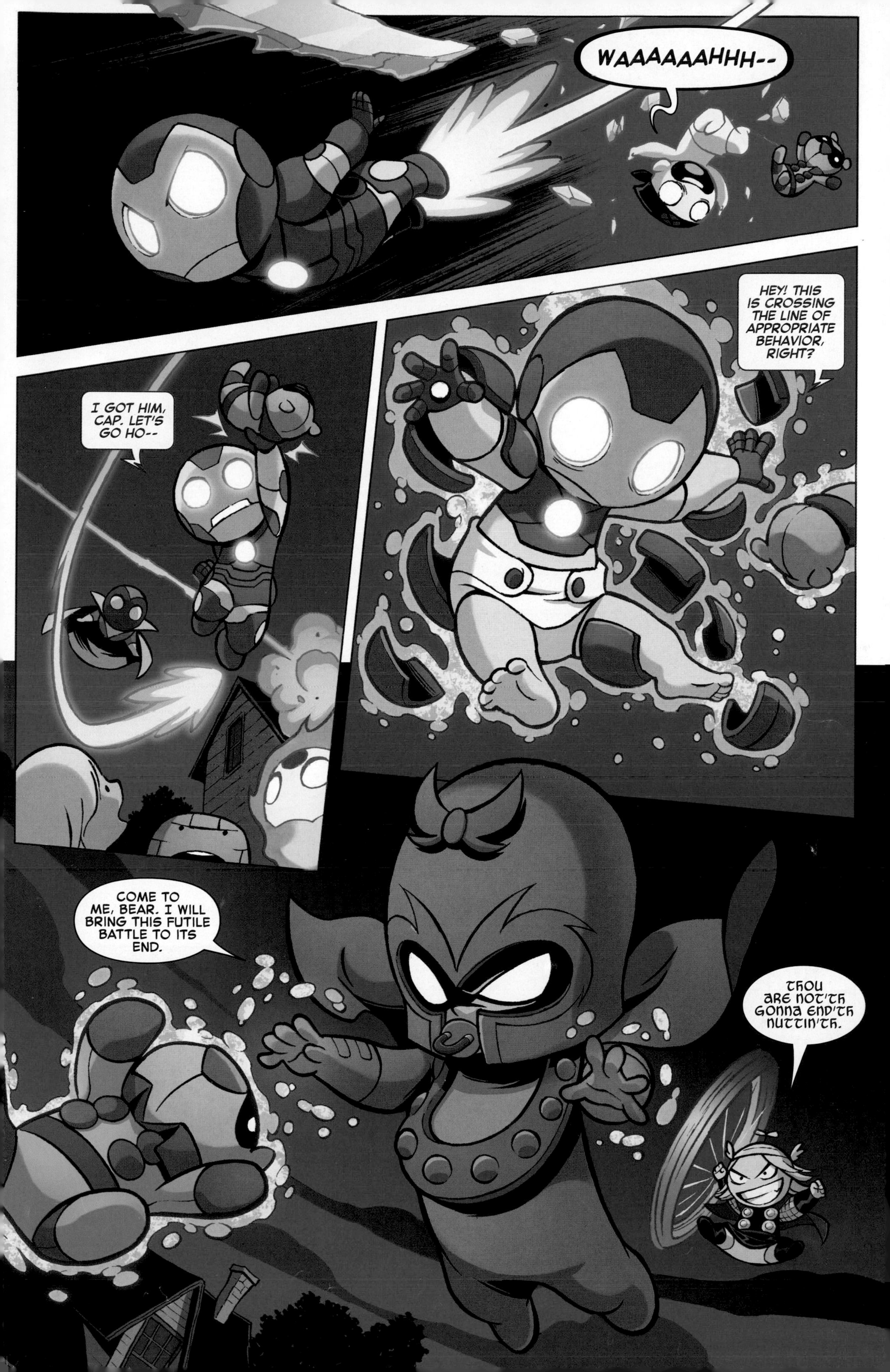

WAAAAAAHHH--
I GOT HIM, CAP. LET'S GO HO--
HEY! THIS IS CROSSING THE LINE OF APPROPRIATE BEHAVIOR, RIGHT?
COME TO ME, BEAR. I WILL BRING THIS FUTILE BATTLE TO ITS END.
THOU ARE NOT'TH GONNA END'TH NUTTIN'TH.

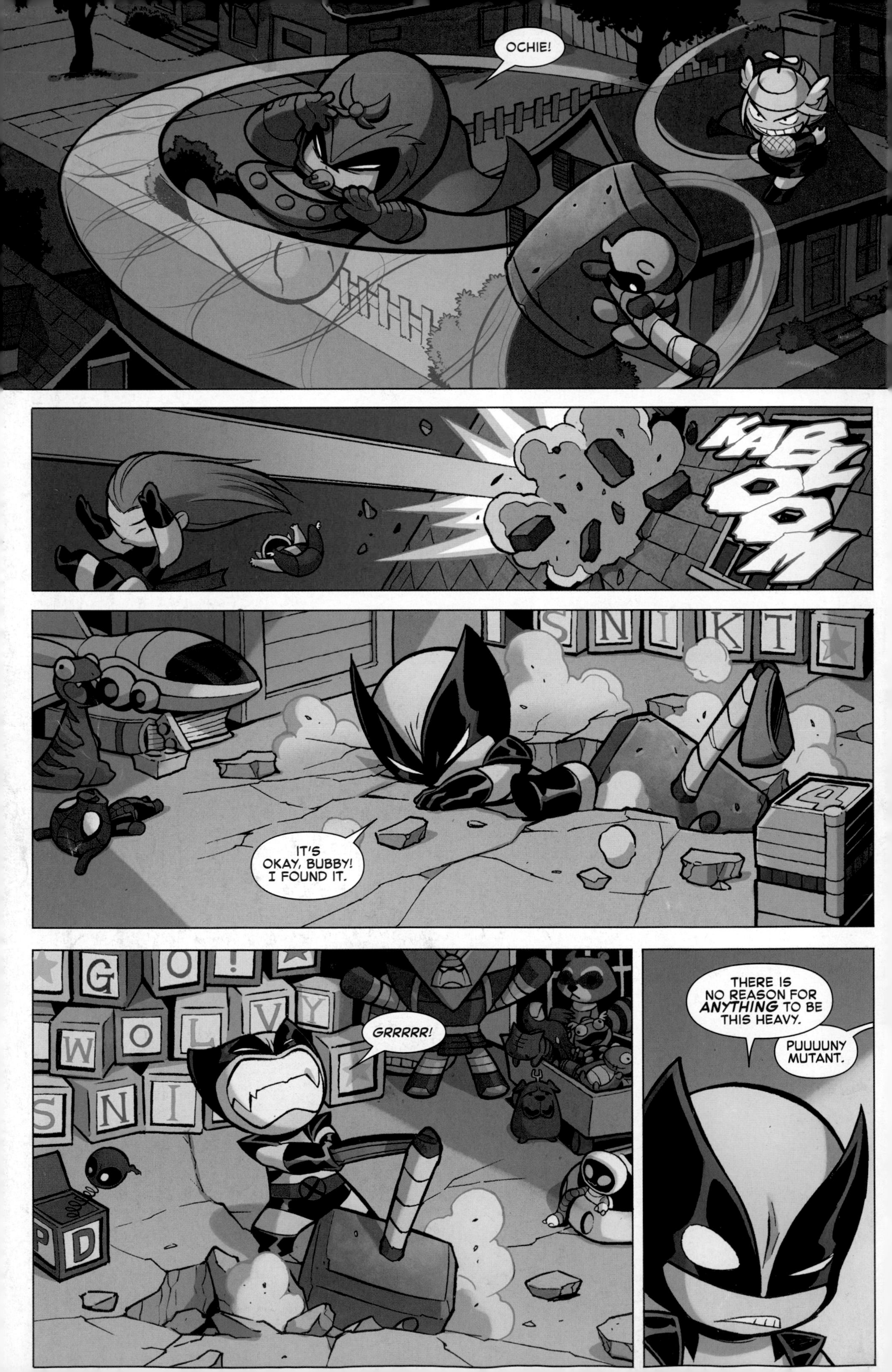
OCHIE!
KABLOOM
SNIKT
IT'S OKAY, BUBBY! I FOUND IT.
GRRRRR!
THERE IS NO REASON FOR *ANYTHING* TO BE THIS HEAVY.
PUUUUNY MUTANT.

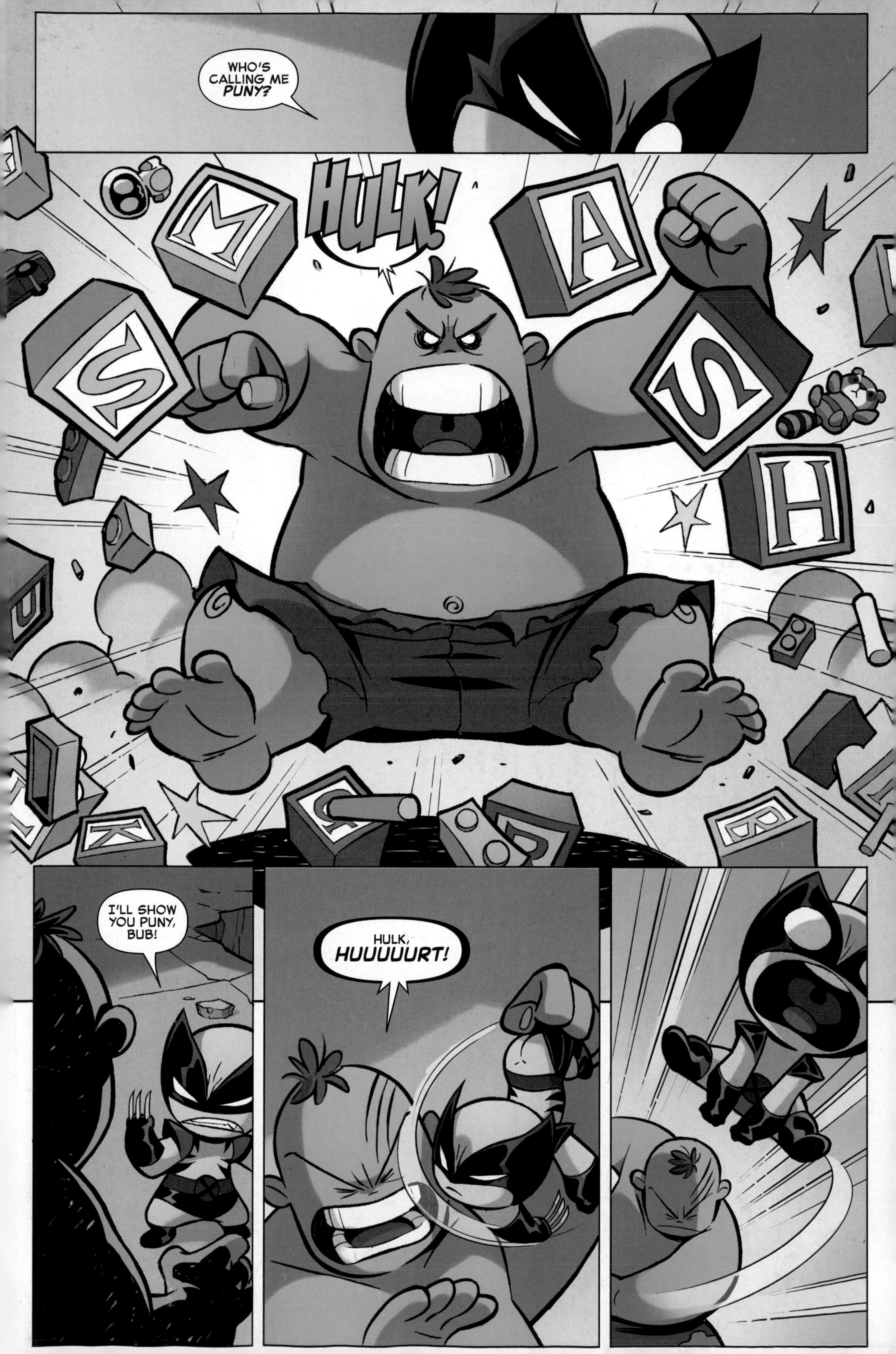
WHO'S CALLING ME PUNY?
HULK!
S
M
A
S
H
I'LL SHOW YOU PUNY, BUB!
HULK, HUUUUURT!

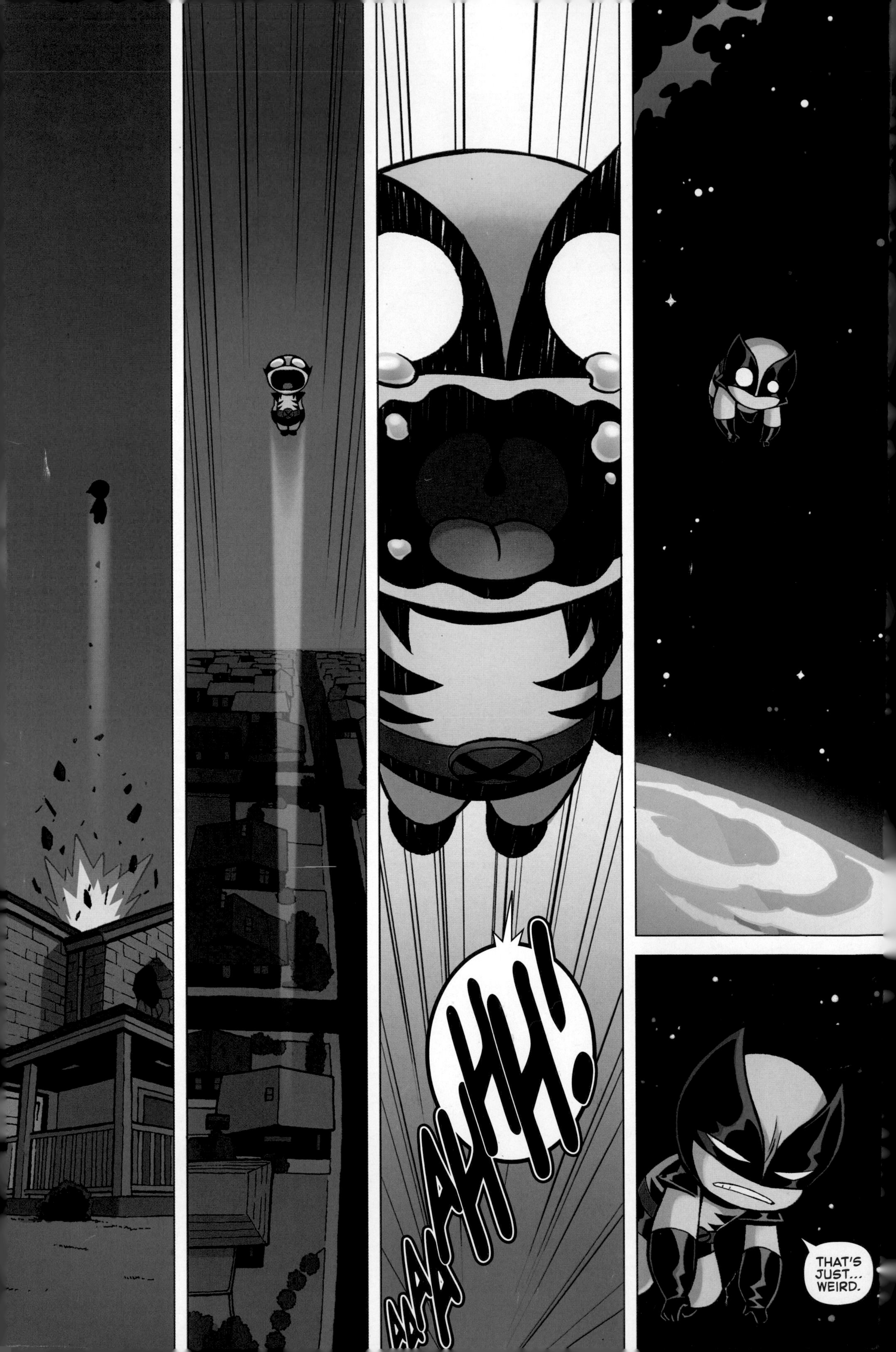
AAAAHH!
THAT'S JUST... WEIRD.

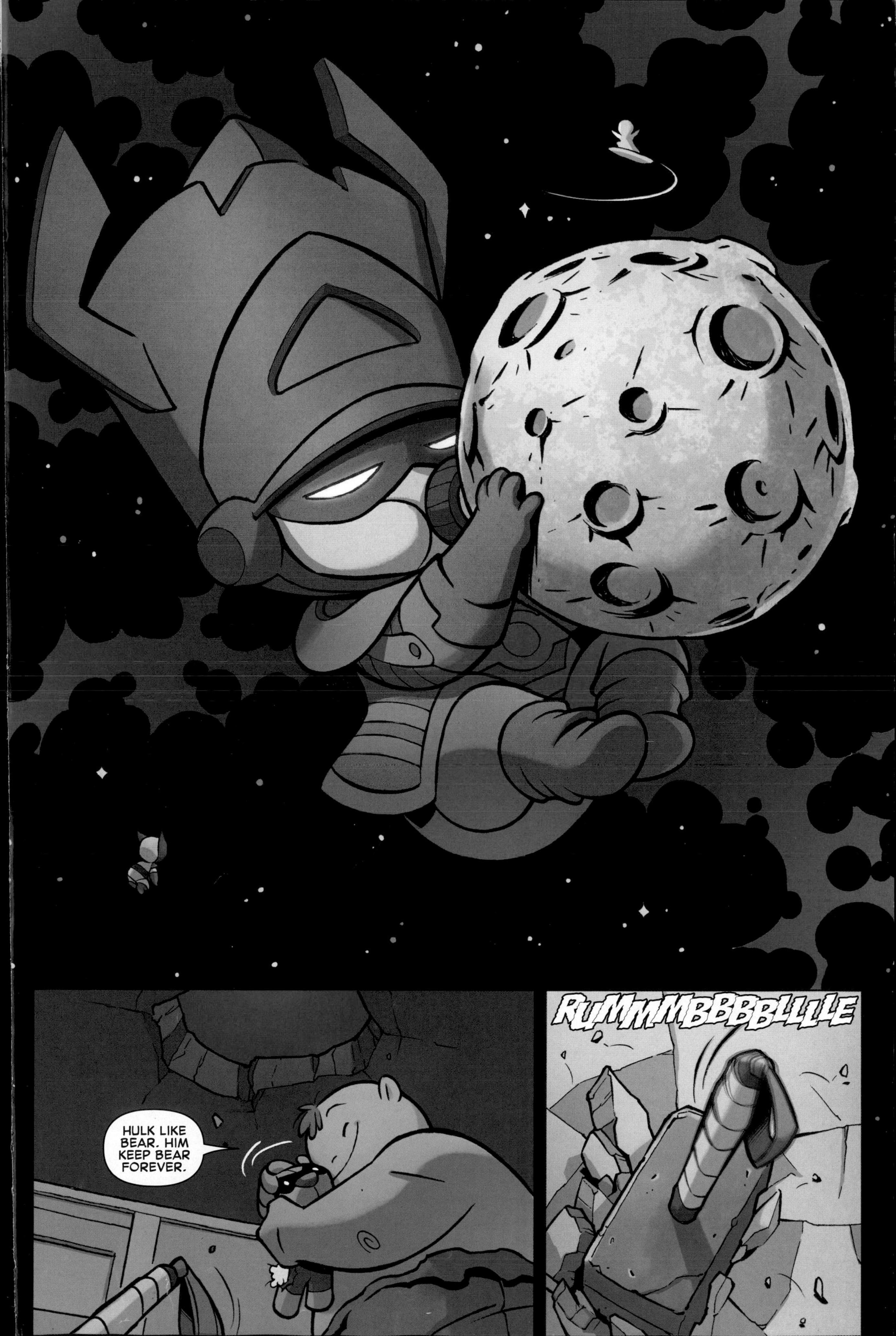
HULK LIKE BEAR. HIM KEEP BEAR FOREVER.
RUMMMBBBBLLLE

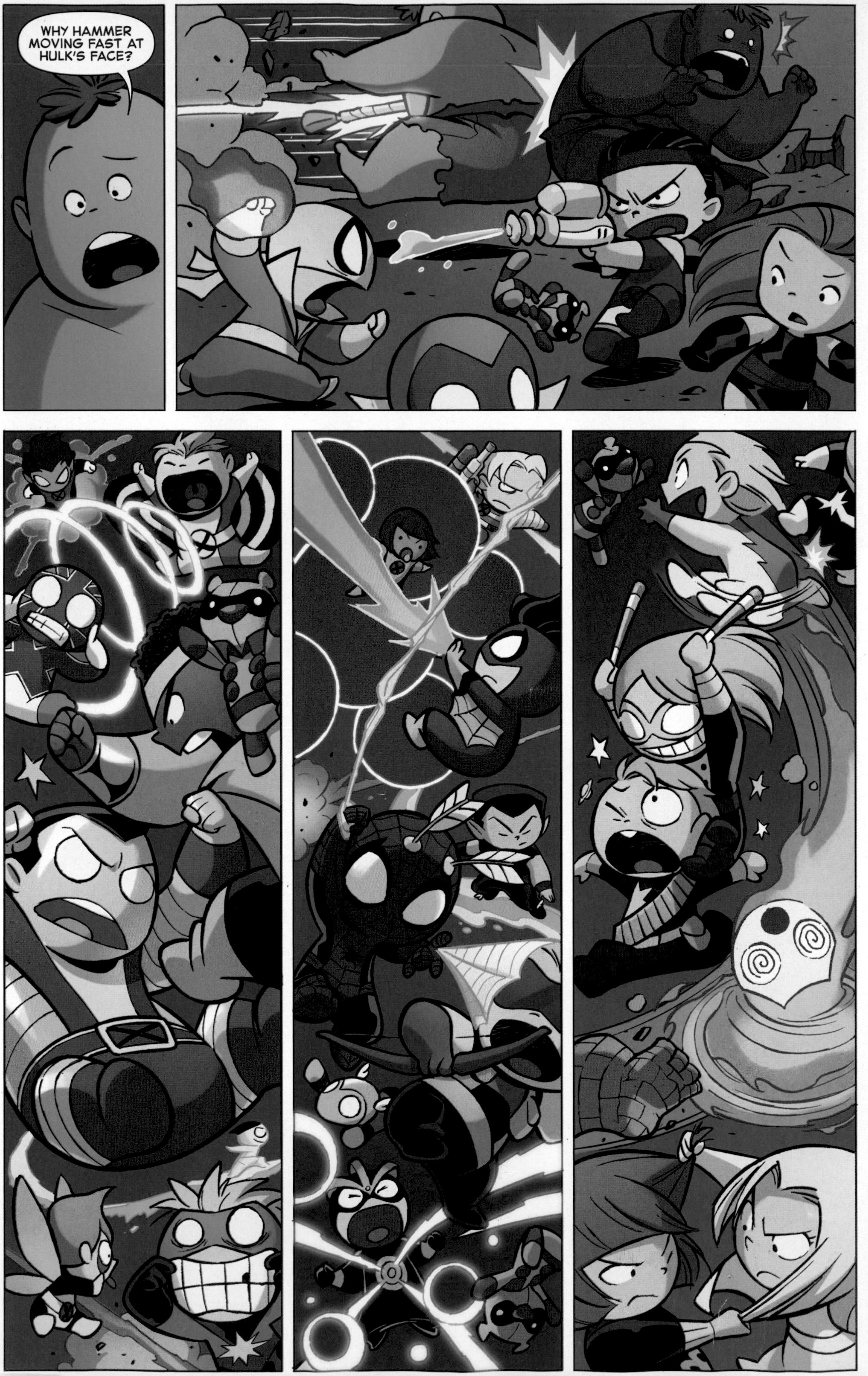
WHY HAMMER MOVING FAST AT HULK'S FACE?

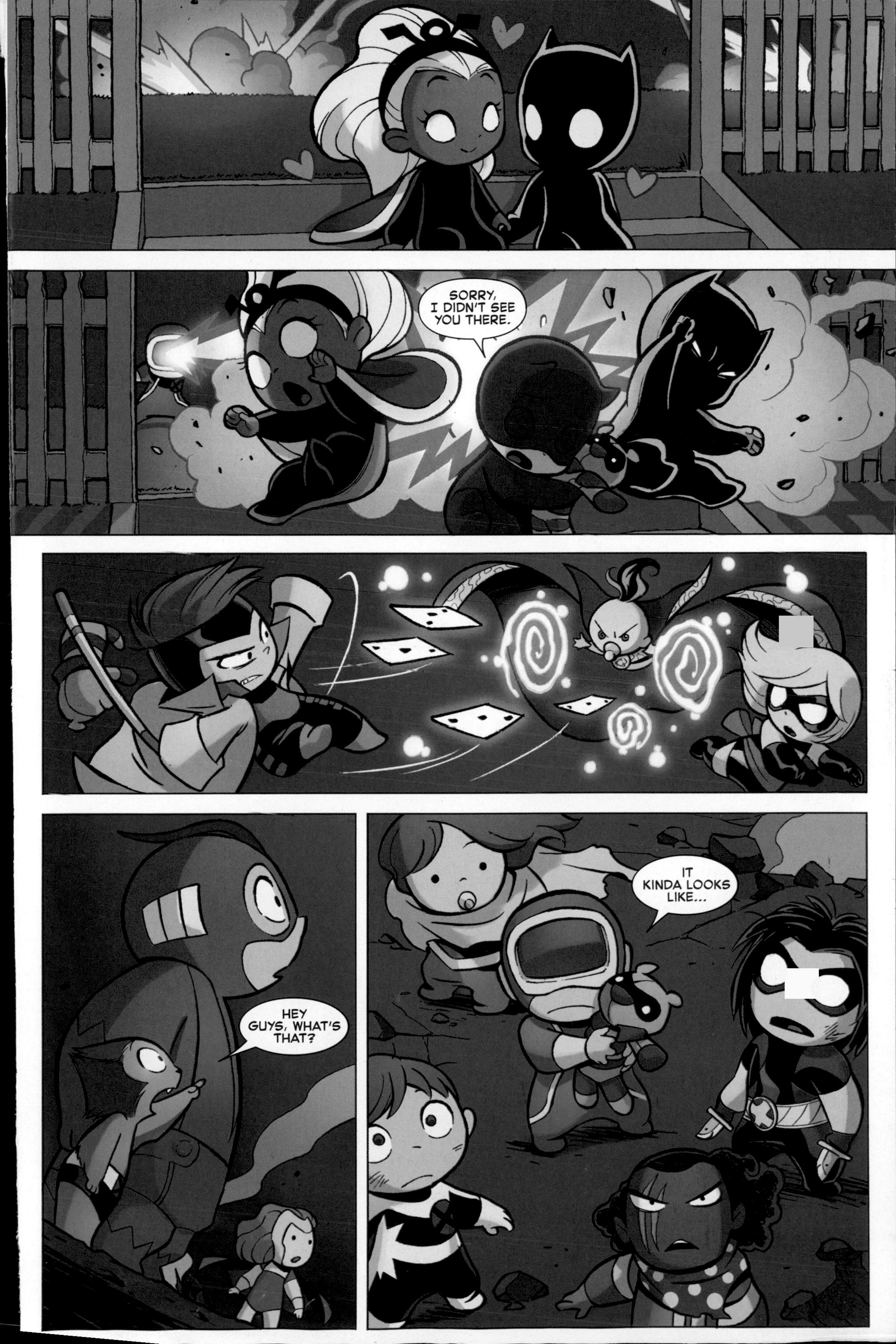
SORRY, I DIDN'T SEE YOU THERE.
HEY GUYS, WHAT'S THAT?
IT KINDA LOOKS LIKE...

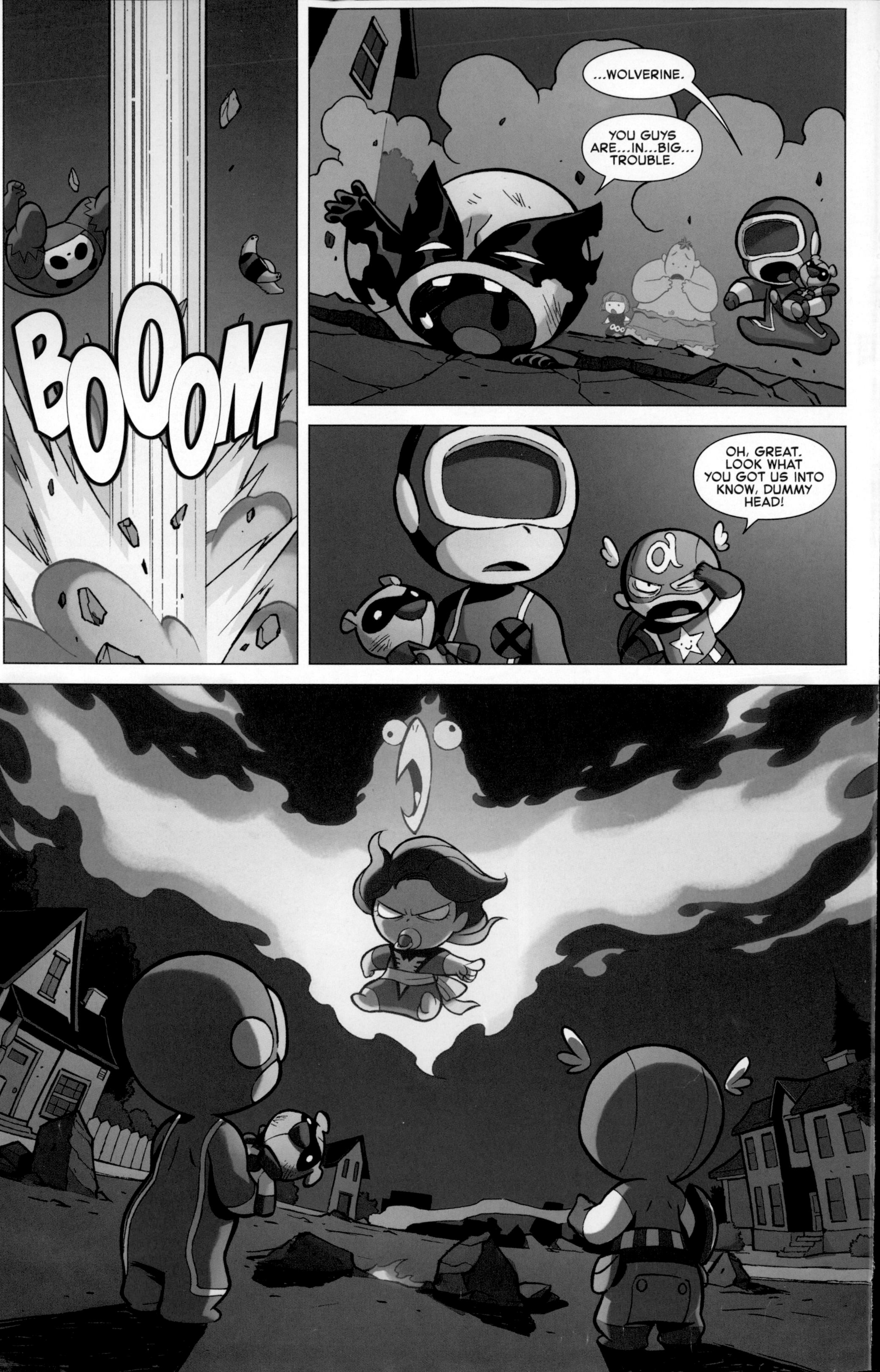
BOOOOM
...WOLVERINE.
YOU GUYS ARE...IN...BIG... TROUBLE.
OH, GREAT. LOOK WHAT YOU GOT US INTO KNOW, DUMMY HEAD!

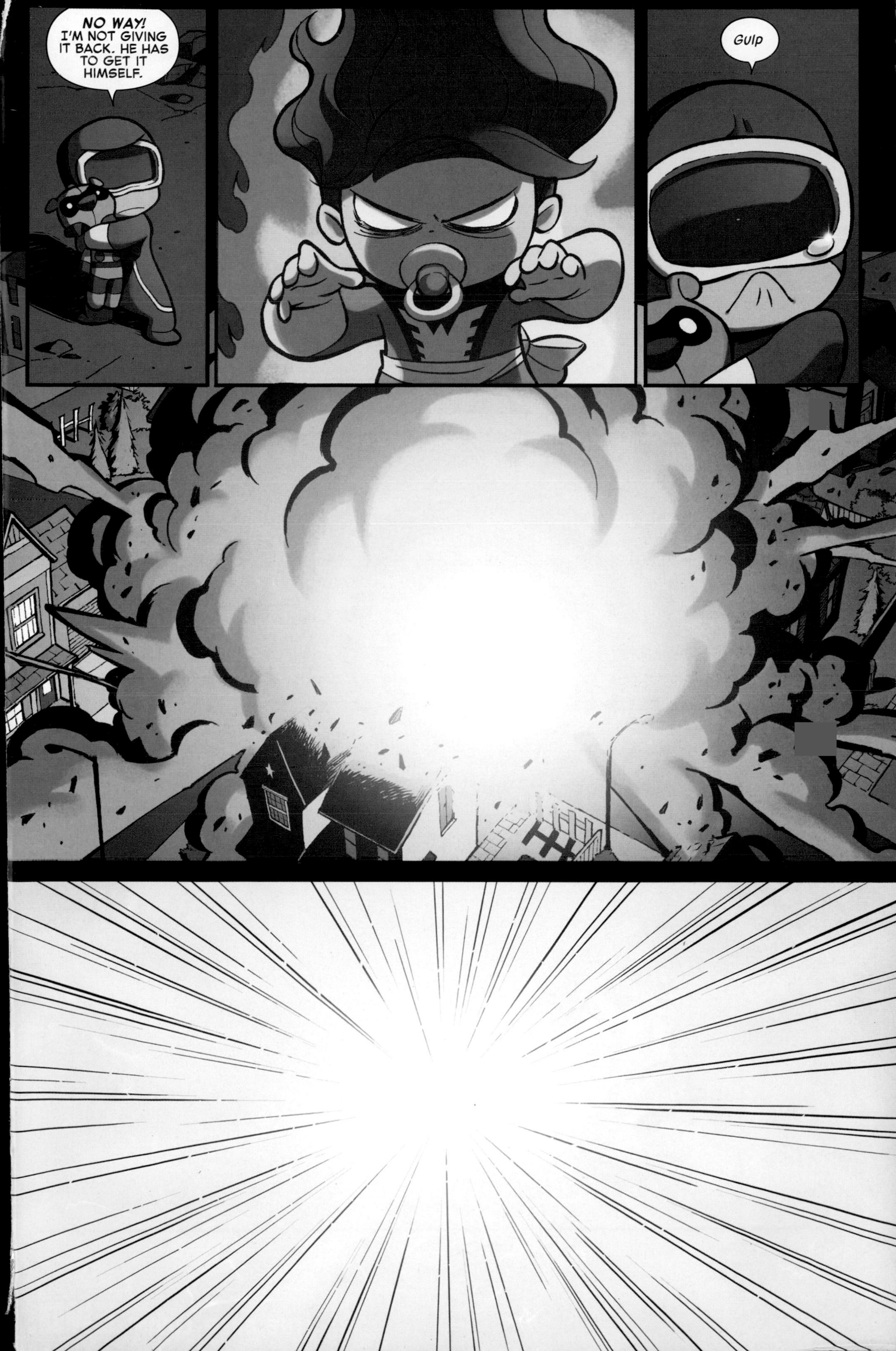
NO WAY! I'M NOT GIVING IT BACK. HE HAS TO GET IT HIMSELF.
GULP

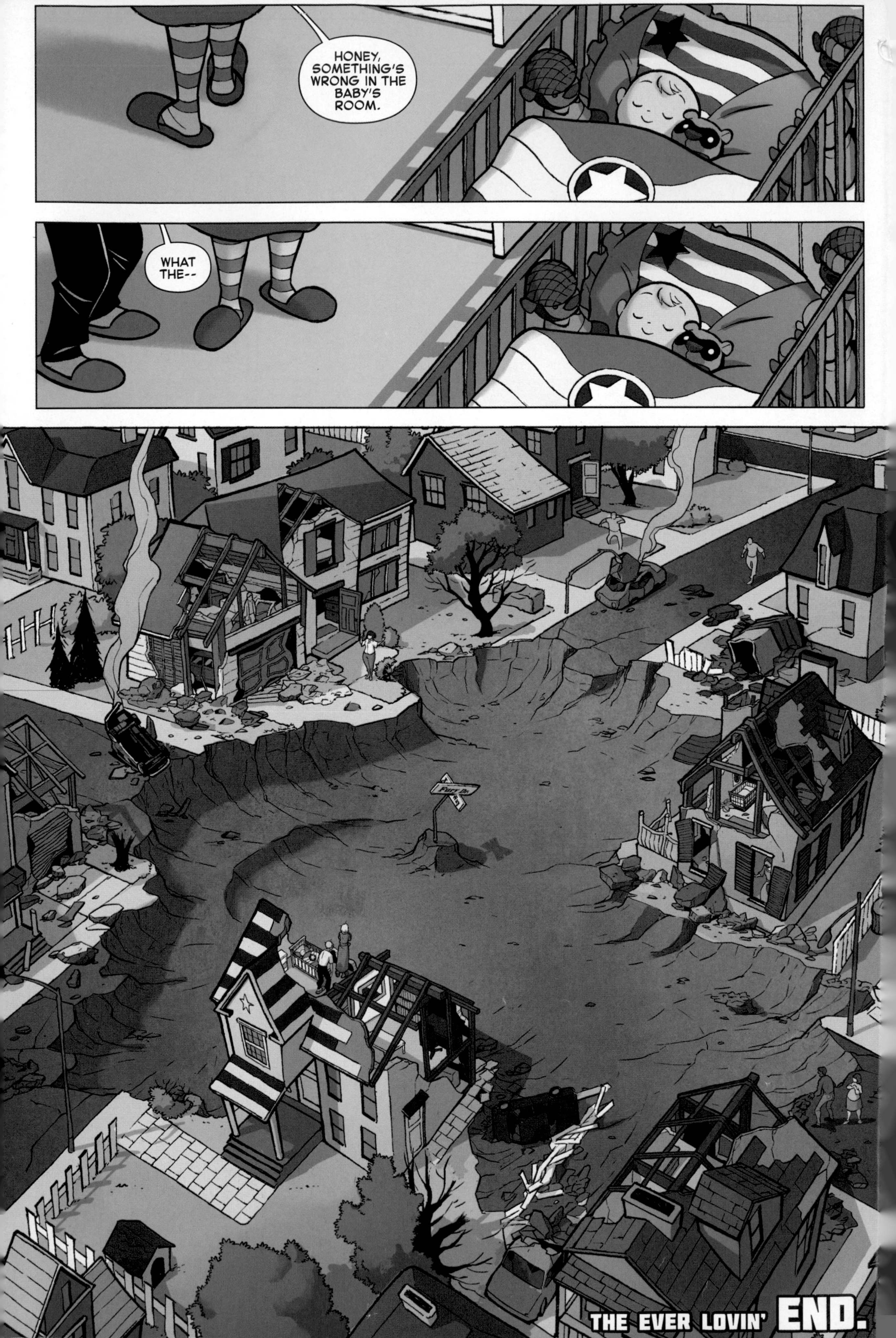
HONEY, SOMETHING'S WRONG IN THE BABY'S ROOM.
WHAT THE--
THE EVER LOVIN' END.

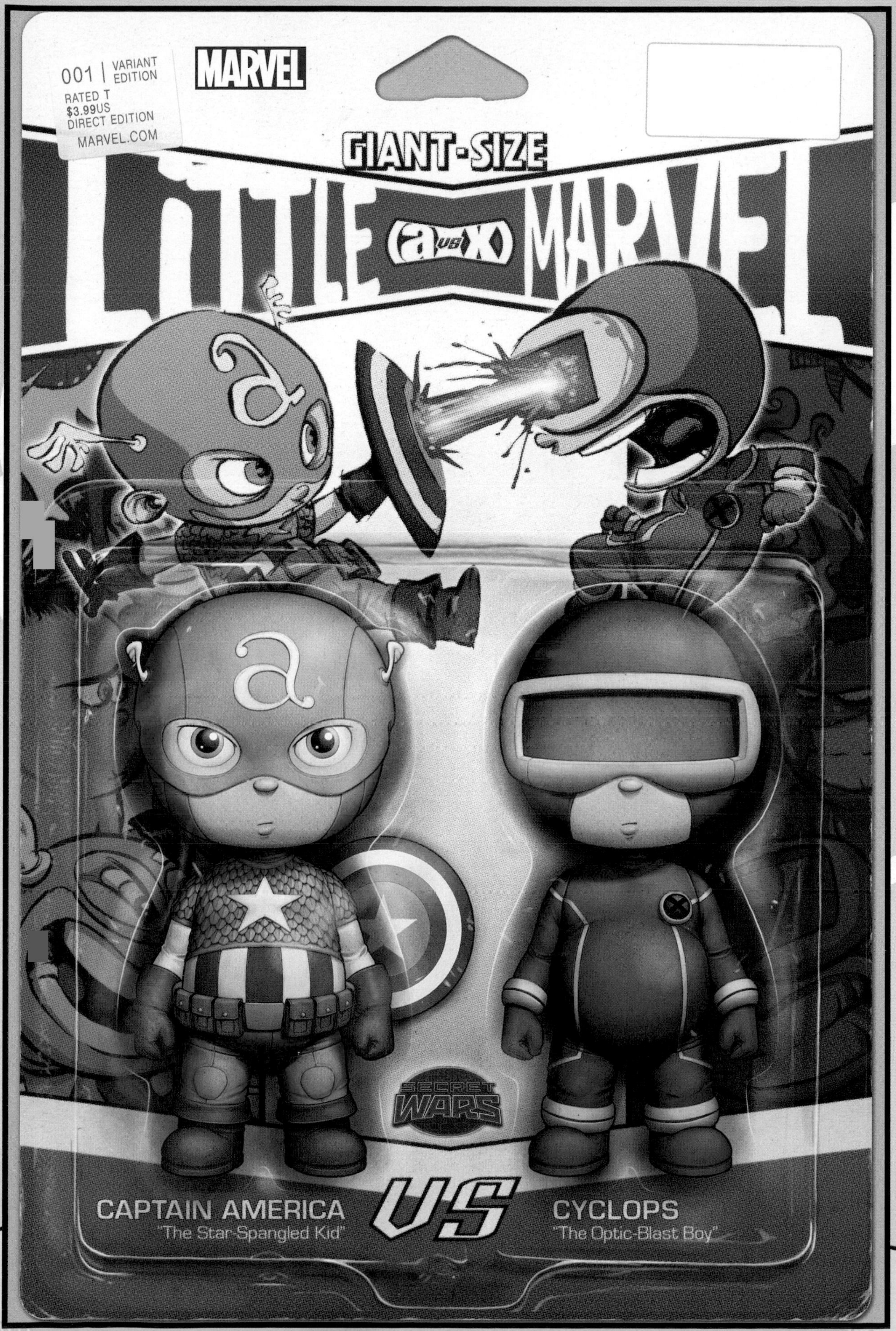
001 | VARIANT EDITION
RATED T
$3.99US
DIRECT EDITION
MARVEL.COM
MARVEL
GIANT-SIZE
LITTLE (a vs x) MARVEL
SECRET WARS
CAPTAIN AMERICA
"The Star-Spangled Kid"
VS
CYCLOPS
"The Optic-Blast Boy"

GIANT-SIZE LITTLE MARVEL: AVX #1 ACTION FIGURE VARIANT BY JOHN TYLER CHRISTOPHER

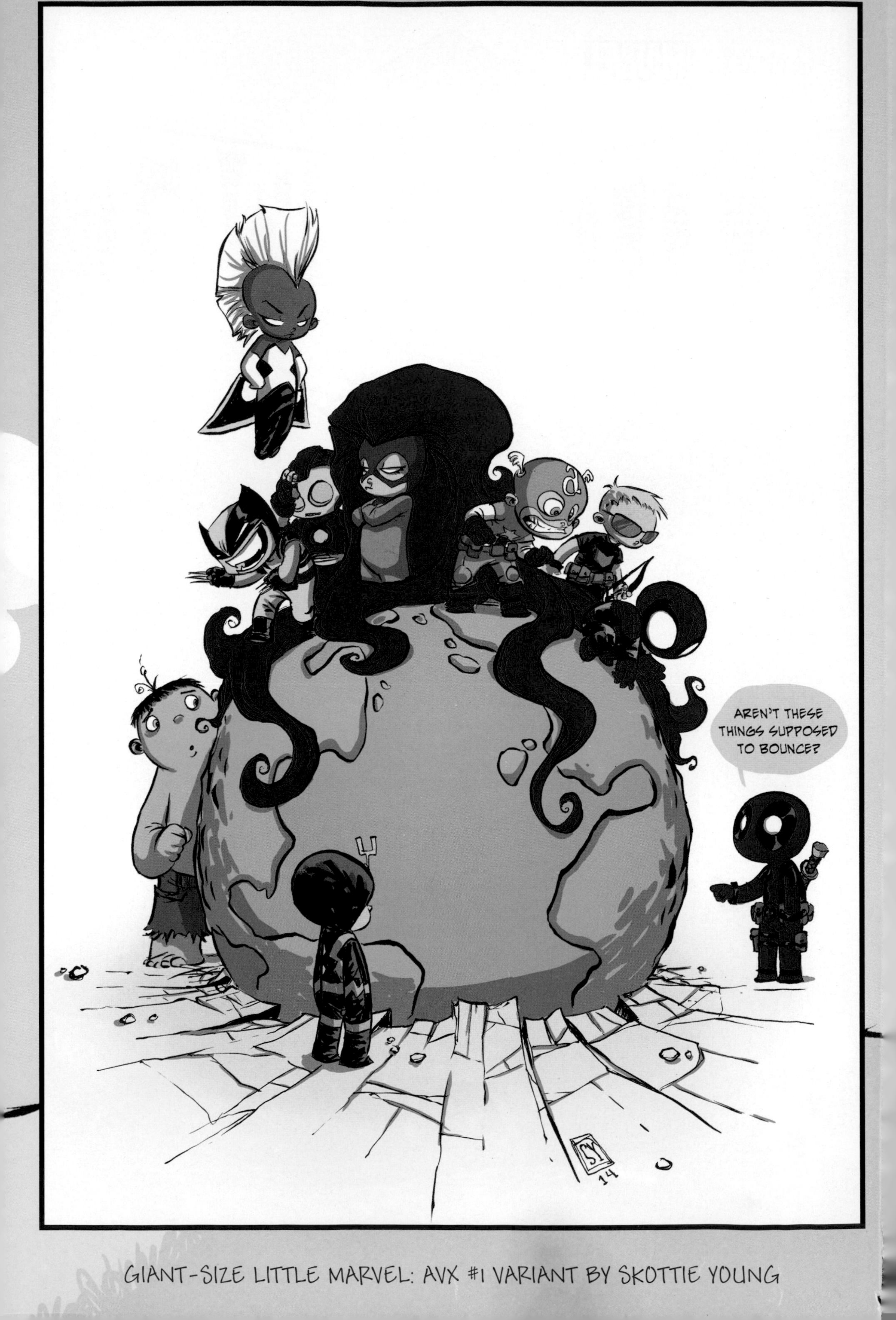
AREN'T THESE THINGS SUPPOSED TO BOUNCE?
SY 14

GIANT-SIZE LITTLE MARVEL: AVX #1 VARIANT BY SKOTTIE YOUNG

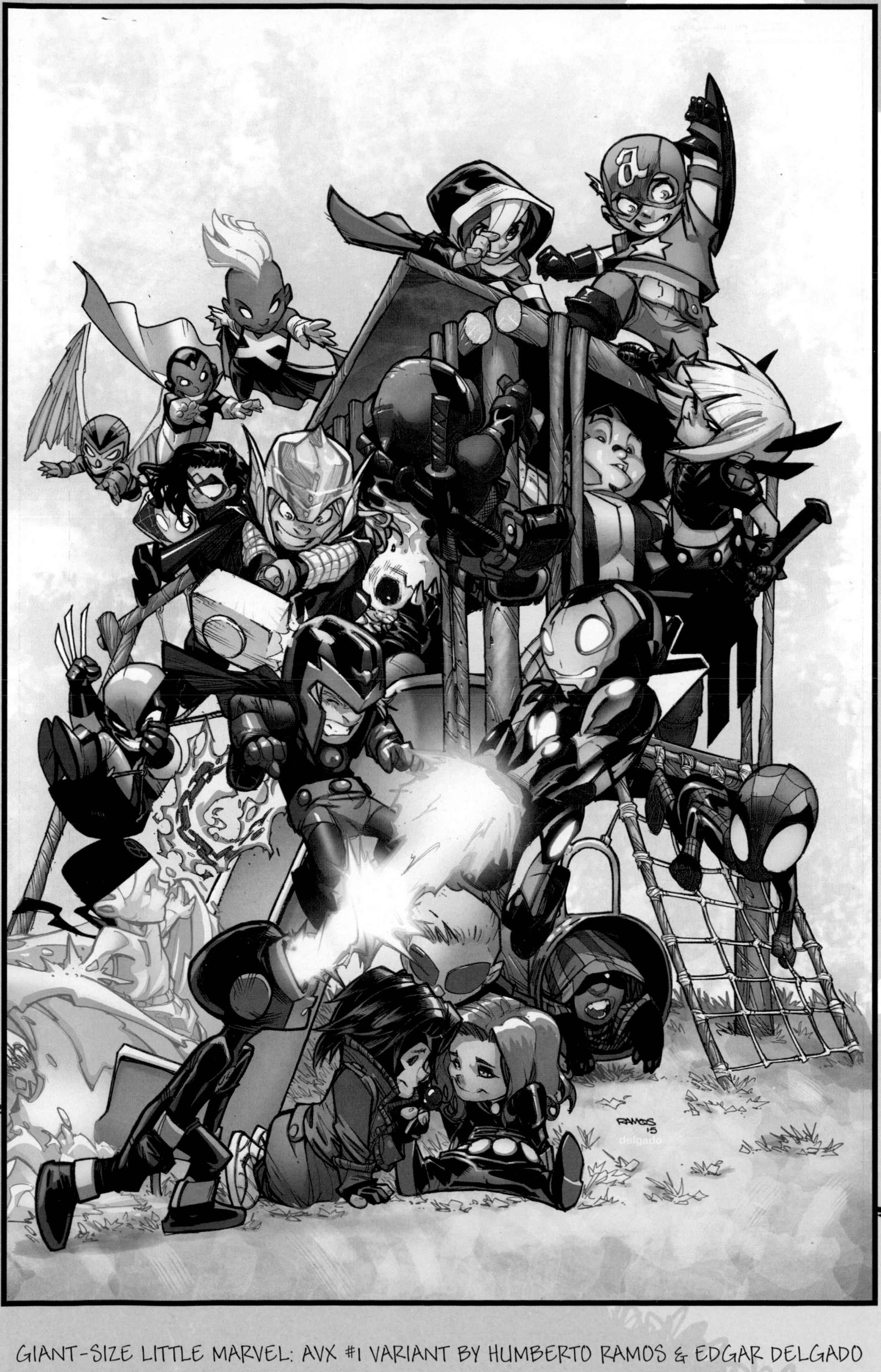
RAMOS
'15
delgado

GIANT-SIZE LITTLE MARVEL: AVX #1 VARIANT BY HUMBERTO RAMOS & EDGAR DELGADO

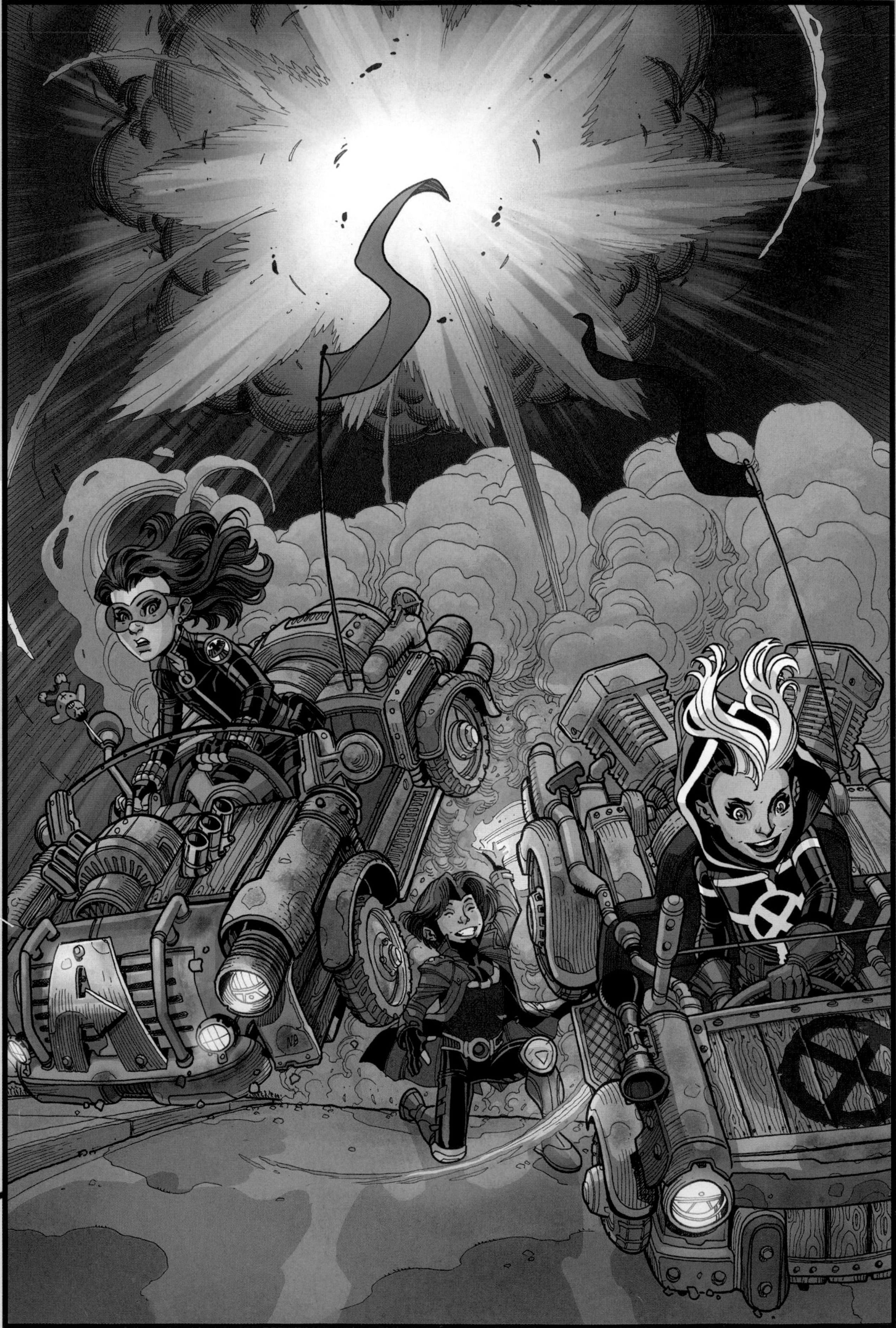

GIANT-SIZE LITTLE MARVEL: AVX #2 VARIANT BY NICK BRADSHAW & JAMES CAMPBELL

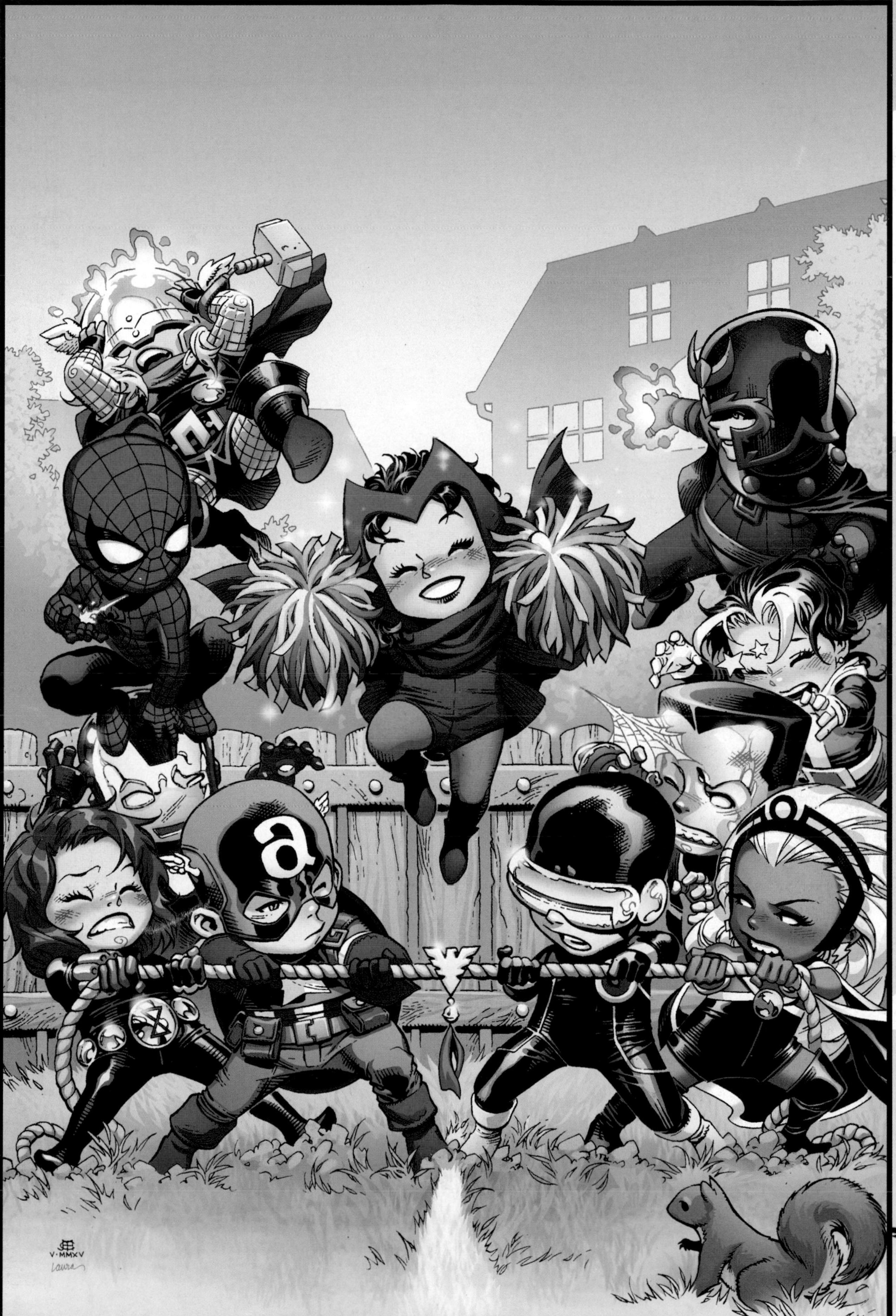
V·MMXV

GIANT-SIZE LITTLE MARVEL: AVX #3 VARIANT BY JIM CHEUNG & LAURA MARTIN

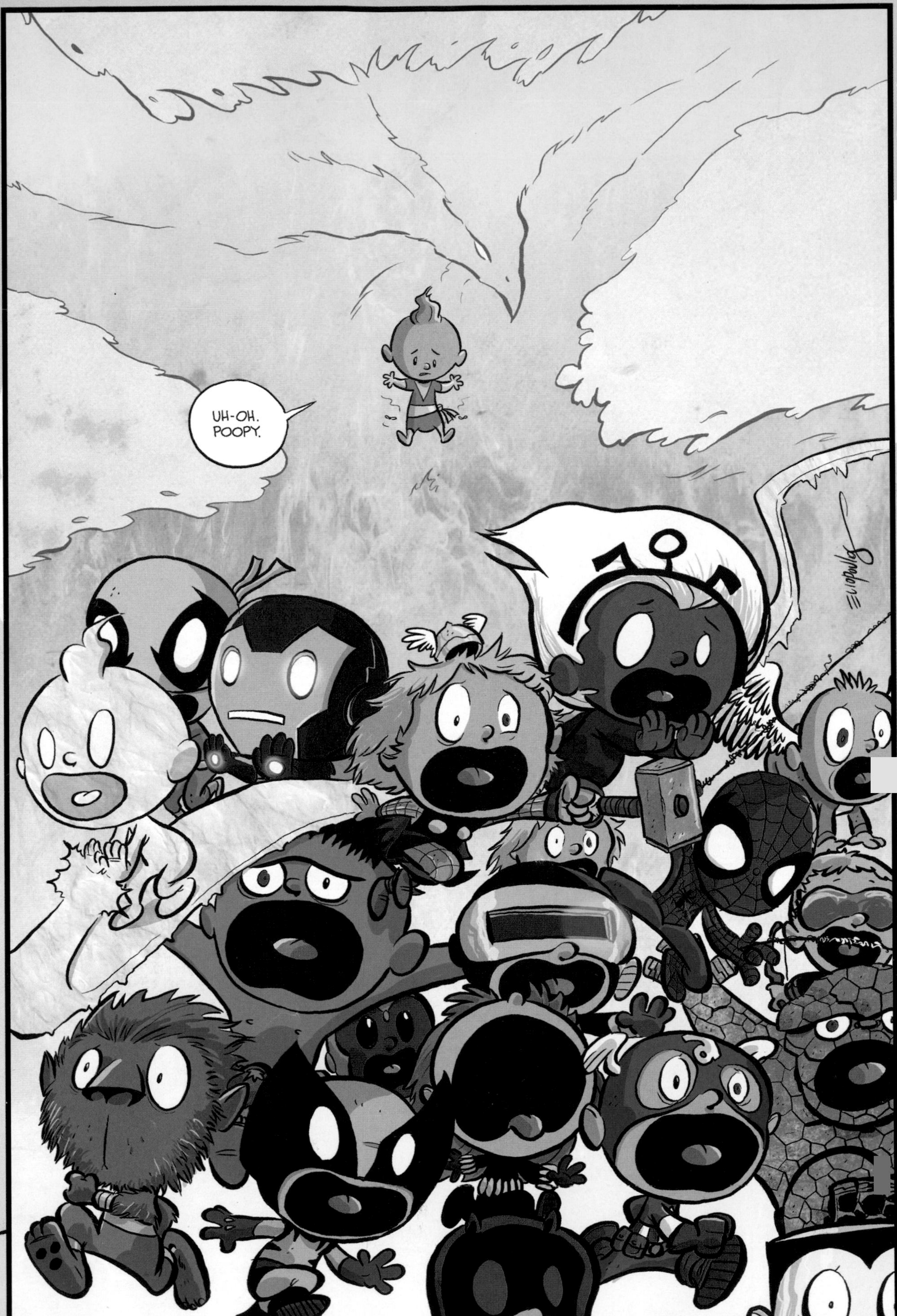
UH-OH. POOPY.

A-BABIES VS. X-BABIES #1 VARIANT BY CHRIS ELIOPOULOS